"In *Messages from the Afterlife*, Mark Ireland raises fundamental questions about the nature and fate of human consciousness. This touching, heartfelt account takes its place in the enlarging body of evidence suggesting that death is not final."
—LARRY DOSSEY, MD, author of *One Mind: How Our Individual Mind Is Part of a Greater Consciousness and Why It Matters*

"Mark Ireland is a soulful, intelligent man who brings higher thinking to mediumship, and he shares with us some of his own thought-provoking stories in his book. As a father who has suffered the loss of his own son, he truly understands the importance of reconnection between the living and those who 'live again.'"
—ALLISON DUBOIS, inspiration for the NBC TV series *Medium* and author of *Talk to Me: What the Dead Whisper in Your Ear*

"If you expect this book to be sombre and extremely sad, it is not. The journey that the author has travelled since the death of his son in 2004 is quite remarkable. He has taken his original grief and raised it to a positive experience of hope for everyone who has lost someone precious.... [A] varied, educational, and interesting journey...."
—TRICIA J. ROBERTSON, psychic researcher and author of *Things You Can Do When You're Dead*

"*Messages from the Afterlife* is a must-read and will bring comfort and peace to thousands. Another great book from Mark Ireland."
—JOHN HOLLAND, psychic medium and author of *The Spirit Whisperer: Chronicles of a Medium*

"Not all books deliver what their titles promise. This one certainly does—and much more. The messages are there, and very impressive many of them are, as is the author's balance between spiritual seeking and a strictly scientific approach.... [F]ascinating reading."
—GUY PLAYFAIR LYON, journalist, broadcaster, and author of *If This Be Magic* and *Twin Telepathy*

I loved this book! Raymond Moody opened the dialogue on NDEs, Brian Weiss did it for past-life memories, Michael Newton for life between lives, the Guggenheims for after-death communications, and now Mark Ireland has done it for mediumship, the capacity of certain individuals to communicate with the spirits of the deceased...."
—JANE KATRA, PhD, healer, professor of public health, and coauthor of *Miracles of Mind* and *The Heart of the Mind*

"In his 2008 book *Soul Shift*, Mark Ireland explained how he was able to overcome the despair he had experienced from the death of his eighteen-year-old son, Brandon, by his research in the area of mediumship. Seeing others grieving the loss of loved ones, Mark Ireland has dedicated his life to helping others move from disbelief or blind faith to a conviction that those loved ones live on and will someday be reunited with us. In this book, Mark provides more intriguing stories of spirit communication and related phenomena, all of which should help the reader overcome grief and the fear of death."
        —MICHAEL TYMN, editor of the *Journal for Spiritual and Consciousness Studies*

"This is a powerful story of development of a 'mainstream business-fueled lifestyle' to one of a deep exploration of life and living. Spurred by the death of a son, Mark Ireland marshals compelling evidence of existence beyond physical death, and records how this knowledge can overcome the grief of the bereaved. It is an important exploration of science, spirituality, religion, and psychic realities."
        —JOHN POYNTON, emeritus professor of biology at the University of Natal,
            South Africa, and past president of the Society for Psychical Research

"Practical, insightful, and poignant, this book is written from the heart of a grieving parent and the brain of a pragmatic researcher. Whether you're interested in psychic-medium abilities, evidence of life after death, or new ways to comfort your grief, Mark Ireland's story and analysis delivers."
        —BOB OLSON, AfterlifeTV.com

"Mark Ireland has created another excellent contribution to afterlife research.... Ireland shares unique information about spirit communication, and eloquently addresses pseudo-skepticism and religious piety—two controversial areas that often contribute to the hindrance of spiritual growth."
        —DONNA SMITH-MONCRIEFFE, afterlife researcher and author of
            Medium7: Evidence of the Afterlife and Predictions

"This is the story of a man's opening up to the world of spirits as they help him recover from the death of his son. We meet the mediums he works with and the spirits communicating through them. We listen as he does battle with materialists who dismiss his point of view with contempt. Above all, we get to know a man who wants us to recognize that we have access to a Divine Source within us and that, as he puts it, 'another realm of being exists beyond this world of physical manifestation.'"
        —STAFFORD BETTY, PhD, professor of religious studies at California State
            University, Bakersfield, and author of *The Afterlife Unveiled*

MESSAGES *from* *the* AFTERLIFE

A BEREAVED FATHER'S JOURNEY
IN THE WORLD OF SPIRIT VISITATIONS,
PSYCHIC-MEDIUMS, AND SYNCHRONICITY

MARK IRELAND

North Atlantic Books
Berkeley, California

Published by
North Atlantic Books
P.O. Box 12327
Berkeley, California 94712

Cover photo © Chepko Danil Vitalevitch/
   Shutterstock.com
Cover and book design by Susan Quasha
Printed in the United States of America

Messages from the Afterlife: A Bereaved Father's Journey in the World of Spirit Visitations, Psychic-Mediums, and Synchronicity is sponsored by the Society for the Study of Native Arts and Sciences, a nonprofit educational corporation whose goals are to develop an educational and cross-cultural perspective linking various scientific, social, and artistic fields; to nurture a holistic view of arts, sciences, humanities, and healing; and to publish and distribute literature on the relationship of mind, body, and nature.

North Atlantic Books' publications are available through most bookstores. For further information, visit our website at www.northatlanticbooks.com or call 800-733-3000.

Library of Congress Cataloging-in-Publication Data

Ireland, Mark, 1958–
    Messages from the afterlife : a bereaved father's journey in the world of
    spirit visitations, psychic-mediums, and synchronicity / Mark Ireland.
        pages cm
    ISBN 978-1-58394-718-0
    1. Future life. 2. Spiritualism. I. Title.

    BF1311.F8I74 2013
    133.9092—dc23
    [B]
                                         2013018430

1 2 3 4 5 6 7 8 9 SHERIDAN 18 17 16 15 14 13
Printed on recycled paper

Contents

Introduction

It was a cruel synergist that moved me to explore life's deepest mysteries. This had been my father's path, but it was not mine—at least not until now.

Reflecting back, I could see that I'd taken for granted the most important things in my life until one of the most precious and beloved among them—my youngest son—was gone. And oddly, it now seemed easier to take risks, following an inner sense that prodded me to pursue a new life course using my freshly recognized gifts to help others.

Prior to January 10, 2004, I could never have imagined that Brandon would die at such a young age. I'd been traveling just before this happened and was grateful to have returned home and spent time with him before the incident.

It was a Saturday morning and Brandon told me that he was going to hike with friends. Their plan was to tackle a particularly challenging mountain. The wind was blowing intensely and something just didn't feel right to me.

A short time later I experienced an unusual "premonition," which included the overwhelming sensation of another presence, as ominous feelings about Brandon's hike suffused me. As a result of my experience I asked my son to stay home. Of course I didn't tell him about the intense feeling that swallowed me up with trepidation and a sense of impending tragedy. Instead, I focused on the *rational* grounds for my request—the windy conditions present that day. In other words, I second-guessed my experience instead of fully trusting it.

Brandon was eighteen years old, adventurous, and determined. When leaving with friends, in matter-of-fact fashion, he uttered his final words to me, "We're going, Dad." Later that day we received a distress call from our older son, Steven, who was relaying a message from Brandon's friends on the mountain. They said that Brandon had become dizzy and passed out, but they didn't know what was wrong. We rushed home to find a swarm of people and emergency vehicles at the base of the mountain, located directly behind our house. Shortly thereafter we were introduced to a Chaplain who informed us that Brandon had died, providing no opinion on the cause of death. A short time later I spoke to Brandon's best friend, Stu Garney, and he told me that Brandon had complained about numb limbs and what seemed to be a rapid heartbeat.

Immediately after learning of Brandon's death I was in a state of utter shock. How was I to accept the death of my child—someone I'd loved since his birth, whose future I longed to see unfold? At that moment it was hard to even imagine going on. How could I function? Would I ever experience joy again?

Fortunately, my family includes members who are endowed with profound spiritual gifts, and this made all the difference for me. I soon contacted my uncle Robert who—like my deceased father—was a minister and gifted psychic-medium, asking him to relay any information about Brandon's well-being that he might receive. Two days later while I was standing in the mortuary making arrangements for Brandon's service, my cell phone rang. It was my uncle calling. He explained that he had tried hard to make a spiritual connection the night before but was unsuccessful. However, his meditation the following morning—that very day—had proven fruitful. My deceased father came to him and shared information about Brandon.

My uncle stated, "Brandon's heart failed due to a lack of oxygen. When he first left his body he was confused, but your dad came to greet him and help him adjust. Brandon also wanted you and Susie to know that you were the best parents he ever could have had."

Less than a week later my uncle's message was validated. When speaking to the physician who performed Brandon's autopsy, I was informed that my son's death was due to a severe asthma attack, which caused his blood oxygen levels to drop, resulting in heart failure.

My uncle's message was the first in a series of connections, validations, and synchronistic events that forever changed me. After spending most of my adult life in the "numb comfort" of a mainstream, business-fueled lifestyle, I was suddenly jolted out of my spiritual complacency. It was a harsh yet vital awakening. Mysteriously compelled by the crucible of my loss, I embarked on an exploration that drew me back to my numinous roots. As I noted, my father had been a deeply spiritual minister and world-renowned psychic-medium, but I had taken a different course in life. Perhaps my father had something to teach me after all.

I am now well into my journey and I've learned many things, but the process will never be complete—at least not in this lifetime. Change is an essential element of life; challenges will continue to arise, as will periods of immense joy and fulfillment. All the while I hope to continue along my path, as I know that I am destined to keep growing.

During my search, I traversed a major precipice and discovered some astonishing things. The fruits of my study have been helpful and reassuring—yielding hope in a world that has adopted materialism as its religion, accepting meaninglessness and chaos as givens. I feel obliged to share my findings, to help dispel this pessimistic worldview that I see as a falsehood.

First, I have culled evidence that physical death is not the end of the road for any of us. I know this message is critical because I've seen people consumed by fear of death or suffering unbearable grief after losing a loved one. Some can draw into a shell, ceasing all efforts to reach their potential, or even give up on life.

Conversely, I've seen people freed from the shackles of despair who were able to rebound and view life from a different perspective. These individuals were filled with a renewed sense of hope and optimism in the face of an apparent tragedy. This doesn't happen every time, because some people choose to hold onto anger or blame and will not release their debilitating thoughts. This choice is ultimately up to each individual. But being able to step back and view life from a larger perspective can change the context of a loss—seeing death as a simple shift to another form of life, rather than the cessation of one's existence.

As someone who has lost a loved one, I can personally attest to the need for healing after such a tumultuous experience. Yet I can also affirm that it is possible for a person to reclaim what can become a most meaningful and fulfilling life. After a time of reprieve, the loss can actually take on a unique and important role—serving as a catalyst for something crucial. Pain can be the ultimate teacher, but only when one is open to the possibility. Eventually the person must learn to move past grief to some degree; otherwise he or she will stand still or even regress.

I've seen afterlife evidence, including psychic and medium phenomena, play a role in easing the anguish tied to loss—advancing and accelerating the healing process. To provide illustration for those unfamiliar with this practice, in these pages I share examples of my interaction with *credible* spiritual mediums. I also provide information to help readers learn more about this field, which is little understood by most people.

CHAPTER 1

The "Why"

People often don't understand the reasons why I—a person they view as grounded and practical—chose to explore and write about psychic phenomena and mediumship. They wonder about my basis for directing bereaved persons to mediums for readings, or "sittings," as they are also called. Apparently I don't exude the sort of vibe expected of someone interested in the "paranormal" or the metaphysical because of my sensible approach to things.

The short answer to both questions is that I have an intimate knowledge of the pain associated with the death of a loved one, having lost my youngest son, Brandon, in early 2004. Losing someone so close—especially a child—is often the most painful event a person will ever experience. For some, the effects of grief can be crippling. They can ripple out for months, years, or even a lifetime.

But I've also seen the healing effects that a *good* reading can have on the bereaved. I've experienced this process firsthand. And I only refer people to the best mediums—the ones who have generated exceptional results on a repeated basis, under controlled conditions.

My father, Richard Ireland, was a highly capable psychic-medium as well as a minister. On many occasions I saw him serve as an instrument of spirit communication, yielding moving, specific validations that infused me with confidence in the reality of the other side of life. I refer to those non-physical realms of being where those we call "deceased" now dwell—with whom a few of those we call "living" are able to communicate, through a variety of channels. Such realms are referenced by various religious traditions.

As noted, I have witnessed the positive effects that a reading can have on someone navigating the turbulent waters of grief—when the medium is able to reveal specific, meaningful information. Observing such individuals before and after readings, I noted that something usually changed. More times than not the end result was positive— the outcome was transformative, accelerating their healing process. In one instance a bereaved father had a breakthrough when medium Tina Powers shared specific, impactful details about his deceased son that he said "there was no way she could have known." Before this, the man had essentially lost all hope, was destitute, and seriously questioning his own faith. Afterward he was relieved, as if a major burden had been removed. He explained that these key pieces of obscure information, communicated by Tina, were his bridge to hope. But rather than *tell you* what I mean, I will share a story to *show you* what I'm talking about.

Days prior to writing this, I received an urgent email from a woman named Linda, a co-worker from California. The subject line of her message said, "I need your help!" The message conveyed little more, except that her brother had died and she was having a hard time functioning. Since another associate had recently informed me that Linda had lost her younger brother, I wasn't surprised to hear from her. I knew Linda was aware of my first book, as well as my overall interest in afterlife evidence. I'd been planning to call her but she reached out to me first. I wrote back that I'd call.

I had already scheduled a visit that afternoon with my friend Debra Martin, a medium, to review my father's soon-to-be-published book on psychic development. During my drive to Debra's home, I called Linda and we spoke for about thirty minutes. She was extremely distraught, and the loss of her brother had pushed her to the edge. Talking between tears and gasps for air, Linda told me that her brother was her best friend and that she didn't know what she'd do without him in her life.

Linda explained that her brother had been riding a motorcycle in Sacramento when a car struck him. The impact crushed his chest and snapped his neck, killing him instantly. Linda also shared that her brother had left behind kids and she was concerned about their well-being. She didn't give me any details about how many children were left behind or their ages.

Linda said that she'd had difficulty sleeping and was suffering from feelings of guilt for failing to call her brother more often before he died. From my experience this is a common phenomenon among people who have just suffered the loss of a loved one. They often harbor a sense of guilt over something they feel they could have done to prevent the death, or for something left unsaid or undone prior to the passing.

She then touched on her disastrous attempt to return to work after spending four weeks away on leave. In her role as a salesperson for a print advertising company, Linda broke down sobbing while talking to clients and co-workers. She was unable to complete even the most basic job functions, such as checking schedules and pricing work.

She then asked how my wife and I had been able to heal after losing our son. I responded with practical advice. I explained that I had written down my feelings, visited with close friends and relatives, and openly shared my emotions with other people. I told her that writing about my son, telling people about his nature as a person, allowed me to purge my feelings—fully exposing them and embracing the essence of my grief. Family members, Brandon's friends, and I each wrote a letter to him, explaining what we loved about him and how much he meant in our lives. I also wrote Brandon's eulogy, as well as a series of "blog-like" notes distributed by email that proved to be the starting point for my first book. I told Linda that I enjoyed reading hopeful books—especially those focused on evidence for the afterlife and other spiritual topics.

Linda said that she had already pursued professional help but it wasn't having much of an effect on her outlook. In her words, "I have been going to a grief counselor but can't seem to pull it together."

She then asked me how long she should wait before pursuing a reading with a medium. I told her that there were differing opinions

on this matter—some people recommend a three- to six-month waiting period while others say there's no problem in proceeding immediately. I explained that there was no pat answer and that it was
ultimately up to the individual. Shortly after the death of her brother,
Linda had paid for a reading with a psychic she'd seen on local TV
but was disappointed with the results. I told her that just because
someone is adept at gaining publicity doesn't necessarily make him
or her a good psychic or medium. Some of the best people I'd met in
this field were relatively unknown.

As I neared my destination, Linda and I wrapped up our conversation, and within a few minutes I was at my appointment saying hello
to Debra. After we greeted one another, I told Debra that I had just
concluded a conversation with a distraught friend who was grieving
the recent loss of her brother. I shared no other details. I then mentioned how odd it seemed to have been engaged in such a discussion
while en route to the home of a medium. Debra followed, "It's no
coincidence that you're here right now—I need to talk to your friend."

Debra didn't elaborate on the reason why she needed to talk to
Linda, but I assumed it was something she felt intuitively. After visiting for an hour, conversing about the upcoming publication of my
father's psychic development book—specifically, discussing what I
might want to write in the Foreword—I asked Debra if she was ready
to speak with my friend.

Time was running short and she needed to pick up her daughter
from school, so Debra said she would first like to try to connect with
the brother. We moved from the kitchen area to the family room,
which was spacious and illumed with sunlight filtering in through
the windows high above. I sank into Debra's comfortable tweed
sofa while she took a seat in a chair positioned ninety degrees to my
left. After picking up a pad of paper and a pen, Debra asked for my
friend's name.

"Linda," I said.

"What is her brother's name?" she queried.

"I don't know," I responded.

Then, within just a few seconds, Debra asked, "Did this involve a motorcycle?" She had dialed in. She followed, "He died immediately—he wants her to know that his soul left his body instantly and he didn't suffer."

I then affirmed the accuracy of Debra's statement about the brother's instantaneous death, based on the information Linda told me earlier.

"There were kids left behind, *the little kids*, he says. He feels that his sister is concerned about them."

Hearing this, I leaned forward and listened intently. Debra was quite focused—sharing validations without hesitation as she tapped directly into a rapidly flowing stream of information. I then confirmed that the brother had kids, but that I didn't know any specifics about them.

Debra continued scribbling on her pad and said, "He wants me to bring something to his sister's attention that has to do with a bath or bathtub." This meant nothing to me so I pleaded ignorance. Debra then mentioned, "He's showing me something red, like a ribbon or banner, at the funeral—possibly used to cover the casket."

Again, this statement meant nothing to me but it made me wonder if there was any significance to her last few statements. I would have to wait to find out.

Debra then said that the brother had specifically mentioned something about a *little boy*. I assumed this must be a reference to one of the kids she'd mentioned earlier, but I didn't know for sure.

It was now time for me to leave, and I promised to share the information with Linda. Debra asked me to have Linda call back later in the evening for a free reading.

I climbed into my car and began navigating the circuitous route out of the neighborhood as I called Linda. When we connected, I made sure to explain that I'd not shared any specific information with Debra—just that a co-worker friend had recently lost her brother and was in mourning.

With this groundwork laid, I started sharing Debra's information with Linda—first reiterating her comments about the brother's death being linked to a motorcycle. I then shared Debra's statement that Linda's brother wanted her to know that he hadn't suffered at the moment of his death. Linda was stunned with the accuracy of what had been shared thus far and was anxious for more validations.

Next I mentioned Debra's reference to "the little kids."

Linda explained to me that her brother had encountered some personal problems many years earlier, and that she had raised his children during that timeframe. And even though the kids were now older, Linda and her husband still referred to her brother's children as "the little kids," something her brother had known.

I was really getting curious about the relevance of Debra's *other* comments, seeing that she'd been on the mark with the things I knew about. I mentioned the "bath" and "bathtub" references. Linda explained that during the time when she was raising her brother's kids, their favorite activity was bath time. She would put them all in the tub at the same time and they would engage in what she called "water wars." This took place when the kids were between the ages of three and eight years. She'd fill the tub with bubble bath and toy boats, put the children in, and laugh as they splashed water about— trying to sink one another's ships.

I then asked about the reference to "the little boy." Linda shared that this was a clear reference to her brother's grandson, recently born to an older stepdaughter named Lindsay—i.e., not one of the "little kids."

It also turned out that Debra's mention of a "red ribbon or banner over her brother's casket" was meaningful. Linda told me that a red banner had indeed adorned his coffin. It was a gift from his motorcycle-riding buddies, intended to signify their camaraderie.

At the end of our discussion Linda expressed deep gratitude for everything I'd passed along and was amazed. Her voice was quivery and she went silent at times, seemingly mesmerized by Debra's comments. All she could do was thank me over and over, saying, "Now I know my brother is okay."

Later that evening Debra gave Linda a reading over the phone and furnished more information. In this session Debra accurately identified the brother's favorite food as pizza. She also passed along a "thank you" to Linda for changing the music at the service—from country-western, which he hated, to the hard rock that he loved.

Debra said that the brother shared the phrase "Live, Love, and Laugh." Linda told me that her brother never said these words to her during his physical life, yet she confirmed owning a piece of art with this very inscription—as well as the fact that she intended to get a tattoo with this exact phrase to honor him.

One day later, I received this message from Linda by email.

> Mark, I cannot thank you enough! I spoke with Debra and she was right on the mark on everything!! There were so many things she told me, things that no one would know. I had been feeling so sad and grieving so much that I started to question if I even believed in the afterlife … then you sent me Debra. It is like a huge weight was lifted from me because I know my brother is here with me. I feel so much comfort and peace. I am so surprised … no tears today and most importantly no sadness. I know he is here … what an amazing thing. You brought my brother to me and I will never be able to say thank you enough. I am forever grateful for the gift you sent me in Debra. The peace I have right now is so comforting.

About a week later I received another note from Linda and she shared some additional affirmations:

> Debra also told me to watch my niece—that she would be touching her head, scratching it as if she had dandruff or something. After the reading I wanted to see if Mary, my niece, was actually having these experiences—but I didn't want to lead her in any way. I recalled how much Mary loved my shampoo whenever she would visit my home. So I asked how her hair was doing and if her mother was buying the brand of shampoo that I use. She responded by telling me,

"Actually, my head has been itching a lot lately—I feel like I have dandruff. I don't know why it's so itchy." Then I asked Mary how long this had been going on; she said about a week.

Linda then shared Debra's information with Mary and it had a profound impact:

Mary now recognizes that her father is around when her head is itchy so she talks to him at those times. Referring to her grandmother, my mother, Mary said, "I wish she could feel the happiness that I feel now—he isn't gone, only his body is gone. He is still here." Mary then said, "Getting the message from my dad by him touching my hair has filled the emptiness I had in my heart. Now I am happy."

Linda wrapped things up by sharing, "I thought that was price-less and wanted you to know the effect Debra's reading had on a sweet twelve-year-old girl who doesn't hurt anymore. God bless you both!"

Dr. Julie Beischel, Director of the Windbridge Institute, a research organization that studies mediums under controlled conditions, recently investigated the possibility that mediumship readings may be helpful in grief therapy. Initial results indicate that this is indeed the case. In her research brief, Dr. Beischel noted the following facts:

- Unresolved grief can cause significant mental and physical distress.
- Traditional psychotherapy provides little to no effect for relieving grief.
- Spontaneous and induced experiences of after-death com-munications (ADCs) dramatically reduce grief.
- Pilot data suggest similar positive effects [as with ADCs] after readings with mediums.

In summary, Dr. Beischel notes, "The combination of traditional psychotherapy and mediumship readings may prove to be more beneficial than either intervention separately. … The potentially therapeutic benefits of mediumship readings warrant further study." [1] Elsewhere Dr. Beischel writes, "Spontaneous and induced ADCs [after-death communications] can have tremendous impacts on the grieving process, and my observations as well as pilot data we collected at the Windbridge Institute suggest similar positive effects after readings with mediums." [2]

I am encouraged to hear about this research and not surprised by the results. I've already witnessed numerous cases, such as the one involving Linda, where the outcome has been overwhelmingly positive. I know that an evidential reading often brings healing to grieving individuals. (Conversely, a bad reading from an inept medium, or a fraud, can do great damage to a bereaved person.)

Many people profess a belief in the existence of a spiritual realm, often aligning with their religious training or background. (Recent surveys indicate that, on average, between 48 percent and 59 percent of Europeans claim to believe in an afterlife, while between 72 percent and 74 percent of people in the United States assert a belief in life after death.[3] But when confronted with the loss of a child, a spouse, or another deeply loved person, one may find that his or her belief set is deeply challenged, and some suffer a crisis of faith. Such individuals may find it difficult to follow church doctrine, where they are often expected to lean solely on blind faith—relying on accounts from other persons, recorded several millennia ago. Questions may arise such as "Why would God allow something like this to happen to me? I've been a good and faithful person."

Ultimately, good mediumship provides evidence that a spiritual dimension exists and that our consciousness survives physical death. Medium communication is a tool that brings healing to people by bridging their "faith gap"—the space that lies between belief and knowing—giving them a reason to have hope and confidence that their loved ones live on and that they will eventually be reunited with them.

CHAPTER 2

The Next Phase

bout a week after Brandon's passing, I set up an appointment with an intuitive named Sandy Canales. (This occurred before I met with any of the other mediums previously mentioned.) I'd been introduced to Sandy a few years earlier at a party where she was giving psychic readings to guests.

Based on my experience, supplemented by positive feedback from others whom I trusted, Sandy seemed accurate and honest. She was also a kind, caring individual whose psychic endeavors were a labor of love; her bills were paid by a career in nursing.

After our initial meeting I rarely spoke to Sandy, but after losing Brandon I felt compelled to reach out to her. I had hopes that a reading might prove helpful therapy for my son Steven and his friends, Stuart Garney and David Butcher, both of whom had been with Brandon at the time of his passing. And frankly, I was hoping for some healing of my own too. We were all hurting deeply, trying to cope with the tragedy, and I felt the encounter might provide some solace.

Some years later, reflecting back on that day with Sandy, I recalled that the process had been helpful although I couldn't immediately remember many specifics. Driven by curiosity, I pulled out the audio tape and played it back. My interest suddenly piqued as it became clear that Sandy had predicted several events that had since come to pass.

Early in that reading, she said to me, "You help a lot of people, and just like your son you help them in a quiet way. I feel like you're going to be a teacher to others, and through that you're going to be touching other people's lives."

I could have dismissed this statement due to its generality, but my life had indeed changed since Brandon's passing. I *had* touched many people's lives—including many who had lost children, spouses, and other loved ones. I'd also had discussions with people who were seeking meaning in their lives and were somehow affected by our interaction in a positive way. And I suppose I was now a teacher of sorts, since I was sharing personal experiences and information that was of value to others. I had branched out by addressing groups in various venues and was often sought by people who wanted to talk after the sessions concluded. Many of these folks related to me because they had also lost someone close to them. By the fall of 2008, I was doing book signings and holding public-speaking events on a regular basis. And in early 2009, I started sharing my father's psychic development materials through instructional workshops in various locations throughout the United States.

As I continued listening to the tape, Sandy targeted something that had since become a most meaningful aspect of my life: "Writing is going to be very cleansing for you, and music is going to be quite helpful to you as well."

As evidenced by the material you are now reading, as well as my first book, *Soul Shift: Finding Where the Dead Go*, writing had clearly become a significant part of my life. Music yielded a curative quality as well—both in terms of listening to music and playing it on my guitar.

Sandy then offered a weighty prediction: "You're going to see Brandon in your dreams. I also feel like within the next six months you're going to make contact with him. It's like he's on the side of your bed, talking to you. And you're going to feel this presence and know that he's there."

She next said, "A song … I don't know if it was a song he wrote, but a song is going to be playing in your mind—and it's going to make the connection for you that he's there."

Hearing this in hindsight was quite startling. Sandy was right in saying that I would see Brandon in my dreams—on multiple occasions, in fact. Her comments about "feeling Brandon's presence on the side of the bed" were even more striking. By implying that I would be the subject of this experience Sandy seemed to miss the mark by a hair, as this episode actually involved my wife Susie. The account was otherwise quite precise—even down to the timing, as Susie's experience took place exactly six months after Sandy's prediction.

In July 2004, we had just returned home from a week-long cruise with Steven and good friend Stuart Garney, who had been Brandon's best friend. Before settling in for the evening, Susie was sitting at the foot of our bed and suddenly felt Brandon's presence. She then saw him to her right side as a "shadow figure," discernible through her peripheral vision. Susie was intensely moved by the experience.

The very next day, Susie received a call from our musician friend, James Linton, who reported a similar episode. James had been alone in his studio, composing and recording music, when he sensed the presence or energy of someone else. Not only did James report seeing a "shadow figure" matching up with Susie's description, he also saw flashes of white light and then felt pushed by a presence to modify a particular song, which later became "The Other Side." James explained that he had simply been a vehicle in the process and the song was a gift from Brandon to us.

As part of her wrap-up Sandy had concluded, "You may be doing training, and during this time you will be helping people. There are many ways to do God's work—you change people's lives and may not realize it. That is God's work."

A few months later I assisted with a training session at work and had some remarkable discussions with two individuals. One chat involved a man who later shared that I helped him repair a damaged relationship with his eighteen-year-old son. He told me that he thinks of me "every single day," because I helped him "see things from a different perspective." Apparently this new outlook helped him bridge the gap with his son, establishing common ground—something that had been lacking. This new approach allowed their relationship to heal. The consistent theme among these encounters was my newfound capacity to assist people—simply by sharing from the heart.

Sandy then brought up my son Steven, saying, "This will change him and mature him. He's going to help people and will do God's work for sure."

Again, this was a somewhat general statement, but since Brandon's passing Steven had changed and matured in remarkable ways. Thrust from his past, he had been transformed from a boy who was primarily focused on his own concerns into a considerate and altruistic young man. These characteristics had always seemed inherent in Steven but for the most part had been lying just below the surface. The loss of his brother apparently drew these qualities out.

Given the option, most of us would choose to avoid suffering, but deep personal growth often results from such events. Perhaps we get too settled and comfortable in aspects of life that are not as important, overlooking or ignoring the underlying reasons why we are here. Just when we feel as if we can put things on cruise control, the universe may remind us in the harshest of ways that physical life is temporal—driving us to reassess our priorities.

In the years that have passed since Brandon's death, more unusual things have occurred than ever before—both to us directly and through mediums. One such story involves a medium, Melinda Vail, and my friend Joe Colucci.

After my first meeting with Melinda I became convinced of her talent and integrity, and I began referring friends to her for personal readings and consultations. During a session with my friend Joe, Melinda brought forth a validation that took him by surprise.

While in the midst of other topics, Melinda stopped in her tracks and told Joe, "Brandon just dropped in." (Melinda had met me on only one prior occasion—approximately three months earlier—and was unaware that Joe's son Michael had been friends with Brandon. In fact, there was no reason for Melinda to bring Brandon's name up because Joe was there solely to discuss his personal issues.) After announcing our son's presence, Melinda indicated that he had a message for Joe to share with Brandon's parents.

The seemingly odd phrase "hummingbirds and butterflies" meant nothing to Joe but made complete sense to my wife when the information was relayed to her. For weeks Susie had noticed and made mention of a proliferation of hummingbirds and butterflies along the path of her daily morning walks in the desert. More amazingly, while Joe was sharing the message with Susie over the phone, she noted that a hummingbird was actually banging into our rear sliding glass door in an attempt to gain entry at that exact moment. After ten years of living in this home, neither of us had ever before witnessed such an odd event.

As she thought back, Susie recalled another unique incident that had taken place a short time earlier. She was watering plants in our backyard when a hummingbird flew close to her and then drank water directly from the end of the garden hose as she held it.

Another unusual incident came to our attention, resulting from a reading given to a different friend. Impressed with comments I'd shared about my reading with Jamie Clark, my friend Jennifer arranged for a reading with him in January 2005. On my advice, she booked her appointment in a blind fashion—not sharing the fact that I'd referred her. Also, to eliminate questions about process integrity, I avoided all contact with Jamie during this timeframe. I wanted Jennifer to have the most credible and validating experience possible, and I thought that this was the best way to ensure such an outcome. It ultimately wouldn't have mattered if Jamie had known her life story, because most of information he furnished was precognitive in nature. In fact, Jamie's commentary yielded some of the most convincing information I'd yet documented, as it dealt with specific predictions about events that had not yet occurred at the time of the session but later came to pass.

Immediately after her session, Jennifer called me and expressed puzzlement. She said that she was unsure about some of the things Jamie shared and was struggling to make sense out of it all. But several months later, the puzzle pieces started coming together, and she was shocked by the precision of several predictions that came true.

Early in the reading, Jennifer was told that her mom was "touching in." Jamie indicated that her mother had been "sad" and "felt bad about how she left," but "was doing much better now" and "was happier." Unbeknownst to the medium, Jennifer's mom had committed suicide years earlier—an event that left her shaken and uncertain about many things. After this opening statement, Jamie's ensuing predictions and comments were even more startling.

Jamie indicated that all his comments were now coming from Jennifer's mother. He went on to say that he would be sharing specific information to serve as confirmation to Jennifer, so she would know this was really her mother communicating.

"A death or a wedding involving a very close friend will occur on February 21," said Jamie, following with: "I see the letter C, signifying cancer, which will be the cause of death, and her body will be cremated." [At this point in the reading it became clear that the references were pointing to a death rather than a wedding.]

Jamie then shared, "At the funeral service, red roses will be everywhere but you will receive a white rose." He continued, "When you leave the service it will be sunny, but then it will be snowy. Your mom says it will be 'snow-funny,' and there is a duality associated with this."

In recapping the reading again much later, Jennifer told me that her best friend from college, Kathy, had been in a battle with cancer for several years, matching Jamie's observation. She then revealed that Kathy passed away on February 21, 2005, the exact date Jamie had given. Finally, her friend's body was indeed cremated.

Jennifer then described circumstances at Kathy's funeral service, where people were handed red roses as they approached the casket. Red roses were indeed everywhere. But as she stepped up near the coffin, the attendant ran out of red roses so Jennifer was given a white rose, as Jamie had forecast. Then, serving as "icing on the cake" for this bizarre set of circumstantial detail, the weather was sunny when Jennifer left the service, but it started snowing almost immediately thereafter. Jennifer said that the unfolding series of fulfilled prophecies seemed so peculiar that she and her sister actually started laughing at the irony. It really was "snow-funny."

After the service, Jennifer and her family returned to a friend's home and watched a video that I'd sent featuring my father's psychic demonstration on "The Steve Allen Show," filmed in 1970. Jennifer told me, "Between Jamie's predictions coming true and watching your father's video, I found it all oddly comforting. I guess it just felt good to know that there's something more out there."

Jennifer shared some other interesting validations from the reading. Jamie said that Jennifer's mom noted, "There are two sisters and both have 'J' names." Jennifer instantly knew that this was a reference to her sister Julia and herself. Jamie followed with "There's an Iowa and Illinois connection with you, like where you're from." This made perfect sense to Jennifer, seeing that her husband was from Iowa and she was from Illinois.

Reflecting on the information contained in Jennifer's reading made me think about other people I've spoken to, who expressed interest in receiving a reading yet failed to follow through because of fear over being told something bad. In this instance, I would not characterize the information about Jennifer's friend Kathy as negative. Jennifer knew that Kathy's condition was terminal, and hearing these specifics served as a point of comfort, perhaps helping her prepare for the outcome—understanding that there is indeed "something more." I would say that most credible psychic-mediums don't share information that might be considered negative unless they feel that a person can change the outcome. I know that was the case with my father.

So, while it's great that Jamie Clark can deliver this kind of detailed and accurate information, what about the rest of us who aren't as psychically skilled? How do we develop the ability to connect, to whatever degree possible?

Through discussions, reading, contemplation, and practice I've come to recognize the importance of subtle feelings and symbols. By paying attention to subtle energy, typically in the form of thoughts and feelings, we begin to tap into our inner capacity to commune with those we've loved and lost, as well as other streams of consciousness and information. It probably won't come to you like a lightning bolt, but it will be there nonetheless. You can detect these communications by *learning the language* and by paying close attention.

Symbols and feelings are often the language of such transmissions; therefore it is vital that subtle feelings and impressions are recognized and not overlooked. Sometimes information of this type may come to us as an understated thought that could easily be disregarded. The lesson here is to learn to acknowledge the validity of such insights because it is through this process of perceiving and trusting subtle information that the psychic muscle is flexed. As we do this, we come to distinguish the *signature* of spiritual energy. Fear tied to the possibility of being wrong can hinder psychic unfoldment. For your "sixth sense" to develop, you must have confidence in your feelings and be willing to take some risks. Don't be too worried about being right every time or overly concerned about what other people might think.

In a world where our senses are bombarded with electronic media messages, cell phones, mp3 players, loud music, action-packed movies, and traffic jams, what I'm suggesting is easier said than done. These distracting factors magnify our need to set aside quiet time for contemplation and meditation, which I would recommend as a sound course of action for anyone interested in being more attuned to subtle information.

With all this said, I must acknowledge that meditation is tough for someone like me who is naturally hyper; I suspect that I'm not alone in this regard. So I also set aside time for creative activities like writing and music. These artistic diversions aid intuitive development because they tap into the same creative aspect residing within us. Keeping a journal of unique events and information perceived can also be helpful since we are able to reflect on the entries at a later time. Such actions can provide us with encouragement, especially when we recognize our "hits," or predictions recorded that ultimately proved to be accurate.

At this point it seems appropriate to note an amusing incident where I actually followed my own advice. It was a sunny afternoon and I was on a lunch appointment with a client named Kelly and an employee named Marcy. While we were driving back from the restaurant, Marcy began speaking to Kelly about a number of subjects and concluded her commentary by asking, "Isn't that right, Kelly Jo?"

In response Kelly chuckled and said, "No, that isn't it."

Kelly then turned toward me to clarify matters, explaining that Marcy had been trying to guess her middle name for the past two months—without success.

Gazing ahead, I quietly contemplated the question and silently asked myself, "Okay, what's her middle name?" I immediately picked up "Kelly Lynn." I did not hear the word, nor did I see it, I just felt that the name was "Lynn." Rather than second-guess myself as I would have done in the past, I opted to trust my feelings. (I know, it sounds a bit "Obi-Wan Kenobi-ish.")

Without hesitation I said, "Kelly Lynn."

Surprised, Kelly turned to me and said, "You're right—how did you know that? Are you a mind-reader?"

Marcy then facetiously blurted out, "Mark is psychic."

I laughed and told them that I'd just asked for the name in my mind and felt it was Kelly Lynn ... no big deal.

In another amusing case, my wife Susie received a call from someone inviting us to attend a dinner party to honor a mutual friend. In relaying the information, Susie told me that we were going to meet at a restaurant called Richardson's.

Two days later, she reminded me about the dinner.

I responded, "Oh yeah, we're meeting everyone at the Fish Market."

With her eyebrow cocked, Susie came back, "No, the dinner is scheduled for Richardson's, but the Fish Market is the backup spot if Richardson's can't accommodate everyone."

Psychic impressions can also touch on unsettling events and tragedies, leaving the percipient wondering why they experienced such a *knowing*—especially in cases where they are unable to alter the outcome.

Not to be outdone by the portrayal of Allison Dubois in the hit TV series *Medium*, I had a vivid precognitive dream on the night of February 1, 2006, which had a tragic twist. In this dream, I could see that a fire had broken out in a room where men were working, causing them to run out in an effort to escape the raging flames. I couldn't tell where the men were, I didn't know the cause of the fire, and I failed to understand the scope of the incident. All I could see was a door opening and closing as men ran and smoke poured out of the doorway. As I woke the following morning, it was with an extreme sense of anxiety because I really felt this would happen but I didn't know when, where, or how.

About a day later I learned that a ferry tragically sank in the Red Sea, taking down about eight hundred people. Initial accounts indicated that a fire had broken out on the ship before it sank, although it was unknown whether fire played a role in causing the disaster. A later account indicated that a car had erupted in flames, and the fire-fighting effort led to water pooling in the garage, which was a lower level on the ship. The pooling of water on the car-deck caused listing and the ship eventually sank. While I cannot prove that my dream was a precognitive event tied to this specific incident, it seemed too closely related to write off as mere coincidence. What I was supposed to do with this information—if anything—I cannot say.

Despite the examples cited I don't want to overstate matters, because I would still characterize my abilities as "sporadic" at best. What has changed is that I've become more adept at recognizing the *feel* of psychic information and am therefore better equipped to single out some of these subtle impressions.

My son Steven also started having more experiences, pointing to his heightening sense of awareness. In one instance, my intuitive friend Sandy Canales came by our home and put Steven and his friend Stuart through a mini psychic development training session. Sandy devised an exercise in which she gave the boys a sealed manila envelope containing a newspaper section. She then asked them to hold the envelope, close their eyes, and share any impressions that happened to come to mind.

After a few moments, Steven spoke of a vision where he saw a clover leaf and a hood ornament, which he felt belonged to a Buick or Cadillac. Upon opening the envelope, Steven found that one of the articles in his newspaper section had to do with Bishop Thomas O'Brien's hit-and-run accident, which had occurred in Phoenix, Arizona. The clover leaf seemed a pretty clear hit for the name "O'Brien." Also, the Bishop was driving a Buick at the time of the accident.

In another instance a few years back, Steven's former girlfriend told him, "There's a movie I'd like to watch with you."

Without delay or contemplation Steven responded, "Oh, that one with Adam Sandler and Drew Barrymore?"

Startled, she replied, "Yes, I want you to see *Fifty First Dates*. How did you know?" Steven didn't know how he knew—he just knew.

In another instance Steven had a vision where he saw the same girlfriend and her friend being fired. At that time, the young women managed two separate retail stores for the same owner. When they were hired, both had signed employment agreements entitling them to accrued bonus money in the event of their resignation—provided they furnished two weeks' advance written notice. Conversely, if they quit without providing notice, or if they were fired, the two would not receive any bonus money. Following Steven's advice, they both gave two weeks' written notice, which enraged the owner, who was clearly caught off guard.

The owner said to them, "Someone must have told you that you were going to be fired, so I will not accept your resignations. As far as I'm concerned you're already fired."

It was remarkable to see other people experience synchronistic events that tied into our family. In one instance, Steven received an unexpected call from a friend with whom he'd not spoken in a year. This young lady had been reflecting on the past, thinking about Brandon and the pain we had suffered, wondering how our family was doing. For some odd reason at that very moment she felt compelled to turn on the television and went straight to the Discovery Channel. As she tuned in, a preview was airing for the show *One Step Beyond*, featuring my participation in a mediumship experiment that dealt with Brandon's passing. Upon seeing the clip, she immediately called Steven, who then contacted me. Had I not received this call, I would have been unaware that the show was about to air. This program was not widely publicized, and to my knowledge it was only shown once in the Phoenix market.

Not long ago, a good friend from Texas brought his wife and grand-children by our home for a visit. Shortly after their arrival, my friend's wife mentioned that their granddaughter was able to see auras around people.

An aura is said to be the electromagnetic field surrounding an object, which can be seen physically and also sensed psychically; it contains information about the item, person, or thing. An aura is defined as an electro-photonic vibration response of an object to some external excitation, such as an ambient light. Russian scientists have observed the aura phenomenon, referred to as the "Kirlian effect," since the 1930s.[1]

After the topic came up, the little girl—who was about seven years old—noted seeing a green aura around my wife Susie.

It has been suggested that the color of an aura can reveal charac-teristics about the generating source. For example, a green aura may signify healing; yellow can denote optimism, creativity, and intelli-gence; blue often ties to sensitivity, caring, and intuition; red will typi-cally symbolize passion, competition, or anger. A white aura is unique, however, in that it includes all the spectral colors. Some sources indi-cate that a white aura represents "spiritual, etheric and non-physical qualities, transcendent, higher dimensions ... purity and truth; angelic qualities."[2] White spots in an aura and around a person are said by some to be angels.

In a related story, I had an unusual encounter during a lunch meeting with a man named Tim who had served as president at a company where I'd previously worked. I had always held Tim in high regard because of his integrity, sincerity, and dedication. I also saw him as completely grounded and rational but open-minded and willing to consider alternate perspectives. Because of his unbiased nature, I was comfortable sharing a copy of my first manuscript during a lunch meeting. About a week later, I received an unexpected follow-up email from Tim that was quite astonishing.

Tim relayed, "I don't know how to say this, but I need to share something that happened during our lunch. As you were speaking about your father, I saw a white cloud or mist around your head. Then, after about thirty seconds I was *hit* with an audible message that said, 'This is a good man,' in reference to you!"

This was some startling metaphysical feedback coming from such a grounded, intelligent, and pragmatic person—someone who had run a billion-dollar company. It seemed that something highly unusual must have been at work for him to be able to receive and share information from such a transmission. After receiving his email, I called and asked if he had ever experienced anything like this before.

He explained that something vaguely similar had taken place on one other occasion but said, "It was not nearly this strong."

I then responded, "You are obviously clairaudient."*

Tim replied, "Apparently only when I'm around you."

A few weeks later I saw my haircutter, Rick Devine, whom I had known since 1988. Our friendship went beyond hair since Susie had provided daycare for Rick's kids when they were young; Susie and I had come to know his family pretty well. Unfortunately, this appointment proved our final encounter, as Rick succumbed to the ravages of liver disease just two weeks later.

---

* The term clairaudience means "clear hearing" and refers to a person's ability to perceive spirit communication in an auditory way.

During this last visit I recalled something Rick had told me a couple years earlier, regarding his innate ability to see auras around people. I shared with him the story about Tim seeing a white cloud or mist around my head. This sparked a memory for Rick, and he responded with a story of his own.

"I know you are aware that I can see auras, but there's something else I never told you. Several years ago you came in for a haircut and I saw a white aura around you. This was one of only two instances where this ever happened."

When I inquired about the other occurrence, Rick responded, "There was a Native American woman whose hair I cut years ago, and I saw a white aura around her too. After that day she left the country to do humanitarian work in South America and I never saw her again."

I knew that I wasn't like my father, renowned psychic Richard Ireland, but perhaps I was beginning to tap into my own kind of spiritual gift. It all seemed to be about healing and required very little of me personally other than to serve as a medium of compassion, talking with people.

In sharing these stories, I am not suggesting that the white cloud or aura mentioned reflect my spiritual standing or that these phenomena fully relate to me. Rather, I believe that I am being assisted by benevolent energies, in support of the work I'm trying to accomplish. I am a bit player, contributing to something larger than myself—helping to facilitate what seems an important transformative process.

So what does this all mean? What is the significance?

Could it be that Brandon's current realm is the true reality and our physical existence is the illusion? Clearly this notion is not new to Hindus, Buddhists, Jewish Kabbalists, Sufi Muslims, and Gnostic Christians. In saying this, I am not suggesting that our world is unreal but rather that our realm may not be the total or *ultimate* reality. Perhaps this physical world is but the reflection of a deeper existence and a more profound reality.

Beginning to recognize instances of psychic phenomena more commonly in my daily life, as well as in the lives of friends and family, all seemed to be part of living in a more synchronistic way, learning to pay attention to the small and the subtle. Also, as I began speaking to more people about these things, I was pleasantly surprised to find that many were open and interested. And as I came to learn, many were accepting of the stories I shared because they had experienced a personal brush with something you could term "paranormal."

CHAPTER 3

Seeing Things Differently

People can fall into habitual programmed patterns of thinking, underpinned by long-held beliefs and blind acceptance of conventional wisdom. Lying beneath such surface thoughts are mental cues that operate on the subconscious level, compelling people to act in certain ways, yielding conclusions that fit within their pre-existing biases. Many people are unaware that these processes are even occurring.

We live in a world where efficiency and practicality are valued, characterized by words like "analyze," "strategize," and "acquire." Conversely, concepts such as "playful," "wonder," "inspire, "mystical," and "quest" may be viewed as less important—even nonsensical to some. I've seen this manifest in the corporate workplace, where people are sometimes treated like soulless robots. With Machiavellian zeal, an executive at a company where I once worked demanded that a group of talented people increase their level of productivity, while simultaneously stripping away their resources to work with. In a move that was unnecessary, the leader laid off staff and added their workload to the plates of the remaining associates—disregarding employee concerns and suggestions about how to achieve greater efficiencies. During this process the leader never showed any true care or concern for these individuals and ignored their creative ideas and suggestions. Underestimating the importance of the emotional component, the executive ultimately paid the price as the team carried out the leader's plan and it resulted in failure. Had an open and innovative environment been cultivated, giving these people a sense that they were valued—along with greater creative license—the employees would likely have generated results far beyond expectations.

Sacrificed through this submission to convention is the joy associated with creative expression and the expansiveness of mind that arises from deep contemplation—especially as related to the mystery of being.

One example of this is the broad field of psychic phenomena. It is frequently rejected as impossible by individuals as well as mainstream science, with no acknowledgment of any truth in its supporting evidence. This often occurs because of boxed-in thinking that is rooted in a materialistic worldview known as *scientism** which dominates much of our society's vision of progress. People are rarely talked out of something ingrained in their thinking, and logical arguments rarely stand a chance against long-held beliefs. If a person has been taught to believe that certain things are impossible, then he or she usually scoffs at their mention rather than weigh evidence in an unbiased way. As an example, consider comments made by psychologist Donald Hebb after he reviewed convincing evidence for psi from J. B. Rhine's research:

> Why do we not accept ESP as a psychological fact? [Rhine] has offered enough evidence to have convinced us on almost any other issue.... Personally, I do not accept ESP for a moment, because it does not make sense. My external criteria, both of physics and of physiology, say that ESP is not a fact despite the behavioral evidence that has been reported. I cannot see what other basis my colleagues have for rejecting it.... Rhine may still turn out to be right, improbable as I think that is, and *my own rejection of his view is—in the literal sense—prejudice.*[1] [italics added for emphasis]

.* Scientism should not confused with "science" or being "scientific." It is more like a religion, albeit an atheistic one, that presupposes certain dogmatic tenets and then treats them like facts. Subscribers to scientism work to protect their doctrines, refusing to consider new or different ideas that conflict with their cherished assumptions. They also want you to believe that they alone represent science and the scientific community.

But some very smart people are now acknowledging the value of a more holistic view encompassing the mind and spirit, as well as the physical body. The average person may be unaware of such new perspectives and the science supporting them that unveil a strikingly new view of the nature of reality and how mind, in fact, can affect matter. Scientist and author Gregg Braden refers to a "field of intelligent energy" that occupies what was previously thought to be the void of empty space—referred to as the "zero-point field" in quantum mechanics—which has been discovered to teem with energy.

Braden notes that this energy "… responds to us—it rearranges itself—in the presence of our heart-based feelings and beliefs…. The revolution is akin to a huge earthquake that registers 'off the scale'— while leveling some of the most sacred beliefs of science."[2]

In alignment with Braden's observations, there are certain "givens" that people have taken as fact which are now being proven incorrect. This applies to assumptions made about the nature of reality based solely on sensory information. People can become conditioned to accept their perceived reality (i.e., the observable physical world) as the totality of what is *real*. But these assessments are based on perceptions derived from physical senses that have inherent limitations and have proven unreliable at times. This is one reason why pilots are trained to fly by instruments rather than by trusting visual cues—their senses can betray them, and sole reliance on physical sight can lead to a crash. Or consider that when you watch a film with 3-D glasses you perceive that you're seeing three-dimensional objects, when you are in fact looking at light being projected onto a two-dimensional screen. People can experience a variety of optical illusions where their perception differs from objective reality—as demonstrated in the following example. In this illustration most people perceive square "A" and square "B" as being two different shades of gray; however, they are in fact the same shade.[3]

If you are baffled by this diagram and don't see how "A" and "B" can be the same shade, I assure you it is so. If you printed and cut out these two squares, laying them side by side you would see it. Or if you covered every part of the diagram except for the two squares in question it would become apparent. The dark squares adjacent to "B," beneath the shadow cast by the cylinder, are actually darker than the dark squares on the periphery. The contrast between the very dark squares and "B," combined with the apparent shadow, tricks your eyes into seeing "A" and "B" as different shades of gray. What we think we perceive isn't always the way things really are.

We are surrounded by energy and forces that are imperceptible to our five physical senses—from radio waves to ultra-violet light—yet we know these things exist. Might there be other types of energy? Could they be so subtle as to be undetectable by our most advanced technological devices yet occasionally register with an intuitive capacity within us?

From where does consciousness arise and from where do things like inspiration and genius emerge? Are we just matter bodies, with all our thoughts, feelings, and emotions merely the firing of neurons in our brain? In their book *The Soul Hypothesis*, Mark C. Baker, Professor of Linguistics and Cognitive Science at Rutgers University, and Stewart Goetz, Professor of Philosophy and Religion at Ursinus College, submit, "Mental life will never be fully reducible to the actions of neurons and synapses. Something will always be left out."[4]

My father's most gratifying reward was opening people's minds to possibilities greater than they'd previously imagined. He told people that they were also capable of perceiving a reality extending beyond the range of the physical senses. During the latter part of the 1960s and into the early 1970s, my father conducted psychic development workshops across the United States that served as the basis for his book, *Your Psychic Potential: A Guide to Psychic Development.*

Perhaps the day will come when Western science is able to confirm the existence of immaterial forces and realms. Compelling research in the field of parapsychology indirectly points to this possibility, yet most people in mainstream science can't bring themselves to consider the implications. Traditional science insists on identifying the "mechanism" that might explain the workings of psi and other phenomena considered "paranormal." Without a material mechanism, psi phenomena and mediumship won't be taken seriously. Worse yet, research won't take place—at least not in any substantial way. Perhaps we would find more answers if we started with the right questions.

At various periods throughout history, scientific advances have presented new truths that flew in the face of conventional wisdom. Unfortunately, those making these key discoveries usually found themselves fighting grueling battles to gain serious consideration for their ideas. In the 1500s Nicholas Copernicus put forth the heliocentric model for the universe, placing the Sun at the center of the solar system rather than the Earth. Less than a century later Galileo Galilei, "the father of modern observational astronomy," proved Copernicus correct—to the dismay of the church. Albert Einstein's theory of relativity was initially dismissed by the scientific community because it challenged the framework of existing thinking. His concepts did not fit within the paradigm of the day, and his assertions contradicted the accepted constructs about the architecture of the universe. Einstein was throwing darts at the Holy Grail of science by questioning the unquestionable, threatening a platform then viewed as a basis of "fact."

Since that time, we have learned that many of these "facts" were no more than widely accepted assumptions.

Now, because of newer findings, even Einstein's Theory of Relativity has come into question. Within the field of quantum physics an odd feature called "entanglement" has been validated, which is forcing scientists to consider the possibility that Einstein's hypothesis may have been incorrect or at least incomplete. Entanglement states that two particles that have become linked in a special way can be separated to any distance—even to opposite ends of the universe—and a change in one particle will be immediately reflected in the other. Entanglement seems at odds with an aspect of Einstein's special relativity, which states that nothing can travel faster than the speed of light. Even though light travels at an astounding 186,000 miles per second, the physical universe is so immense that it would still take about 15 billion years to traverse the entire distance at this rate of speed. Entanglement also seems to imply a universe that is highly interconnected rather than comprised of a multitude of disparate parts.

This ongoing churning of ideas and theories reinforces an important point. We simply do not understand the full scope of the universe and life. To learn and progress, we must encourage unconventional thinking and challenge existing standards.

Some scientists and scientific communities point to assumptions as if they were fact. This requires any new theories to fit within their limited schema. Sadly, this practice discourages people from conducting a sincere and open search for the truth in unsanctioned areas, resulting in a perpetuation of convention and a diminished number of significant discoveries.

The human desire for certainty is so strong that we will take any action necessary to protect our worldview. This proclivity has reared its ugly head in most human endeavors: science, religion, and even business. We prefer the comfort and predictability of a universe that we think we understand.

At this point, readers who are not interested in science or are already comfortable with psychic phenomena and mediumship may choose to skip ahead to chapter 4. But if you'd like some more thoughts on how modern Western culture has limited our spiritual understanding, read on.

Returning to my earlier point about individual perceptions of reality, I now turn to a scientific discipline that offers more questions than answers: quantum mechanics. Thanks to modern physical science, we know that the "stuff" of the material world is nothing but energy in vibration manifesting as the physical objects we observe. Einstein demonstrated that matter and energy are interchangeable ($E=MC^2$), therefore we know that items that appear solid are essentially the same as light or electricity.

In my eighth-grade science class I learned that matter could appear as a solid, a liquid, or a gas. I was also told that the underlying components of matter could be examined with powerful instruments like the electron microscope. My teacher talked about the cellular level, the molecular level underneath, and the atomic level underneath that. My textbook featured a diagram of an atom with a solid core, surrounded by series of streaking, orbiting electrons that resembled a miniature solar system.

In recent years I was surprised to discover that my eighth-grade teacher omitted some important facts about this subject. Perhaps she was unaware of them. For one thing, atoms are not compact at all. They are actually 99.99999 percent empty space.[5] As difficult as it may be to conceive, the things we see and touch in this world are physically more "nothing" than "something."

Nor are atoms the smallest units of matter. Atoms are made from subatomic particles such as protons, neutrons, and electrons, which themselves are comprised of even smaller particles such as quarks and neutrinos, down to a level where you really can't even call the constituents particles anymore. And at this level such particles can also manifest in wave form in seemingly interchangeable fashion in a phenomenon known as "wave-particle duality." This is where you and

I come into the equation, because the physical system will manifest as one or the other (a wave or particle) only when observed. This is called the "observer effect" and seems to have strong implications in the "mind vs. matter" debate.

String theory attempts to bridge classical physics, which deals in the realm of large objects, and quantum physics, which addresses the realm of the very small. String theory suggests that tiny vibrating strings of energy infinitesimally smaller than subatomic particles are the basis for everything that exists in the universe. The resulting manifestation of any physical object is said to be dependent on the vibratory rate and shape of the underlying energy strings. Mysteriously, this explanation bears a great similarity to information conveyed by wisdom teachers throughout the ages who have used the term "vibration" when speaking about the matrix of the universe, the fabric of reality, and the essence of being. Some, like the Buddha, also alluded to the transitory and illusory nature of physical reality, which seems to aptly describe our world when considered from the quantum realm up. Is it possible that these wise sages have been clued into the true nature of the universe all along, through intuitive rather than analytical means? If we are all universally connected through an underlying matrix, as I suspect is the case, then it follows that sensitive individuals would be aware of this knowledge through subtle means.

After discovering this information, I suddenly perceived the foundation of "the real world" more like a flashy, unstable façade than a solid, tangible "something" or "someplace." Through quantum physics it has also been demonstrated that the universe is not comprised of a multitude of disconnected objects. Instead, it has been revealed that there are underlying processes at the quantum level that play a role in how the physical universe manifests on the macro scale. We play an integral part in this progression.

While it may be difficult for some to accept, science has proven that the "observer" (you or me) assumes a role in bringing the physical universe—an observable state that we call physical reality—into being. As a result of our observation, underlying subatomic components (electrons) move from a state of potentiality into fixed positions, producing the everyday objects we observe and our perceived reality. Could it be that reality is a subjective rather than an objective phenomenon?

Ultimately the seemingly solid objects we see are made of the same stuff as a photon of light, a radio wave, or a thought. All are forms of energy manifested in different ways. I would offer that the same may be true with other forms of energy tied to unseen realms. Electrons appear and then disappear at times, but no one knows where they go when they are not here.

Perhaps people are mistaken when they look out at the physical world and assume that they perceive the full depth of reality with a high degree of accuracy. Instead we are utilizing our senses to capture a narrow bandwidth of information that our brain deciphers to create an interpreted reality.

There is a quote, widely attributed to Einstein, that states, "It is entirely possible that behind the perception of our senses, worlds are hidden of which we are unaware." Whether those were in fact Einstein's words I cannot say, but I resonate with the sentiment and with the possibility open, it's not too difficult to imagine other realms of existence where the deceased may flourish with their consciousness untouched by the process of physical death.

In his book *Phantom Walls*, Sir Oliver Lodge—a physicist, writer, and one-time president of the Society for Psychical Research—writes:

> The marvel is that we are associated with matter at all … I used to say that death was an adventure to which we might look forward. So it is; but I believe that really and truly it is earth-life that is the adventure. It is this earth-life that has been the strange and exceptional thing. The wonder is that we ever succeeded in entering a matter body at all. Many fail.[6]

In 2007 Dr. Robert Lanza, Chief Scientific Officer at Advanced Cell Technology and Adjunct Professor at Wake Forest University School of Medicine, authored a theory called "Biocentrism" which challenges the existing paradigm accepted by most in science and academia today. According to *U.S. News and World Report*, Lanza's "mentors described him as a 'genius,' a 'renegade' thinker, even likening him to Einstein."[7]

Biocentrism calls out flaws in the existing model, offering a new way to view consciousness and reality. In a 2010 radio interview Lanza noted, "Space and time are not external things." Rather, he indicated that "the mind—through the process of observation—brings space and time into being."[8]

Speaking to the possibility of other dimensional realities and an afterlife, Lanza said,

> According to the "many-worlds" interpretation of quantum physics, there are an infinite number of universes—known as the multiverse—associated with each possible observation. Biocentrism extends this idea, suggesting that life has a non-linear dimensionality that encompasses the multiverse. Experiments show that measurements an observer makes can even influence events that have already happened in the past.[9]

On his website Lanza offers the following:

> Life is an unfolding adventure that really transcends our linear way of thinking ... although our bodies self-destruct, that "me" feeling is just energy that operates in the brain. And we know that energy doesn't go away at death. One of the surest principles of science is that energy never dies—it can never be created or destroyed. Life has this non-linear dimensionality that transcends any individual history or universe. It's sort of like a perennial flower that returns to bloom in the multiverse. Death doesn't really exist in a timeless, space-less world.[10]

Psi and mediumship research, near-death-experience cases, and other unusual phenomena point to the possibility that mind or consciousness is primary. Our self-awareness is more than the mere byproduct of brain function. There is evidence suggesting that other realms exist where the consciousness of previously living individuals now thrives.

In his book *The Psychic Yellow Pages*, renowned paranormal researcher and author Dr. Hans Holzer reports:

> The gift of being a psychic "reader," a medium, a clairvoyant depends on a force within that person that Professor Joseph Rhine of Duke University called extra-sensory perception or ESP for short. Some people possess more of this energy force, some less, but it is neither miraculous nor "supernatural" in nature; it is merely puzzling to those who cling to the belief in a universe that can be perceived only by using the ordinary five senses.[11]

Speaking about his own psychic function, my father mentioned listening to "the small still voice within." This statement implies the existence of an inner capacity possessed by each of us in varying degrees that can be utilized to access information without the use of physical senses. Might this faculty reveal something about who or what we really are at a deeper level? Is this how we access our *true self*—the essential spiritual aspect of us beyond the physical body we now inhabit?

There is actually a massive body of information supporting the reality of these phenomena, derived from serious scientific studies conducted since the late 1800s. Despite all this data, the skeptic mantra remains "One hundred years of nothing," speaking to their ignorance, or irrational denial, of evidence derived through experiments conducted during that timeframe. H. H. Price, a philosopher known for his work on perception and parapsychology, once said, "The greatest skeptic concerning paranormal phenomena is invariably the man who knows the least about them."[12]

The pervasive materialist worldview severely curtails current research into these areas of exploration. Sadly, there is but a handful of scientists doing research on paranormal topics today because funding is hard to secure and such work can result in ridicule from colleagues and what essentially amounts to career suicide.

Early work in the paranormal field was conducted by the Society for Psychical Research, commonly known as the SPR. Published records about the origins and mission of this organization state, "The SPR, the first learned society of its kind, was founded in London in 1882 for the purpose of investigating 'that large body of debatable phenomena designated by such terms as mesmeric, psychical and spiritualistic,' and to do so 'in the same spirit of exact and unimpassioned enquiry which has enabled Science to solve so many problems'."[13]

The SPR's first president was Henry Sidgwick, Professor of Moral Philosophy at Cambridge University. SPR records indicate that Sidgwick's initial colleagues included Frederic Myers, "a classical scholar but also a man of lively and wide-ranging interests," and Edmund Gurney, primary author of the psychical research classic, *Phantasms of the Living*.[14]

In entering this area of research, SPR members quickly learned to identify fraudulent mediums—separating true anomalies from cases of deception. Referring to this issue and the work of their founders, the SPR now states, "With their scientific ideals and experience in investigating paranormal claims, they were fully aware of the tricks, the illusions, and the dangers of wishful thinking."[15]

In their early days, the SPR began collaborating with foreign scientists like William James, frequently referred to as "the Father of American Psychology." James was a progressive thinker who taught at Harvard until his retirement in 1907. He studied and wrote about diverse topics ranging from human emotions to religion and spiritualism. James also conducted a number of experiments with renowned American medium Leonora Piper. In an article appearing in a 1909 issue of *Science*, James said of his work with Piper, "In the trances of this medium, I cannot resist the conviction that knowledge appears which she has never gained by the ordinary waking use of her eyes and ears and wits."[16]

James later published the book *Expériences d'un Psychiste*, providing a more extensive account of the many experiments he conducted with Miss Piper. The work with Piper and more specifically the "cross-correspondence experiments" yielded what some consider the most compelling evidence for life after death or for telepathy. Piper's abilities were studied as well by other prominent scientists including Gardner Murphy, James Hyslop, Sir Oliver Lodge, and Dr. Richard Hodgson, the latter an avowed skeptic. By virtue of the overwhelming evidence Piper furnished, these scientists came to believe in life after death.

In her study of Piper's abilities, Eleanor Sidgwick, a proponent of higher education for women, former Principal of Newnham College, and one-time President of the SPR, wrote, "Veridical communications are received, some of which, there is good reason to believe, come from the dead, and therefore imply a genuine communicator in the background."[17]

"Cross-correspondence" cases yield some of the best evidence that mediumship is facilitated by communication with discarnate spirits rather than through telepathy with a living person. Such cases involve the receipt of multiple fragmentary communications, typically from several mediums located in different areas, that make no sense independently but which collectively fit together like puzzle pieces to convey a meaningful message. These communications are usually unsolicited and unexpected, and therefore appear to be directed by an independent intelligence. The first recorded case appeared in spontaneous fashion—ostensibly designed by the deceased Frederic Meyers, a founding member of the SPR, to eliminate the telepathy theory from consideration in such communications. This took place in 1901, a few weeks after Meyers's death. In this instance the cross-correspondence was detected by SPR research officer Alice Johnson.

The case involved multiple mediums located in various places across the globe, receiving information at roughly the same time. After the mediums recorded their impressions, the entries were examined. They initially appeared fragmentary and meaningless until brought together and examined as a whole. The seemingly incomplete messages formed cogent ideas that implied engagement with an external intelligence. As reported in the Sir Oliver Lodge classic, *The Survival of Man: A Study in Unrecognized Human Faculty*, Alice Johnson of the SPR said in reference to messages originating from two of the participating mediums,

> Mrs. Forbes' script, purporting to come from her son, Talbot, stated that he must now leave her since he was looking for a sensitive who wrote automatically in order that he might obtain corroboration of her own writing. Mrs. Verrall, on the same day, wrote of a fir-tree planted in a garden and the script was signed with a sword and a suspended bugle. The latter was part of the badge of the regiment to which Talbot Forbes had belonged and Mrs. Forbes had in her garden some fir-trees, grown from seed sent to her by her son. These facts were unknown to Mrs. Verrall.[18]

Summarizing her view of this and other cross-correspondence evidence, Johnson said,

> We have reason to believe that the idea of making a statement in one script complementary of a statement in another had not occurred to Mr. Myers in his lifetime—for there is no reference to it in any of his written utterances on the subject that I have been able to discover. Neither did those who have been investigating automatic script since his death invent this plan, if plan it be. It was not the automatists themselves that detected it but a student of their scripts; it has every appearance of being an element imported from outside; it suggests an independent invention, an active intelligence constantly at work in the present, not a mere echo or remnant of individualities of the past.[19]

Speaking to the significance of the cross-correspondence experiments, British researcher Montague Keen reported,

All serious psychical researchers are aware that the most formidable body of evidence for discarnate communication resides in the cross-correspondences. These began shortly after the death in 1901 of Frederic Myers, one of the principal founders of psychical research in the UK. The aim appeared to be an attempt by ostensibly discarnate intelligences, whose identities were apparent from the scripts, to defeat the theory that information conveyed could be attributed to the exercise of paranormal faculties of a single medium.[20]

By the early 1930s, J. B. Rhine's parapsychology testing laboratory at Duke University was getting the most attention in the field of psychical research. In the early stages of his work, Rhine's primary area of interest was investigating evidence for consciousness survival after death, but he soon realized that this was too controversial a subject to tackle—and that he would struggle for support within the scientific community. Rhine is said to have "concluded in the end that anecdotal research on postmortem survival would always be open to scientific challenge and ambiguity."[21]

Rhine then shifted his focus to exploring the potential for ESP and psychokinesis (the ability of mind to influence physical objects) in controlled laboratory experiments. Starting with telepathy experiments, Rhine utilized Zener cards—a special deck containing five different design symbols, with five cards of each design. The idea was that a "sender" would view a card and then try to telepathically send the image to a "receiver," while the two were physically separated. Since there were five "suits" and twenty-five cards in a deck, the receiver's correct identification of five cards would represent chance results.

Rhine's most successful endeavor in studying telepathy was undoubtedly the "Pearce-Pratt" telepathy experiments, using the protocol noted above, which generated positive results that were 22 billion to one odds against chance. Perhaps the most impressive single aspect of this series of experiments was that on one occasion Pearce had twenty-five consecutive hits.[22]

During his forty years at Duke, Rhine's research established significant statistical evidence for the existence of ESP in its various forms. At the same time, the strict focus on ESP and psychokinesis contributed to survival research being back-burnered.

More recently, other researchers have focused on answering the most basic question about mediumship. Tricia J. Robertson and Professor Archie Roy[23] conducted a series of unique experiments, three of which were reported in the peer-reviewed *Journal of the Society for Psychical Research* (JSPR). This particular research took place over a five-year period.

The initial experiment was designed to test the hypothesis, "All statements made by mediums are so general that they could apply to anyone." Yes, this was the actual hypothesis—it was literally an attempt to see if the results would warrant any future assessment. The results were very encouraging—in fact, millions to one against chance—so with this initial effort under their belt, Roy and Robertson were motivated to take a deeper dive.

A strict protocol was developed for their next round of experiments. Among key restrictions, the mediums and sitters were physically separated prior to the experiment. In this process, one researcher remained with the medium while the other stayed with the audience of forty "sitters" in another room.

A few weeks prior to the experiment, one of the researchers selected certain numbers to be randomly placed on seats that would identify the people who should receive a reading. The scientists did not intend for any particular person to receive a reading. Rather, whoever happened to assume a seat with a number became an intended recipient.

Before the sitters were admitted into the room where the experiment was to take place, one researcher randomly numbered the seats. The seating arrangement was then recorded on a piece of paper and sealed in an envelope to ensure that the researcher could not be accused of altering seat numbers after the process had concluded.

When entering the room, sitters were handed random cards with numbers written on them indicating their seat. The researcher who numbered the chairs was not the same one handing out numbered seat assignments as people entered the room.

After everyone was seated, one researcher tapped on the door of the adjacent room to cue the medium to begin making statements. Communication was facilitated via a microphone that piped the medium's voice into the sitters' room. During this process the mediums received no feedback and were simply required to share any impressions they might receive. This was the protocol for multiple experiments of this type. There were typically six such readings conducted in a normal experiment, per medium, who was encouraged to make no more than thirty statements for each reading. Representative statements included things like names, physical details, professions, etc.

When all six readings were finished, the researchers made copies of the medium's statements and distributed them to the sitters. All attendees were then instructed to grade each reading as if it were intended for them. In this process sitters were to assess the accuracy of each statement made, as either applicable or not applicable to them.

When the sitters completed the task of grading papers, the researcher, who had not numbered the seats, collected them and subsequently checked to determine the specificity of each statement. The researcher who had numbered the seats was not allowed to handle the papers until the other researcher had completed the initial reduction of the data, a process that could take many hours. The first statement might apply to twenty of the forty sitters, while the second statement might apply to only one person in attendance, and so on. These statements were graded by specificity by a tick for correct and no tick for incorrect, those applicable to a single sitter were deemed highly specific, while those applicable to twenty sitters were highly general. Robertson mentioned an example of a correct and highly specific statement made by medium Gordon Smith during the research experiment: "The intended recipient of this message lives at Christmas Cottage."

When a session had been completed and after the data had been initially reduced by the researcher who did not know the intended target seats, the researchers met and exchanged data to get the full picture.

One would receive a copy of the seat numbers, and the other would receive a copy of the results, so it would become clear if the intended seat numbers had shown the greatest relevance in the reading.

The following key points related to the controls:

- No one could know who the intended recipients of any message would be.

- The researcher who reduced the initial data did not know who the recipient was.

- The medium could not see, hear, or read body-language response from a sitter.

- The medium did not know anything about the sitters including gender.

Despite these controls, including up to triple-blind protocols—meaning that there were three levels of separation between medium and sitter—the researchers found that accurate, specific information was delivered to the intended recipients at disproportionately high rates when compared with other sitters.

After five years of experiments, Robertson and Roy concluded that when good mediums are used, the aforementioned hypothesis is proven false.[24]

Another researcher, Dr. Julie Beischel, directs the Windbridge Institute in Tucson, Arizona, a private research organization that tests mediums under controlled conditions. Through her work, Dr. Beischel has validated the Institute's primary hypothesis that qualified mediums are able to report accurate, specific information about deceased people—tied to a living sitter—without any advance knowledge about either party and no sensory feedback.[25]

In 2007, I was privileged to serve as a sitter in a multiple-blind mediumship experiment conducted by Dr. Emily Kelly of the University of Virginia's Division of Perceptual Studies. Experimental protocols required mediums to furnish readings to proxy sitters—people who assumed the place of the actual sitters during the sessions, providing an additional level of control. None of the sitters knew the identities of any mediums nor did we know any of the other participants.

During the readings, which were conducted by phone, the proxy sitter recorded medium statements and then transcribed them. After the readings concluded, written transcriptions were distributed to each of the participating sitters. At this point the other sitters and I were instructed to grade the papers for accuracy. We measured the applicability of each statement to our intended deceased loved one on a point-by-point basis. I was given six readings to analyze—one intended for me and five intended for others. Through this process I arrived at an overall grade for each reading, ranking them from most accurate to least accurate. I presume that the process was identical for the other sitters.

Dr. Kelly did not explain her overall methodology to me, but I assume there were likely thirty or more readings conducted, broken into five groups of six, or something along those lines. If that was the case, a chance result would have five of the thirty readings being correctly identified by sitters as belonging to them. Anything more—ten or fifteen correctly identified readings—would indicate a statistically significant result. Dr. Kelly may have established a deeper level of statistical analysis, including a measurement for readings rated below number one.

I do not know the specific outcomes of this experiment, and I am not at liberty to share any specific information about my reading or rating process since Dr. Kelly is presently pursuing publication of an article in a science journal. But I can tell you that she was enthusiastic about the results and referred to them as "embarrassingly good." I took this to mean that the experiment generated results far exceeding chance.

Unfortunately, the handful of bold researchers like Dr. Kelly who conduct such experiments with stringent controls encounter great difficulty in getting their work published in science journals, especially when the results are positive. I am hoping that she will succeed in this endeavor.

Does good mediumship prove survival? For those aware of the compelling evidence for psychic phenomena and mediumship—satisfied with the reality of their existence—one question remains, dating back to the Society for Psychical Research's earliest investigations more than a century ago. Presupposing that mediums operating under controlled conditions are able to provide relevant and specific information about deceased persons, this query focuses on the underlying question of how such phenomena occur.

Most mediums, the majority of people who consult mediums, and some researchers subscribe to the "survival" hypothesis. This theory, also referred to as "survival of consciousness," implies that information furnished by mediums comes from deceased persons communicating from some adjacent realm of existence. Further, it is asserted that these communications are usually conveyed telepathically.

There are other hypotheses that endeavor to explain how mediums do what they do, each offering vastly different explanations. Before delving into these alternative models, let's start by exploring the various forms of psychic phenomena—the ways people access information without utilizing their five physical senses.

Because parapsychologists observe so many different types of psychic phenomena, they have devised descriptive categories based on certain characteristics. Within the branch called "mental phenomena" (as opposed to "physical phenomena"—dealing with manifestation of things like "independent voice" and materialization, which won't be addressed here), five categorical definitions have been established:

- **Clairvoyance:** "Clear-seeing"—to see beyond the limits of time and space, past and future.

- **Clairaudience:** "Clear-hearing"—auditory reception of information, often voices.

- **Clairsentience:** "Clear-sensing"—perception of information through smell or feelings.

- **Telepathy:** Thought transfer between two minds.
- **Psychometry:** The ability to read energy/information emanating from physical objects.

Because no one knows the *modus operandi* for these phenomena, it cannot be established whether some forms of psi may be facilitated by spirit communication. So with these issues in mind, following are some alternate theories that attempt to explain how certain mediums are able to provide accurate and meaningful information about discarnate individuals.

Proponents of a model often termed "Super-psi" presuppose that mediums are actually talented psychics who utilize a sort of *supercharged* psi ability—presumably leveraging any of the aforementioned faculties, allowing them to access any information anywhere, anytime. Expanding on this, the previously mentioned Tricia Robertson of the SSPR explained to me, "Super-psi, according to its supporters, allows a person to access every book, human thought, every journal, etc., everywhere in the world. It has no limitations, as anything can be accessed." She went on to say, "Super-psi cannot be seriously considered a scientific theory, as any theory must have boundaries that can be tested. Super-psi has no boundaries and no explanation."[26]

So while this model has adherents, it may never be proven. By the same token, it may never be disproven until an alternate theory is accepted that renders Super-psi infeasible.

Another hypothesis, referred to as the "archive theory" suggests that mediums tap into a sort of universal database or energy field. This cosmic storehouse of information, akin to the Akashic field referenced in Eastern traditions (and in the work of "The Sleeping Prophet," Edgar Cayce), can be thought of as "God's memory." This schema suggests that a medium tunes into a subject—be it a question, a person, a place, an object, or something else—then culls pertinent information from the aforementioned non-physical database.

In such a scenario, one might envision a medium conducting a reading for a bereaved person who wishes to hear from a deceased loved one. Let's assume that the medium has a striking number of hits and the sitter is pleased with the quality of information shared. In this situation, the archive-theory proponent would argue that the medium has tapped into the universal database or energy field and is simply reporting on information contained there.

Another argument asserts that mediums use telepathy to read the mind of the sitter and then report back pertinent information. One might assume that addressing this concern would be as simple as separating the medium and the sitter, but telepathy cannot be eliminated as an explanation even in controlled readings where the sitter and medium have no direct contact. This is because telepathy's boundaries are not known, and distance does not appear to be a limiting factor (as with entanglement). But such controls are useful in removing normal sensory information, thereby eliminating other explanations such as "cold reading," the term for a process whereby body language and other cues taken from the sitter are interpreted, and then guesses are made and subsequently modified based on sitter reactions. The practice of separating medium and sitter by two or more levels is commonplace among today's researchers at the Windbridge Institute, the SSPR, and the University of Virginia's Division of Perceptual Studies.

Speaking about the viability of telepathy as an explanation for the aptitude of talented mediums, Tricia Robertson of the SSPR notes, "Telepathy does not cut it ... although telepathy exists. It is a very weak faculty between living persons."[27]

Let's now return to the survival hypothesis—the theory that mediums are able to obtain relevant information via communication with discarnate persons. One such case involves George Pellew, a Harvard graduate, writer, and journalist who had worked for the *Boston Journal*. Four years prior to his death (caused by a fall down a flight of stairs), Pellew moved to New York City and joined the ASPR (American Society of Psychical Research). Subsequent to joining the ASPR, out of what appeared to be intellectual curiosity, Pellew met Dr. Richard Hodgson, who had been studying the medium Leonora Piper. As Michael Tymn noted in a 2013 article, Hodgson had "… gained a reputation as a debunker of fake mediums, [and] was hired to manage the affairs of the ASPR and especially to further investigate Mrs. Piper."[28]

Through the course of his investigations, Hodgson came to the conclusion that Piper's abilities were legitimate; however, he did not understand the mechanism behind them. At about the same time, Hodgson and Pellew had several discussions about the possibility of life after death. Despite his incredulous attitude toward the subject, Pellew was sufficiently open-minded to agree to attempt making contact with Hodgson if should he die first and find himself "still existing."

About a month after Pellew's death, Hodgson brought some of the deceased man's friends to Piper for a sitting. Convincing communications ensued immediately—initially through Piper's "control" and then directly from Pellew, who assumed full control of the medium. Highly specific information was provided that could not have been researched and which was pertinent to the sitters. This sort of information, supplemented by the fullness of personality, assured the sitters that they were indeed communicating with Pellew.

But what makes this case so strong in supporting survival is that Hodgson conducted many such sittings over an extended period of time, and Pellew, communicating through Piper, only recognized and acknowledged those sitters whom he had known during his physical life.

Michael Tymn writes:

> Hodgson noted that during the time Pellew communicated, he brought 150 sitters, 30 of whom were known to Pellew when he was alive. In each case, Pellew greeted them by name. The non-recognition of the other 120 was contrary to the telepathic and cosmic soul theories. That is if Mrs. Piper's secondary personality [the control] had been reading minds or searching in some cosmic computer, she/he would have known the names of all of them.[29]

Some of the most compelling evidence for the survival hypothesis comes from what are referred to as "cross-correspondence" experiments, which I touched on earlier in this chapter. Early cases of this type, documented by the SPR, involved messages from multiple mediums situated in various locations. Each medium received fragmentary information including drawings, sentences, geometric designs, and even Chinese characters, which were immediately corroborated by phone and telegraph. This enabled the message to be deciphered by joining the fragments into a whole. Individually the messages seemed meaningless but when combined, a mosaic effect became apparent and a complete meaning was revealed. The complexity and elaborate nature of these experiments suggested that information conveyed to the mediums had been disseminated as the product of intention from an intelligent source.

One of the most exceptional cross-correspondence cases ever documented involves apparent transmissions from SPR researcher F. W. Myers to different mediums shortly after his death. Renowned authority Montague Keen explains:

> Following Myers' death in 1901, a voice claiming to be his spirit communicated through the entranced medium [Leonora Piper] who was undergoing rigorous investigation by George Dorr in Boston. Aware that Myers had been a distinguished classical scholar, whereas Mrs. Piper was not, Dorr invited "Myers" to say what the word *lethe* conveyed to him. A considerable number of references emerged. Many were unknown to Dorr, whose classical knowledge was modest, but investigation showed that nearly all of them were accurate, if usually oblique, references to persons, incidents, descriptions, and places found in Ovid's *Metamorphoses* which gives an account of the mythological Hadean stream of Lethe bounding the shores of the Elysian fields and from whose waters the newly dead must drink to purify themselves and wash away all earthly memories before re-birth.[30]

When Sir Oliver Lodge learned of this, he decided to pose the same question through another medium known as Mrs. Willett, with whom he was having sittings in London. She was a very intelligent, well-educated woman but had not pursued classical knowledge. She was also Myers's sister-in-law, and she too had been transmitting messages purporting to come from him. In response to the same question, she communicated a long series of references, many of them unknown to Lodge or his fellow classicists Piddington and Mrs. Verrall, the latter being a University classics lecturer. Virtually all of these were found to derive not from Ovid but from an entirely different account connected with Aeneas's visit to Elysium with Anchisis, his father, as described in Book Six of Virgil's *Aeneid*, on which Myers had once written a scholarly commentary. The references were equally accurate although many were clearly allusive and some were linked to the Ovidian messages received three thousand miles away via Mrs. Piper. When Lodge asked why "Myers" had not given the same responses, Mrs. Willett's automatic writing replied that, had he done so, critics would have dismissed the evidence as mere telepathy between the mediums.[31]

There are other occurrences similar to cross-correspondence, involving what are called "drop-in" personalities. In such cases, the medium connects with a discarnate that is unknown to the sitter, and the information relayed seems meaningless. However, that information is later validated as accurate and meaningful to a party not present at the reading (but who is apparently known to the discarnate). Cases of this sort eliminate sitter telepathy as a possibility and also render super-psi a highly unlikely explanation, pointing instead to the conscious intent of some intelligence.

As noted earlier, Dr. Julie Beischel, Director of the Windbridge Institute, studies mediums under controlled conditions, using experiments up to quintuple-blind in format. As part of her study, Dr. Beischel has sought to understand what mediums experience while doing their work, and she has uncovered an interesting dichotomy between the psychic experience and the mediumship experience. In an interview with the popular *Daily Grail* online magazine, Beischel reported:

... because the proof-focused research [a triple-blind study published in a journal] cannot differentiate between survival and psi, we are also engaged in process-focused research in which we are examining the mediums' experiences during mediumship readings compared to psychic readings for the living in which telepathy, clairvoyance, and/or precognition are used. Our Windbridge Certified Research Mediums (WCRMs) perform psychic readings for clients as well as mediumship readings and, when asked, report being able to clearly distinguish between the two experiences. My favorite quote about this from a WCRM is "a psychic reading is like reading a book ... a mediumship reading is like seeing a play." Dr. Adam Rock and I have published both qualitative and quantitative studies in this area and are currently attempting to find support for the next step: a blinded, quantitative study of mediums' experiences during the two types of readings.[32]

At a seminar I attended in 2009, Dr. Beischel reported that mediums often feel the presence of others during mediumship readings. The mediums also report sensing a loss of volition, as if another personality assumes some measure of control over their thoughts and feelings. These experiences stand in stark contrast to what mediums report during standard psychic readings, which are typically far less emotional.

Another consideration is that the personality, mannerisms, and sense of humor of the deceased person often come through in readings. This phenomenon takes things to a more personal and subjective level—going beyond the mere reiteration of data. I've experienced this in numerous sessions with top mediums where my father's personality was clearly evident in the communication.

Most touching, though, was an occasion when medium Tina Powers spoke to me in the exact style and intonation as my deceased son, Brandon. The words chosen and the manner in which they were delivered precisely mirrored my son's mode of conversation. While speaking in a "channeled" sort of way, Tina addressed a difficult working relationship I'd experienced with another person—an individual I immediately recognized from the details she furnished. After the person's identity was established, Tina parroted Brandon as she stated, "She didn't get it, *Dad*."

As noted, Tricia Robertson and the late Professor Archie Roy postulated two theories in a paper that is currently awaiting publication. They tested pragmatic data against several theories—one of which was the survival hypothesis. And from their research, Robertson and Roy formulated some of their own theories.

In my communications with Tricia I gained the sense that she and Roy have seen strong evidence for the survival hypothesis, but she also noted, "I don't think for one minute that *all* mediums are connecting with discarnate beings." I took this to mean that some research cases may point to survival while others apparently lead to alternate explanations. Those interested in learning more about research conducted by this team should read Tricia Robertson's book, *Things You Can Do When You're Dead!*, published in 2013.

On a personal level, apart from scientific experiments, I have witnessed events that could serve as evidence to support the survival hypothesis. As an example, let's refer back to the case I noted in chapter 1, where medium Debra Martin shared a good deal of relevant information about my friend Linda's recently deceased brother.

First, you may recall that Debra correctly identified that the brother had been killed on a motorcycle. But Debra also specified that "he died instantly—his soul left his body immediately and he felt no pain. *He wants her to know this*." If Debra had been receiving information via clairvoyance, it seems she would have simply reported that he died instantly, yet she also was compelled to let Linda know that her brother didn't suffer when he died. So *who* was doing the prodding?

Refer back to Debra's mention of Linda's brother's kids and how they loved taking baths together when they were little. I knew nothing about this so Debra couldn't have read my mind. If one were to assert that this was a case of clairvoyance, I would ask why Debra referenced something so touching and relevant to both persons as opposed to a more mundane piece of information. Could it be that an active intelligence was guiding Debra, ensuring that she would share the kind of information most likely to bring healing to Linda?

Next, recall Debra's mention of a red ribbon or banner over her brother's casket. I had no knowledge of this information, so telepathy with me would be an impossible explanation. Further, the red banner was placed on the casket *after* Linda's brother had died, suggesting the possibility that his "soul" or "spirit" may have been aware of events that transpired after his death and that he may have communicated these things to Debra.

Remember too that Debra indicated that Linda's brother shared the phrase "Live, Love, and Laugh." Linda said that her brother never said these words to her while physically alive but noted that she owns a piece of art with this inscription and also intends to get a tattoo with this precise phrase to honor her brother. (Linda decided to get the tattoo after her brother's death but prior to the reading.) Might this point to the possibility that Linda's brother was aware of things taking place in his sister's life after his death?

After meeting many qualified mediums, experiences like these have become almost commonplace in my life, yet they never cease to amaze me. While most of these events did not occur under controlled conditions in a lab, it doesn't diminish the validity of what I witnessed. In fact, psi phenomena and mediumship tend to work best outside the rigid lab environment, where the medium is relaxed and able to interact with the sitter. It is an emotional process and works best when the feelings of the medium and sitter are not stifled. Technically, a face-to-face reading opens up the possibility for cold reading, i.e., educated guesses based on sitter reactions and other cues interpreted by the medium. But if a person consults a medium who has a solid reputation, this shouldn't be a concern. The type of specific information shared by top mediums, akin to what I received from Debra Martin, could never be produced through cold reading. Most importantly, an excellent reading with a good medium can be very helpful to someone coping with grief; they will recognize and cherish the rare gems that come through, confirming a real connection.

Aside from information provided by mediums, there are numerous other areas yielding compelling evidence of life after death. In my opinion, two of the best examples are the following cases of post-mortem apparitions.

In 1925, four years after the death of a farmer named James Chaffin, one of his sons began having visions. The son, named J.P., said that he'd seen an apparition of his deceased father, who appeared standing at his bedside. J.P. indicated that his father communicated to him that his last will and testament had been modified prior to his death, something unknown to any family members. In one of his visions, J.P. received instructions to look in the pocket of his father's black overcoat. He subsequently asked his mother the whereabouts of the coat and learned that she had given it to J.P.'s brother John. J.P. then traveled to John's house and examined the coat, finding a piece of paper sewn into the lining which said, "Read the 27th chapter of Genesis in my daddy's old Bible." J.P. then asked a neighbor to serve as a witness as he searched for the Bible. After locating the book, he opened it and found the modified will inside (which was newer than the original one already in use). As a result of this mysterious relay of information and the subsequent discovery of the later will, the court honored it as the final one. This case is among the most thoroughly investigated and confirmed of its type, having been scrutinized by the SPR and judicial court judges, who deemed the will legitimate and enforced it. Ten court witnesses indicated that they recognized the signature on the will as belonging to James Chaffin.[33]

Then there is the case of British Lt. David McConnel, who died in a plane crash on December 7, 1918. It was established that impact occurred at precisely 3:25 PM because McConnel's wristwatch was frozen on that time. At about the same time as the crash occurred, Lt. J. J. Larkin, McConnel's roommate, saw him enter the facility and asked if he had a good flight. McConnel answered, "Yes. Got there alright. Had a good trip." Then he left. About fifteen minutes later another friend asked Larkin when McConnel would be back. He was hoping the three of them might have dinner together. Larkin explained that McConnel was already back. Later that day both men learned that McConnel had died in a crash. Larkin reported the experience to his commanding officer the following day and his friend corroborated his story.

Regarding the McConnel case, author Michael Schmicker notes, "The SPR examined the case and it remains one of the best stories of its kind in their files. It had a reliable, no-nonsense witness whose claim was confirmed by another independent witness, and the details themselves were written down shortly after they happened when memories were very fresh."[34]

Maybe someday science will "prove" the existence of the afterlife, but for now the matter falls into the category of subjective belief, depending on your own experiences. With that said, some individuals have undergone remarkable occurrences—ranging from near-death experiences to lucid dreams and apparitions—rendering what we label "belief" as something closer to "knowledge" from their perspective. Maybe we can learn something from these people. Perhaps all reality is subjective, and the notion of a purely objective reality is the fantasy.

CHAPTER 4

Interviews with
Two Psychic–Mediums

Some contemporary mediums dislike the term "psychic" because they feel it carries a negative connotation, leading people to associations with crystal balls, tea-leaf reading, fortune-telling, or other stereotypes. Among many who practice or study mediumship, the phenomenon is most commonly considered a form of telepathy with the deceased. However, unusual in this regard is prominent medium George Anderson, who gained acclaim from appearances on a New York radio talk show on which he gave readings to anonymous callers; he subsequently participated in controlled scientific tests at the University of Arizona and was featured on HBO's special "Life-Afterlife." His abilities are said to be facilitated exclusively through clairvoyance (clear-seeing), clairaudience (clear-hearing), and clairsentience (clear-sensing).[1]

But whether a medium's abilities are tied to telepathy or any of the other noted faculties, it follows that the individual must be psychic in order to be a medium, as telepathy and all the aforementioned "clairs" are forms of psi. Ultimately, it's about the transfer of information, and a variety of means exist by which mediums receive messages from those in spiritual realms.

It's been said that "All mediums are psychic, but not all psychics are mediums." This means that some individuals are able to garner information without use of their five physical senses—through psi—but connecting and communicating with discarnate individuals is a more refined and highly developed skill, requiring greater sensitivity and discernment.

In the end, maybe there is nothing wrong with the word "psychic" and it just needs to be freed from the shackles of inaccurate typecasts and misinterpretations. After all, it is just a word, and words help us express abstract concepts and ideas. Various forms of psi have been validated through scientific studies and scrupulously detailed anecdotal accounts. In fact, the scientific evidence is so strong that some diehard skeptics have softened their stance on this topic. As parapsychology writer and Oxford graduate Chris Carter notes, "Recently, journalist Steven Volk was surprised to discover that leading skeptical psychologist Richard Wiseman has admitted that the evidence for telepathy is so good that 'by the standards of any other area of science, [telepathy] is proven.' Mr. Volk goes on to write, 'Even more incredibly … another leading skeptic, Chris French, agrees with him'."[2]

In terms of evidence, one of the most compelling cases involves renowned medium Eileen Garrett and the ill-fated British airship R101. Two days after the airship crashed, an entranced Garrett brought through the soul/personality of H. C. Irwin, the deceased captain of R101. While in this altered state, Garrett served as a mouthpiece for Irwin and furnished a highly technical account of the crash and its cause, which was submitted to the Air Ministry and was subsequently validated as accurate in every detail. Not only was the information beyond Garrett's level of knowledge and understanding, it had been well guarded by the British Air Ministry for reasons of national security. For a most interesting and meticulous account of this scenario, I recommend John G. Fuller's book, *The Airmen Who Would Not Die*.

Given that the existence of psychic phenomena is considered a well-established fact, especially among those who have studied the evidence, I return to my initial question: Must we coin a new term for someone who demonstrates psi abilities—calling them an "Intuitive," a "Sensitive," or an "Anomalous Information Receptor"? Or is it possible to simply remove the stigma tied to the word "psychic"?

I suggest that spirit communication is a sacred gift that has long been misunderstood. The field has been disparaged by pseudo-skeptics and damaged by fraudulent mediums; it's time for the matter to be viewed in a new and positive way. To this end, I've furnished a body of evidence supporting the hypothesis that qualified mediums are capable of receiving and sharing accurate information from discarnate personalities. But I thought that readers might also appreciate a glimpse into the nature of these experiences from the perspective of the medium. To gain these insights, I interviewed two top mediums.

I first spoke with renowned English medium Linda Williamson. Mediums often say things like "spirit tells me this," or "they're showing me that," and the layperson may not understand exactly what is transpiring, much less gain a sense for what that medium is experiencing. So I asked her to explain what it means to "hear spirit."

"It's an inner voice," Linda said. "And I can tell if it's a man or a woman or if they have an accent, but it's really mental communication. Sometimes I get it as a definite voice, while at other times it's an impression of the words or of a thought."

I then asked about the process by which she sees spirits. Linda explained that at one time she limited herself by making statements such as "I can't do this" or "I can't do that." But once she stopped thinking in those terms, Linda found that she was able to see more and more over the years. "My technique now is to take some quiet time in advance of when the sitting is scheduled. I then tune into the guides and ask them to bring to me the spirit communicators that the sitter wants to hear from. Then I concentrate and try to see them. I ask that they show themselves to me. I don't see them as if they were flesh and blood. But I do see them—rather like a hazy outline—so I have an idea of the person's height and build, for instance."

I'd often wondered whether mediums see spirits through their eyes, just like you would see another living person, or if they were detecting a strictly mental image. So I asked her.

"I do see them with my eyes open—they are definitely there, outside of me. And although I'm not seeing them as if they were physically present, I definitely see them. I know that I'm looking at something outside of myself because if I close my eyes I am unable to see them."

Speaking about variations in visual quality, Linda said,

> I find that the clarity varies. Sometimes I see things very clearly, sometimes I just get a mental picture, and sometimes I don't see anything at all. But I need to explain that it works on different levels. I'm always using my inner senses, not the outer ones. I tune in, asking the deceased to show themselves to me. If you're talking to someone, you look at them, and it's the same with the deceased person. I need to look at them in order to establish a link. In my mind I say, *Tell me who you are, what you want to say, and explain your relationship to the sitter.* So I'm listening, but the words are not actually audible. I'm getting a sense of the communicator, feeling what kind of personality they have. I feel their emotion: if they're very eager to get through or if they want to share an answer to a particular question. So I'm working with all three things— seeing, hearing, and sensing—all at the same time.

Linda begins her preparatory process in advance of the sitter's arrival. During the course of this pre-reading progression, one or two "communicators" will usually come through. And oddly, on those occasions when a spirit communicator fails to appear, the sitter is often late or does not show up at all. This seems to indicate that the discarnate spirit is aware that their loved one is going to be a no-show. Maybe this indicates that the deceased person has a broader view and sense of awareness than we do. And likely that view is not bound by limitations of time or space.

When the sitter arrives, Linda makes sure that the person is relaxed by explaining her process in an attempt to demystify things. She then asks a spirit communicator to come forward. When there is more than one communicator, she requests that they form an "orderly queue" because things become "muddled" if they talk at the same time. In most cases, Linda becomes connected with one communicator, typically the one with whom she connected in advance of the session. She concentrates on that person and listens intently:

> After tuning in, I look at them to determine if I can see them more clearly. At the same time, I'll begin to sense their personality or receive a message from them. Very often it will be just a few words, which I will share with the sitter. I ask the sitter if they understand the phrase or word. I don't really know what I'm talking about, in the sense of meaning—I'm just passing on the words. The sitter usually understands but if not, I go back to the communicator and ask for more information.

Linda knows that it's important for her to not "embroider" the information because it can lead to misinterpretations and misunderstandings. So she always tries to report exactly what she is hearing and seeing. "There was a lady that came yesterday. I was seeing pictures of fruits and vegetables. I wondered if they indicated something about her diet." But Linda simply relayed to the client, "I'm seeing fruits and vegetables." As it turned out, the woman's husband worked for a fruit and vegetable supply company.

Linda learned that there can be hazards associated with delivering unfiltered messages. "Sometimes you have to be a little bit tactful [when relaying information to the sitter]. They're not always terribly polite on the other side of life because they're just the same people that they were here."

Linda has to discern when to deliver a message directly and when it needs to be couched: "I think you need to learn to trust when to say exactly what you're receiving and when to wrap it up a little bit—when it's too blunt. Sometimes I've said something that was quite direct and thought, 'Oh dear, should I have said that?' because I wouldn't have chosen to say something like that myself. But then the sitter will often convey, 'That's exactly what they were like—that is precisely what they would have said.' And that is what I needed to hear for my confidence."

Linda explained that this is not about being arrogant or saying 'I'm always right'—which is impossible because "mediumship is never an exact science." But she told me that she gains confidence through confirming feedback, which tells her to trust the information she's receiving and relaying.

Linda also indicated that some messages come through in a rather humorous manner. In one example, she had made a connection with a deceased man just prior to the arrival of a female sitter. After determining that the man was the father of the sitter who was en route, Linda asked whether he'd ever done this before. "No," he said. "I've never died before."

Linda then explained the phase that normally follows: "When I have received all the information I can get from the particular communicator, they [typically] step back and someone else will come forward." Discussing the impact of different personalities in the process, Linda noted,

> The way in which people communicate often tells you a lot about the personality. A forthright person—a strong character—will communicate much more easily than someone who was reserved. I remember an occasion when the lady who came to me really wanted to hear from her father and I sensed her father there, but every time I tried to speak to him another member of her family would come forward and say a few words. It was almost as though every time he was about to speak somebody else cut in front of him. Eventually I got to her father and she said, "Well, that was like him, because he was a very polite person, and he would always stand back and let everyone else go first."

Finally, I asked Linda about the time she read for celebrated medium John Edward. In a well-known case documented in his bestselling book, *Crossing Over*, Edward came to Linda after consulting with two other mediums—hoping to hear a secret phrase from his deceased mother. Where the first two mediums failed in this endeavor

Linda successfully delivered the phrase, "The Guiding Light." John Edwards's mother was a fan of soap operas and *The Guiding Light* was her favorite show. I asked Linda how she received the information, whether it had come to her as a symbol or if she heard the words.

"I heard the words but didn't realize they were significant. I didn't know it was a code. As far as I can remember—and it was quite a few years ago—the words came to me, 'Your mother is your guiding light' and that was said twice."

Linda then went on to talk about other readings where a short phrase would prove meaningful.

"Sometimes just a few words can be very significant. I was once reading for a woman and I said, 'Your father is telling me that he's *had a good rest.*' And she said, 'The last words my father said to me before he died were *now I'm going to have a good rest.*'"

I brought up an exceptional reading I had with the medium Tina Powers, who took on my son's persona. Her delivery gave me the sense that I had a direct line of contact and communication with Brandon. In regard to this Linda said, "If you are tuning very closely to the person who is communicating, you then take on their mannerisms. In fact, you may even use their gestures while not even being conscious that you're doing it. This is when it's working really well." She continued:

> I usually listen to what the communicator is saying to me, and I sense what they're trying to convey. I will tell the sitter, and then I wait for the next bit. But when it's flowing really well, it's like you become that person. You don't have to think about it; the words just come out. And you tend to take on the characteristics of the person who is coming through. That is when you get the clearest evidence.

When Linda was young, she always felt that there were "people" around her. Linda heard voices and was unsure if they were *real* or not. As she got older the voices told her about things that were going to happen, so she had validation. For example, the voices told Linda that an aunt was coming to visit—and the aunt did arrive, unexpectedly. She knew that the voices weren't caused by her imagination, although she didn't really understand what was going on.

Linda read all kinds of books on psychic phenomena, leading to her growing interest in the subject. When she got a bit older, Linda attended a spiritualist church and really felt at home there because people understood her. While attending the church, she participated in a development circle primarily focused on meditation. Linda found these sessions helpful, but her group leader didn't teach how to develop mediumship. She had to work it out for herself.

Linda calls her technique "tuning up." It starts with entering a passive meditative state where she is very quiet and her mind is still. When seeking to communicate with spirit, she notes, "You actually need to reach out to them. You're honing in on that person who is trying to communicate with you, and you're building a mental bridge with them—a link through which they can put into your mind thoughts and impressions they want to convey." And, she said, "It's necessary to hold the link strongly, to concentrate, and as you do you'll feel the communicator coming closer and closer. And if it is working well, it's as if you become that person—you'll know exactly what they're like and what they want to say." Linda noted that she often picks up on physical ailments that the person may have experienced prior to their passing. If, for example, a person died of a heart attack, Linda might feel a slight pain in her chest but receives only enough pain to comprehend the meaning.

Linda had been given a lot of comfort from another medium when her father died. During her reading the medium correctly stated her father's name, sharing, "He says that when he was dying he told you that he wasn't afraid." And it was true. Said Linda, "That kind of proof really helped me at that time." This was a key factor in Linda's desire to become a medium, because she saw how much a good sitting could help a bereaved person.

&.

Jamie Clark is one of the most accommodating people I know. No matter what I throw his way, whether it's a crazy question or an experimental idea, Jamie is always willing to play ball. So when I asked if he'd be willing to sit down and discuss his psychic and mediumship abilities in great depth and detail, he said "Yes" without pause.

Were it not for some unusual spiritual art and a large collection of philosophical books in his living room, Jamie's home would be indistinguishable from just about any other American household. As we started our dialog I could tell that Jamie's youngest son was excited to have a visitor in their home, because he hung around waiting to see what would develop.

Jamie and I sat down in his kitchen area as the afternoon sun poked in through the sliding glass door at the back of the house, illuminating the room with diffused light. I started out by asking if he would share his perspective on the difference between a psychic and a medium. Based on his answer, I got the impression that he uses both faculties interchangeably.

Said Jamie,

> Anyone who can connect with the other side can read vibrations. [Deceased] loved ones will send you telepathic messages and make you feel things. So you become more sensitized to changes in vibration or frequencies, as I call them. From there you can pull out and go into a psychic mode, connecting with the sitter's soul energy. For me psychometry is good. I'll shake their hand or ask to hold something of theirs and then I can get that vibration—the mental atmosphere around the physical body. And I can see what's in their past, where they are at the moment, and most likely where they're heading if they stay in the same direction—usually with a high degree of accuracy. So there is a difference and also a similarity [between the psychic process and mediumship process] in that it's mental atmosphere for the physical person and mental telepathy for the spiritual person.

Jamie told me that there are times when he uses mediumship and psychic abilities simultaneously, yet he knows which is which. He noted that during a mediumship reading, most of the information comes from "the other side," but the picture can sometimes be "filled in" with psychic information. He said that he makes a mental request of the sitter's deceased loved ones to please come through with validating communications, including speech, mannerisms, dates, times, names, and experiences.

I brought up the Super-psi theory, asking Jamie how he knows that he is truly communicating with a deceased person rather than reading the mind of the sitter, picking up on residual energy, or unknowingly using his psychic abilities alone to provide validating information.

"I would say it's actually a little bit of all those things," he responded, "where the person from the other side helps pull me in a certain direction to read that sitter's vibration so I can give them the most accurate information. But ninety percent of it is the mediumship."

I then asked how he can know that he is connected to an individual on the other side.

"You feel and see them. They create a picture—an energy form. They put themselves on a level where they will be recognized. For me they vibrate as a male energy, strong and powerful, or a female energy, softer and more contemplative. Sometimes you'll get a more sensitive male or a more powerful female, but I let the client hear that and decide. That accuracy—in identifying this personality characteristic—needs to be there."

I stated how the very nature of my questioning was to some degree an effort to box a nearly indescribable experience into a human explanation. Jamie seemed to agree. "The other side is expanded and you feel everything—I get little glimpses of that. It is like an overlaying of dimensional frequencies."

I followed by asking if he hears an audible voice during readings, just as if he were talking to another person. "Yes, but it's mainly in my mind's voice. That's how they communicate most of the time. Sometimes it will be right here [in the ear] and they're whispering things, but

I would say that ninety percent is the 'inside' communication." Jamie's sense of clairaudience seemed similar to what Linda experiences.

I asked Jamie whether he ever sees spirit with his eyes open or if it is more of a vision that occurs while his eyes are shut.

"I've trained myself to eyeball you [the sitter] and *here we go*. I look at you and I then have what is like a screen superimposed on your physical being. For example, I may be looking at you but then I see a train go by, or I'm viewing a baseball field, or I see a horse with your dad sitting on it." Jamie noted that when he tunes in this way he will typically look away from the sitter and try to get a clearer picture and not be distracted by the client's emotions. And in describing how the pictures form, he noted, "It's like little bubbles—like tiny cells of light that coagulate together and form a picture. It's not always clear but I can sometimes see facial features—hair, nose, and mouth—while other times it is obscure." This sounded a bit like Linda's experience where she saw in varying degrees of clarity from sitting to sitting.

Jamie indicated that clairsentience, the ability to feel things, was another key mode of communication for him. Each reading is different in terms of which abilities he uses to communicate. He hones in on whatever will work best for that particular personality—hearing, seeing, or feeling.

In terms of preparing for his mediumship readings, Jamie always takes protective steps to keep negative influences away. He wants to receive only genuine communication from desired sources. This is accomplished through a mental statement of intention, including a visualization process where he surrounds himself with light and angelic energy.

Jamie noted that a medium must be balanced to do good work, avoiding stress in other areas of their life. And he expressed the value of having a mentor in the development process. In his case it was Jamie's mother who helped him develop—studying various religions and conducting exercises designed to ramp up his understanding. Again, this was similar to Linda's experience, although her mentoring environment was the developmental circle at her church.

Chapter 5

The Skeptical Neurosis

In previous writings I have shared my perspective that skepticism is a healthy attribute for any intelligent person. It is normal to question things that don't make sense, and it is wise to ask for validation of extraordinary claims. But the "open-mindedness" of some skeptics is akin to birds that don't believe in air because it can't be seen, or fish that swim to the surface of the ocean—certain it is the edge of the universe. It seems interesting that most science-minded individuals today believe in the existence of dark matter, which cannot be observed or measured, but they quickly deny other phenomena that can be deduced yet are likewise physically immeasurable.

By definition, a skeptic is one who assumes an open-minded position—not pre-judging claims without impartial inquiry and investigation. But the skeptic who really isn't a skeptic at all has already subscribed to a particular worldview and will fight to the end to defend a pre-disposed stance. Such individuals have been called "super skeptics," "extreme skeptics," and "debunkers." Rather than openly investigate without bias, examining such claims with earnest effort, the debunker works in backward fashion—seeking to discredit information that conflicts with his position. I suggest that this type of behavior is actually anti-science because, as Alex Tsakiris, host of the "Skeptiko" Internet podcast show, puts it, "Science is a method, not a position."

I didn't write this chapter to go to battle with debunkers, but rather to make readers aware of their own mindset and methods so they can see past them and remain unbiased on their path of personal exploration.

And before firing a full quill of arrows at skeptic-debunkers, I note that we all display similar behavior at times. Consciously or unconsciously, people often seek to protect their turf. Being purely objective can be difficult, but when you claim to be a skeptic, a scientist, or both, detachment is a prerequisite, not an option.

Dr. Don Watson, a neuroscientist and MD with a strong interest in the open exploration of unexplained phenomena, suggested that I employ the term "pseudo-skeptic" to describe self-styled "debunkers." As Dr. Watson explained:

> You can dialogue with true skeptics, because their minds are open, and they are happy to engage in rational discussions of data and theory. On the other hand, you can ignore the knee-jerk nay-sayers. Using the term "skeptic" or "extreme skeptic" to describe debunkers obscures the issues—in fact, it turns them upside down. The skeptical mindset holds that we can never possess certain knowledge. Because the dogmatic mindset claims certain knowledge, dogmatism is the exact opposite of skepticism. It's clear from their pontifications that the most vociferous critics of psychical research are dogmatists, not skeptics.... Further, those who make money as debunkers should be identified as "professional pseudo-skeptics." This term indicates that as long as the money flows, they will never change their positions.[1]

He then expounded on why it is so difficult to find impartial people when broaching the subject of controversial research:

> Because science can never provide certain knowledge, skepticism is the legitimate mindset for scientists. However, dogmatism is deeply embedded in the academic cultures. Many academic scientists, perhaps the majority, write and talk as if they have certain knowledge about the world. Rather than maintaining open minds about facts they don't know, these persons dogmatically deny or ignore them.

Arthur Koestler knew these academics well. He wrote, "Innovation is a two-fold threat to academic mediocrities: it endangers their oracular authority; and it evokes the deeper fear that their whole laboriously constructed intellectual edifice may collapse."[2]

In closing his argument, Dr. Watson offered the following:

> The history of science shows that scientific revolutions inevitably invite reactionary cynics. Every scientific revolution from Copernicus through Newton, Maxwell, Einstein, Planck, Freud, and Darwin have unearthed counter-revolutionaries. Today we laugh at such nay-sayers if we pay any attention to them at all. In the future, others will ridicule today's pseudo-skeptics.

Debunkers quickly dismiss research into the paranormal, characterizing such efforts as "pseudo-science." (Given this, I suppose it's only fair to call them "pseudo-skeptics.") Why do they scoff at serious scientific study of paranormal phenomena, deeming such research unworthy of consideration? On the surface, there seems no reasonable response to this query because, at its core, science is predicated on the unbiased exploration of the unknown. A man named John who responded to a blog I'd written offered some insights, pointing to a possible answer. In my article I had suggested that most skeptic-debunkers are married to concepts founded in material reductionism and are therefore proponents of a mechanistic universe based in seventeenth-century science. John saw things a bit differently and had a fairly extreme reaction to the topic:

> This attack is not being perpetrated by those advocating the 17th-century science of Newton or touting a mechanical versus metaphysical universe. These are advocates of 20th-century science, citing Karl Popper and the use of his theories to determine what constitutes science and what constitutes pseudo-science. Pseudo-science is presented as the stuff of self-deluded mouth-breathers. In the interests of protecting

the delicate minds of our children and preserving the integrity of our educational institutions, they demand its eradication.

John's words made me wonder ... have we reached a point in society where it is no longer possible for people to hold different perspectives? Where no tolerance exists for variation from accepted norms? Taken at face value, John's comments seem to suggest that the adversaries of paranormal research are so certain about the accuracy of their position they are willing to employ authoritarian tactics in an effort to maintain control.

John also made me wonder about the roots of this movement, and his response offered a few clues. Mainstream science apparently became hostile toward certain subjects considered "fringe" in the mid-nineteenth century, as evidenced by the appearance of the term "pseudoscience" in the *Northern Journal of Medicine* in 1844.[3]

Following this trail, I learned more about Karl Popper and his mid-twentieth-century theories. Popper proposed the standard of "falsifiability" to differentiate "real science" from non-science. "Statements such as 'God created the universe' may be true or false, but they are not falsifiable, so [according to this conjecture] they are not scientific; they lie outside the scope of science."[4]

Acceptance of this standard essentially eliminates the serious examination of anything non-physical—including the domains of things considered "metaphysical," or beyond the realm of conventional physics. By "boxing in" what is viewed as *real* science, a broad range of phenomena was shut out from study, as it became taboo to do so. This seems rather odd, considering that the universe is big and diverse—and we haven't figured it all out yet. Also, deciding what is testable and falsifiable seems a highly subjective matter.

Afterlife research advocate Victor Zammit offers an interesting perspective on the word "skepticism," noting its original connotation in ancient Greek language:

Skepticism allowed for possible confirmation of some hypothesis or belief ... this meant being open-minded to ideas, concepts, and other new phenomena to be considered. But the closed-minded debunkers unfairly hijacked the term "skepticism" and used it to mean nothing but being closed-minded, unqualifiedly negative, [implying] that any new phenomena—unless it is materialist—cannot be validated.

Being a debunker means having a belief that nothing exists after this physical life. But these debunkers have never produced any evidence to show that what they believe has any empirical substance at all. This means they have a personal belief [which is] no different from a religious person with a personal belief—it is a subjective belief. And all subjective beliefs are subject to invalidation, whereas all afterlife evidence has the substance of being empirically elicited.[5]

My father welcomed legitimate, open-minded skeptics in the course of his work and also submitted to testing. During his public psychic demonstrations he allowed people to examine all aspects of his process, from scrutinizing blindfolds to making sure that the adhesive medical tape was sealed tightly around his eye sockets and nose—thus preventing physical vision. I always viewed this as a rather humorous aspect of my father's demonstration since his eyesight was extremely poor, even with his glasses on. Aside from that, he typically furnished additional information of a specific nature to audience members, going above and beyond the written questions. So ultimately the blindfolds seemed mainly for effect.

In referring to "legitimate skeptics," my father was speaking about individuals who questioned the phenomena but were willing to reassess their existing views given sufficient evidence. Conversely, my father had little patience for those who sought to undermine the process in order to preserve their preconceptions while simultaneously ignoring the evidence.

Several years ago, I met a gentleman named Jim Samurin who exemplified the true meaning of the term "skeptic." Jim and I met over lunch in the summer of 2006, and he shared some fascinating stories pertaining to life experiences that reshaped his thinking. One such event took place the first time Jim witnessed my father's psychic demonstration. Relaying his story, Jim told me, "I have to preface this by saying I was a non-believer … unequivocally."

Jim made no bones about his skepticism prior to this event—he assumed that psychic phenomena was folly. And he would probably never have been there on that particular evening except for his friendship with Tony Deprima—my father's attorney at the time.

Tony Deprima had also been quite skeptical when he met my dad in 1967, but his doubts faded after hiring my father to work at his restaurant/nightclub. He and his partners wanted to hire "entertainment" to infuse the business with new patrons, but Tony soon concluded that my father's abilities were more than a mere entertaining novelty. Since the partners were in control of the showroom facilities, they knew that everything was on the "up and up." So it was this first-hand and up-close view that enabled Tony to reconcile his skepticism and accept the legitimacy of my father's unusual gifts.

Interestingly, Tony and his partners were occasionally maligned by belligerent patrons who wrongly alleged that management was in cahoots with my father. This gave the men a tiny taste of the world my dad lived in every day. Actually, the owners often tried to trick my father in a variety of ways but consistently failed in their efforts. One mischievous stunt they carried out involved the movement of my father's wastebasket, mid-stream during the demonstration while his eyes were fully taped and blindfolded. According to Tony, my father would always adjust his aim and continue discarding used papers into the relocated target without missing a beat.

More impressively, Tony and his partners took a twenty-dollar bill, recorded the serial number, and then wrapped the currency in aluminum foil—placing it in a sealed envelope. Then during the middle of the demonstration, Tony sent the envelope up to my father, asking that he state the serial number. Per Tony, my father was tested in this manner on three separate occasions and performed flawlessly each time—correctly stating the serial number, as requested, before opening the envelope.

Setting the stage for Jim Samurin's account, I must first share a related background story.

On a sunny Saturday in 1980, Tony Deprima ventured to a Phoenix-area lake on a fishing excursion and reeled in an unusually large catfish. When it came time to return home, Tony felt conflicted over what to do with his prized trophy. On one hand, he didn't want to kill the fish and eat it—yet he couldn't bring himself to release it back into the lake. Eventually Tony decided to fill his ice chest with lake water so he could take the fish back to the city, where he would deposit it into a pond near his workplace.

Upon arriving home, Tony met his wife in the driveway, and she was angry with him because he was late and they had planned a double date that evening with the Samurins. Tony cleaned up quickly and they left to pick up the other couple en route to the venue where my father was appearing that evening. When they arrived at the establishment, my father's demonstration was well underway—his eyes were taped and blindfolded and he was sharing messages with members of the audience. Soon after the couples were seated, my father spoke to Jim.

"Pull out any bill you like and I'll tell you the denomination and serial number. You don't even have to send it up."

Jim told me that he took this as a challenge. "So, I'm looking around thinking there has to be a gimmick and I go at it like this." Jim then showed me his hands folded in a manner intended to conceal his money, reminding me of a professional gambler hiding his cards during a poker match. "I didn't want any cameras to pick it up, so I held the money so there was no way anyone could see this but me."

Then Jim shared, "And I always used to carry a lot of hundred-dollar bills. So I'm saying to myself, *This guy might guess a one, a five, or a twenty, but he's not going to guess a hundred-dollar bill.* I'm looking around and I have my hands folded just like this—and I'm not exaggerating."

Jim showed me how his hands had been tightly clasped over the currency that night.

"No one but me could see what I was holding and I'm saying to myself, *Okay, I've got this guy nailed*. What he was suggesting was impossible—it couldn't happen in a million years."

Jim then recalled what proved to be the first in a series of puzzling revelations, as he recounted my father's next words: "It's a one-hundred-dollar bill." Before Jim had even digested the fact that a one-hundred-dollar bill had been specified, my father followed by accurately calling out the entire serial number.

Befuddled yet highly intrigued, with his skepticism possibly waning, Jim then began to take notice of the people around him, initially focusing on an Air Force Lieutenant and his pregnant wife. Jim noted that my father picked up their paper and called out the wife's name.

"You're going to have a child and it's going to be a boy," my father said.

Baffled, the woman followed with a rhetorical question, "How could you know that?"

My father came back, "You're going to give birth on November 12th."

As he was explaining the story, Jim interjected, "I'll remember this forever … The woman responded, 'Well, the doctor says it's going to be November 13th or 14th.' Your dad followed by telling her, 'You'd better tell your doctor to be ready on the 12th, because that's when he's coming.' If you had seen the look on this lady's face when your dad said November 12th. Never mind that he said it would be a boy. I'll bet you a million dollars that's when she delivered the kid—I don't have any doubt about it."

By this point it was clear that Jim Samurin's view of reality had started to change and his skepticism was diminishing. Yet the surrealistic events of that particular evening had not yet concluded. Jim continued, "Nearing the end of the demonstration, your dad turned his attention to Tony and held his throat, as if he were gasping for air."

Per Jim, my father said, "There's something in your car—it's not human—it's dying…. It's having trouble breathing—it's suffocating."

Suddenly remembering the catfish he'd left in his trunk, Tony looked at Jim with a sense of dire urgency and said, "My God, it may be out of water."

Tony explained things to Jim as they rushed into the kitchen, borrowed a large pot, and filled it with water. The two men then ran downstairs to the car and opened the trunk, where they found the fish struggling to survive with gills exposed, flopping around in about an inch of water. Without hesitation, Tony emptied the contents of the kettle into the ice chest, providing immediate relief to the suffering fish.

On further examination Tony noticed a small leak in the ice chest that had apparently been dribbling for hours. The men then traveled to an office complex where Tony had intended to place the fish in a pond, but the access gate was locked. Instead, they ultimately settled on a lagoon at a nearby park.

The evidence presented to Jim Samurin that evening was highly compelling—likely beyond what most people could ever hope to observe. Yet the key point is that Jim was open to reconsidering his position based on the new evidence that he witnessed. This is something pseudo-skeptics are not prepared to do. No amount of evidence will make a difference to a person of the debunker mindset if the implications conflict with their existing worldview.

Pseudo-skeptics often attribute the apparent success of mediums to a technique called "cold reading." In this process, body language and other cues taken from the sitter are interpreted—then guesses are made and subsequently modified based on sitter reactions. No doubt, cold reading occurs and fraud does exist in this field. There are unscrupulous people with zero psychic aptitude who are eager to take money from the vulnerable.

But just as there are con artists, there are also legitimate mediums capable of facilitating high-quality readings under controlled conditions. Cold reading can account for general statements made by mediums facing or interacting with a sitter. But when mediums provide highly specific, detailed information—especially in multiple-level blind experiments, as executed by the Windbridge

Institute, the Scottish Society for Psychical Research, and University of Virginia—cold reading is rendered an untenable explanation. Controlled readings of this type have generated results far beyond chance, testing the hypothesis that mediums can (under said conditions) provide accurate and specific information about deceased individuals.

Expanding on this topic, Tricia J. Robertson, Immediate Past President of the Scottish Society for Psychical Research, wrote:

> Having examined paranormal phenomena for approximately twenty-five years, I have concluded the following:
>
> 1. Various forms of paranormal phenomena do occur.
>
> 2. Many of the sceptical [or "skeptical" in U.S. spelling] arguments fail to hold water, as they do not address all the facts.
>
> 3. Media sceptics choose a weak example of a particular phenomenon and dissect it for TV/ magazine/etc.
>
> 4. They do not address the wealth of evidence already on record.
>
> 5. Psychological interpretations are not always the answer, as sceptics suggest (although they may sometimes be).
>
> 6. Paranormal phenomena may not be parapsychological—they could possibly be para-physics, para-biology, etc.
>
> 7. The explanation for paranormal phenomena will not have a "one size fits all" answer—that is for certain.
>
> 8. The avid sceptic will never look at these events and examine the evidence with an impartial eye; they KNOW what is possible or not possible before they examine the evidence. *This is a belief system.*

9. I am not a religious person with a fixed belief; I examine evidence and carry out research (over years) on claims of the paranormal.

10. The half-hour or one-hour sound bite seen on TV is worthless. This end-product only reflects how a producer/director chooses to shape a programme.[6]

Pseudo-skeptics often characterize all mediums as "fakes" and "frauds." And while fraud does occur, there are also some uniquely gifted people who possess abilities outside the bounds of what is typically considered "normal." In truth, for every big-name psychic in the public eye there are hundreds of virtually unknown mediums working in anonymity—compelled by a deep spiritual desire to help others. Many of these mediums eke out a modest living, working for nominal fees or for nothing at all, without concern for personal riches or fame. Some such mediums serve as ministers or parishioners in churches that embrace and even revere their unique gifts. What, say the cynics, is the motivation of these humble mediums operating on meager means?

Debunkers claim that greed-driven mediums willfully deceive vulnerable and dim-witted people. Yes, attacks on mediums also spill over to those interested in paranormal phenomena, and this interest is typically characterized as gullible or unintelligent. This unwanted portrayal clearly serves as a deterrent for anyone concerned with their self-image, steering them clear of the fray—as well as any expansion of understanding they might gain from interacting with a credible medium.

Some of the pseudo-skeptics casting stones at mediums are compensated by groups bent on subverting concepts failing to fit with their ideologies. One such organization, formerly known as "CSI-COP" (Committee for the Scientific Investigation of Claims of the Paranormal), recently changed its name to CSI, or "Center for Skeptical Inquiry." On the surface both names sound harmless enough—as if to imply a mission based in fostering the free exploration of all phenomena—but names can be deceiving. According to Guy Lyon Playfair, a respected journalist and investigator of psychic phenomena, "CSICOP's greatest achievement was to persuade much of the scientific community, the media and the general public that it was a genuine scientific organization devoted to a search for scientific truth. In reality of course it was nothing of the kind. It was, and its successor no doubt still is, a vigilante-lobby group promoting the cause of fundamentalist secular humanism."[7]

An early criticism of CSICOP came from one of its own, founding member Marcello Truzzi, who left the organization shortly after its start. Truzzi coined the term "pseudo-skeptic," noting, "I call them scoffers, not skeptics." As Truzzi put it, "Since 'skepticism' properly refers to doubt rather than denial—nonbelief rather than belief—critics who take the negative rather than an agnostic position but still call themselves 'skeptics' are actually pseudo-skeptics."[8]

Expanding on the theme in another forum, Truzzi stated, "They tend to block honest inquiry.... Most of them are not agnostic toward claims of the paranormal; they are out to knock them.... When an experiment of the paranormal meets their requirements, then they move the goal posts. Then, if the experiment is reputable, they say it's a mere anomaly."[9]

One may wonder why some debunkers may have muffled facts and hidden evidence supporting paranormal phenomena. If their case is so clear, why would they resort to distorting information rather than allowing the full set of facts to reveal the truth? Perhaps a partial answer is found in the words of those who have scrutinized CSICOP from the inside. In examining the scientific status of CSICOP long ago, sociologists Pinch and Collins (1984) described the Committee as a "scientific-vigilante" organization. Engineering professor Leonard Lewin noted that in articles published by *The Skeptical Inquirer* (CSICOP's mouthpiece), "the rhetoric and appeal to emotion seemed rather out of place." Sociologist Hans Sebald (1984), now retired from his post at Arizona State University, described contributors to SI as "combative propagandists." Robert Anton Wilson (1986) labeled

CSICOP the "New Inquisition." R. A. McConnell, PhD, author of *Parapsychology in Retrospect*, who spent the first forty years of his career in the Physics and Biological Sciences Department at the University of Pittsburgh, wrote, "I cannot escape the conviction that those who control CSICOP are primarily bent upon the vilification of parapsychology and parapsychologists."[10]

Television programs have been produced under the guise of openly investigating paranormal claims in a fair and impartial manner when they were actually influenced by pseudo-skeptics. The late Montague Keen, a prominent English parapsychology researcher, attended one such production and afterward offered some interesting insights into the process. Contrasting what he and the live studio audience actually saw with the edited program, Keen noted a severely slanted angle to the production, stating, "There was a deliberate suppression of important and relevant material."[11]

One such example of exploitation involved a female medium, whose taped interview was intentionally edited to wrongly portray her as a fraud—including only the more general statements from the reading while omitting valuable, compelling footage. Upon seeing the final version of her excerpt, the woman was reduced to tears. As the audience viewed the edited version of the woman's reading, they saw that "Her statements were interlarded with comments [from debunkers] … showing how each [of the assertions she made] could be reasonably deduced from responses, facial expressions, guesswork, etc. The medium … protested most vehemently [that] … by omitting much more evidential material [through editing] the extract of her filmed sitting had given a false impression, stigmatizing her as a fake."[12]

Keen also reported that the debunker James Randi attempted to cold-read audience members in an effort to replicate the medium's work. Randi failed miserably in this endeavor, yet the awkward footage was omitted from the final production. Said Keen, "The edited version omitted his first extended but futile attempt at cold reading which was so unsuccessful that the embarrassed floor manager had to announce a technical fault and stop the show."[13]

Keen reported what appeared to be the most serious charge of all: "The editing omitted what was probably the single most impressive piece of evidence—an anonymous and untraceable booking made by a grieving father for a private reading with Keith Charles, the medium, who described to him the detailed contents and design of a sealed letter that had been placed, unbeknown to the father, in the coffin of his daughter by her sister."[14]

The exploitive efforts were not lost on the live audience, who by and large sided with the mediums and their supporters. Prior to the start of the program, an audience poll indicated that 44 percent of the attendees were "believers," 19 percent were "non-believers," and 37 percent were "uncertain." After the program concluded another poll was taken, revealing a clear shift in audience perspectives. At this point, 54 percent were now "believers," 24 percent were "non-believers," and 22 percent were "uncertain."[15] Given this backdrop, it seems clear that someone viewing only the edited version of the program could come to a far different conclusion than a person who witnessed the entire program.

Some poorly designed mediumship experiments have yielded less than favorable results. Do these failures indicate that mediumship is unfeasible, or were the results reflecting the underlying motivations of the scientists involved? Were these cases of scientific sloppiness or the execution of processes designed to confirm pre-existing biases of the experimenters? Addressing the importance of experimental design, Julie Beischel of the Windbridge Institute indicates that several factors are critical to executing an optimal mediumship test:

> I think people fail to understand that proper research design includes optimizing the possibility of achieving positive results. If you want to study plant growth, you don't put a dry seed on the bench top in the lab and then say, 'Plants can't grow.' You use soil, water, sunlight, and then you study the growth of the seed.[16]

While thumbing through my father's autobiography, *The Phoenix Oracle*, published in 1970, I found a strikingly similar statement on this topic:

> Actually, you can compare it to the planting of a flower. To make something grow and blossom you need the right kind of soil, water, and "tender loving care." Like the creative person—the artist, or musician—the psychic is an extremely sensitive human being.... I do not mean that scientific, clinical conditions should be sacrificed; instead, newer and more interesting test methods should be used. It is important that the psychic receive acceptance on the same level as the scientist—with dignity, respect, and understanding. To test ... in the most productive manner, the proper setting is required.[17]

This leads us to a consideration that appears even more critical than the environmental and experimental conditions. During a public presentation I attended in 2009, Dr. Beischel shared information from an earlier paper she had written indicating that the single most important factor in conducting these types of experiments is the quality of the mediums participating in the research:

> In addition to optimal experimental conditions and well-chosen sitter and purported discarnate participants, the quality of the medium participants is of paramount importance for a successful mediumship study. [David] Fontana emphasizes the "obvious necessity to have trial runs with mediums when developing experimental methodologies" and then to "work only with those mediums who appear to perform well under these methodologies." Also, this is one factor that may have been responsible for the negative results of one recent mediumship study (O'Keeffe & Wiseman, 2005). The medium participants in that study "were recruited via a list of certified mediums provided by the Spiritualists Nationalist Union" with no apparent trial

runs to ensure that the mediums could perform under the stringent conditions of the experiment. To ensure that this is not an issue in our studies, we have developed a rigorous screening protocol for medium participants. In addition, we prefer to replicate results across numerous skilled mediums rather than to use repeated trials with one "star" medium as was often the case in historical research (e.g., Thomas, 1928; Saltmarsh, 1929).[18]

When looking at the protocols involved with the O'Keeffe and Wiseman study noted by Dr. Beischel, one might ask if this was an innocuous case of shoddy experimental design or a deliberate attempt to ensure a negative outcome. Psychologist Richard Wiseman is a fellow of the Committee for Skeptical Inquiry (formerly CSICOP) and considers himself a skeptic-debunker, so one is left to wonder.

In a separate instance Wiseman agreed to collaborate with Dr. Rupert Sheldrake on a test intended to ascertain whether certain dogs intuitively know when their owners are coming home—i.e., without sensory information. This collaborative effort was to follow on the heels of Sheldrake's own experiment, which yielded compelling results that Wiseman drew into question.

In the original experiment conducted by Sheldrake, a videotape camera was used to determine when the test dog, "Jaytee," went to the front window—ostensibly in anticipation of his owner's return home. Sheldrake's experiment was repeated more than *one hundred times* and revealed that Jaytee went to the window far more often when his owner, Pam Smart, was returning home than when she was away. This phenomenon held true even in cases where Pam came home at random or non-routine times. Also, no auditory cues—such as the sound of an automobile engine—could have been heard by Jaytee.

Sheldrake offered to assist Wiseman and his assistant in their efforts to replicate the earlier experiment. In addition to sharing his protocols, Sheldrake gained Pam's approval, allowing Wiseman to use Jaytee for his test.

Wiseman subsequently conducted only four videotaped tests, three of which occurred at the home of Pam's parents. In these tests, Jaytee went to the window 78 percent of the time when Pam was on her way home, but only 4 percent of the time when Pam was away. Wiseman's results were strikingly similar to those from the earlier experiment. In this regard, Sheldrake noted, "When Wiseman's data were plotted on graphs, they showed essentially the same pattern as my own. In other words, Wiseman replicated my own results."

Since Wiseman's results seemed to corroborate his own experiment, Sheldrake was stunned to later read that Wiseman had claimed the experiment a bust.

"I was astonished to hear that in the summer of 1996 Wiseman went to a series of conferences, including the World Skeptics Congress, announcing that he had refuted the 'psychic pet' phenomenon."

In unraveling the case, Sheldrake found that Wiseman had altered the experimental protocols without speaking to him, which seemed a breach of their agreement. Were these changes designed to ensure a negative outcome? Among the alterations made, Wiseman revised the time-window when Pam was considered to be "coming home," which affected the data analysis.

As Sheldrake shared, "The difference between our interpretations of these experiments arose because Wiseman et al. had a different agendum from mine. I was engaged in a long-term study of this dog's anticipatory behavior, whereas they seemed more interested in trying to debunk a 'claim of the paranormal.' They themselves defined an arbitrary 'claim' for Jaytee's 'signal' and judged this by disregarding most of their own data. They argue that since they specified their criterion in advance (or rather criteria, since they changed the criterion as they went along), the agreement of their pattern of results with mine is irrelevant."[19]

Wiseman eventually admitted that his results were similar to Sheldrake's.

Outside the lab, one ploy used by debunkers to discredit psychic-mediums involves the apparent offer of a million-dollar prize to anyone who can "prove" the existence of psychic or other paranormal phenomena. Such an offer generates the desired effect by creating an impression that "no one has yet won the money, therefore no one must be capable of providing proof." In practice, this offer seems to be more fluff than substance.

When probing the underpinnings of the "James Randi Million-Dollar Challenge," it becomes clear that the definition of what constitutes a "successful" demonstration is a subjective matter, and test data can be used in any way desired by JREF (the James Randi Educational Foundation.) Experimental results that would be considered a success under scientific standards could still fall far short of this program's requirements and could therefore be deemed a "failure." Worse yet, the requirements aren't clearly stated and can seemingly be adjusted at the whim of JREF.

Greg Taylor, author of the *Daily Grail*—a popular site featuring articles on anomalies and unusual science—wrote the following about the James Randi challenge:

> It seems quite obvious that the Million Dollar challenge does not offer—and has not offered in the past—a fair scientific evaluation of paranormal claims. Rather, the statistics employed are primarily based on ensuring the million dollars remains safe. Other rules further stack the deck against participants, by handing control of publicity to the JREF.[20]

In a communication to Taylor on this matter, Suitbert Ertel, Psychology Professor Emeritus at the University of Göttingen [Germany], noted:

> Randi and those who offer a large monetary prize for psi effect demonstrations are entitled to demand unachievable psi effects. It's their money and they must be careful not to lose it. Everybody must admit that this is reasonable economically. But careful reasoning about money and property is quite a different thing than careful scientific reasoning.[21]

An additional deterrent to potential participants hoping to land the prize is a stipulation requiring them to surrender all rights to legal action, regardless of any emotional, professional, or financial damage sustained. As Taylor notes, "Applicants give the JREF/Randi virtually absolute license to use the data as best suits their publicity needs, without any legal recourse for the participant. Not exactly enticing for an applicant...."[22]

There is a commonly held notion that most debunkers are scientists, but this is simply not the case. Some debunkers are actually stage magicians who feel compelled to dismiss all things paranormal—vilifying such cases as examples of chicanery, whether or not they can support their assertions. Perhaps these people are driven to discredit such claims because of the nature of their vocation, which requires them to deceive others while simultaneously forging a mindset of mistrust.

Might there be a deeper issue with debunker-type magicians? Although most such magicians are not scientists, many are backed by powerful people married to mainstream science and academia. So one may ask why these academic types are bent on stopping or discrediting research into controversial areas such as psi phenomena. Addressing this question, Tricia Robertson offers the following insights:

> Sociologists Harry Collins and Trevor Pinch conducted a study to evaluate the manner in which parapsychology has been treated by critics in the main scientific journals. They found straightforward statements of prejudice; pseudo-philosophic arguments to the effect that parapsychology ought to be rejected simply because it conflicts with accepted knowledge; accusations of fraud without any evidence to support them; attempts to discredit scientific parapsychology by association with cult and fringe activities; and emotional dismissals based only on grounds that the consequences of its acceptance would be too horrible to contemplate. They

concluded that the ordinary standards and procedures of scientific debate were being seriously violated. This fear, in the minds of some sceptics, seems to stem from a perceived threat to the structure of science.[23]

Continuing, Robertson notes,

However, physicist Henry Margenau has demonstrated that it is impossible to identify a single scientific law actually threatened by the reality of paranormal phenomena. He points out that the Law of Conservation of Energy and Momentum has already been broken by discoveries in quantum physics, which address non-locality or action at a distance; and he notes that nothing in parapsychological discoveries contradicts either the Second Law of Thermodynamics or the Principle of Causality. The only contradictions that seem to exist are with our culturally accepted view of reality based on such laws.[24]

In his book, *Beyond Supernature*, author Lyall Watson paraphrases psychologist Charles Tart, PhD, suggesting,

… the emotional nature of the debate might be due to the fact that discoveries in parapsychology offer a more personal kind of threat that operates through unconscious fears of the subject…. Science is not so much a body of undisputed fact as a set of perceptions about facts that are, on the whole, very useful but occasionally harden into dogma.[25]

Further, Watson notes,

Normal science is guided by a substantive set of beliefs, held both consciously and unconsciously by the scientific community. And anything that starts out by defining itself from the beginning as paranormal is likely to be dismissed as irrelevant.[26]

Consider Dr. Rupert Sheldrake's comments on this topic, captured during an interview in 2008, striking at what could be the very heart of the pseudo-skeptic movement: "These are mainly people who are committed to a kind of militant/atheist worldview. As far as they are concerned, if you allow any psychic phenomena to occur you are leaving a door open a crack and ... within seconds you could have God back again and, even worse, the Pope. So, I think, for them, it's almost like a kind of religious struggle. It's like a crusade."[27]

Pseudo-skeptics speak as if there is no scientific evidence supporting the existence of psychic phenomena, but nothing could be further from the truth. In actuality, significant data have been amassed since the 1880s from a wide range of research initiatives, which have yielded compelling support for psi in many forms. According to Dr. Dean Radin, "There are a half-dozen psi effects that have been replicated dozens to hundreds of times in laboratories around the world."[28]

But there is no doubt that ongoing research into the paranormal has been significantly handicapped by pre-existing biases. To quote Dr. Radin again, "The same scientific mind-set that thrives on high precision and critical thinking is also extremely adept at forming clever rationalizations that get in the way of progress. In extreme cases, these rationalizations have prevented psi research from taking place at all. If serious scientists are prevented from investigating claims of psi out of fear for their reputations, then who is left to conduct these investigations?"[29]

In the realm of skeptic debate, Near-Death Experience (NDE) phenomena are worthy of consideration. Today, because of media attention, most people are familiar with the term "NDE" and they know that such cases involve people who have had a close brush with death or were considered "dead" in a clinical sense—meaning they had no heart beat and in some cases no brain or brainstem activity— but were revived at a later time and reported lucid experiences that occurred while clinically "dead." NDE encounters typically include visitations from deceased loved ones, meetings with a "Being of Light" or significant religious/spiritual figure, and then transport through a "tunnel" into an alternate-dimension reality.

Debunkers usually respond to these reports by labeling them products of a distressed brain. But such dismissals don't fit with certain cases when patients had no brain or brainstem activity—where these persons furnished accurate details about events that took place in the operating room when their brain was considered "dead" by all accepted scientific criteria.

Debunkers attempt to refute these facts by asserting that such patients are able to make educated guesses about events that took place while they were unconscious. Dr. Penny Sartori of Swansea University in England unveiled evidence from a five-year study (1998–2003) that runs counter to such claims. Well-known for her work with the largest long-term clinical study of Near-Death Experiences in an Intensive Therapy/Care Unit, Dr. Sartori compared cardiac-arrest survivors who had reported an OBE (out-of-body experience) with a control group, the latter comprised of patients who had undergone resuscitation but did not report an OBE. There was a marked difference in the responses of these two groups.

First, findings reveal that the closer a patient was to death, the more likely it was that they would experience an OBE. Further, those patients who had an OBE were more accurate in their reporting of information regarding their surroundings than those who did not experience an OBE.

> When contrasted with the control group, who had undergone resuscitation but did not report an OBE, many discrepancies were discovered. Having been asked to re-enact their resuscitation, the control group's reports were very inaccurate and demonstrated misconceptions and errors between the actual procedures performed, as well as equipment used. Many of these patients either had no idea as to how they had been resuscitated or made guesses, based on what they had previously seen on television.[30]

We also have the case of Anita Moorjani, who accurately repeated a conversation that took place between her doctor and husband during the time she was experiencing an NDE. What makes this account remarkable is that the discussion occurred outside the room where her cancer-ridden body lay comatose, about forty feet down a corridor. In her book *Dying To Be Me* Anita describes how she observed and then reiterated this discussion in which the doctor told her husband Danny that her organs were shutting down and she would likely die within a matter of hours.[31]

Finally, lab-based science is not the only method by which knowledge is gained or understanding expanded. Outside the laboratory we enter the domain of personal experience—which may be termed "anecdotal" evidence by others but is first-hand experiential evidence for an individual. I don't discount the value of personal experience because that is where life is lived. Like most people, I have observed many unusual things in my life that will never be published in a science journal. And just because my experiences didn't occur in a lab under controlled conditions doesn't diminish their reality or impact on my life. If a golfer hits a hole-in-one but has no witnesses, it doesn't lessen the truth of what took place, particularly for him or her—even if the feat is never again repeated.

One of the biggest down sides of the pseudo-skeptic agenda manifests as a lack of funding for research into controversial areas of science. Aside from a handful of independent researchers, barely surviving on shoestring budgets, and a few brave universities that have chartered a limited number of initiatives, virtually no research is being done in fields related to psychic phenomena and mediumship. This scenario is even more frustrating when considering that tax-supported funding goes to initiatives such as studying the sexual behavior of the whiptail lizard, hormonal mechanisms in the brains of rats that make them want to eat salt, and the mate-selection process of red-winged blackbirds.[32]

I would suggest that research into the survival of consciousness after bodily death is likely near the top of most people's wish list, yet taxpayers typically have little say about such matters. Perhaps this would change if people stood up to leaders in government and academia and told them the type of research they wanted to see.

I also hope that the next generation of scientists will step forward and embrace this challenge—not succumbing to peer pressure or fear of reprisal. I know that some brave explorers have already taken on this mantle, and ideally more will join them.

Perhaps the time is right for a change. Standard scientific norms do not answer our deeper questions, and the starkness of materialism does not fulfill the human soul. I suggest that we should work together, initiating a fresh search for meaningful answers to age-old questions.

CHAPTER 6

Reflections

I retain many fond memories from the early years of my life that have had a pronounced influence on my outlook today. I suppose my upbringing was highly unusual, although it didn't seem like it to me at the time; other kids didn't have clairvoyant parents uncovering the secret details of their daily lives, but I never felt like my life was particularly unique. My father allowed me to go through a full array of normal childhood activities without intervening—even when he knew I was on the verge of a painful event.

In the early 1960s, my father and I shared a remarkable dialog when I was between three and four years old that he later related to me. We were driving one day, before the advent of mandatory seatbelts, when he noticed that I was sitting against the car door. He urged me to move closer to him in case the door happened to accidently open.

I responded to my father, "If that happened I would break my head and be all broken up into a lot of little pieces. Then I'd go up to heaven and wouldn't cry anymore. They would make a new body for me and make me come down here again."

"Have you been here before?" my father asked.

"Of course," I said.

"How did you get over there? Were you in a war?" my father queried.

"Yes, but I wasn't killed in a war," I replied.

"But how did you get over there?"

"I just got old and tired and went," I responded.

"How old were you when you died?"

"Eighty-three. My mama was my mama in my past life but I never saw you before!" I told my father.

"Did you have any brothers or sisters?" my father asked.

"Nine," I answered.

In recapping this conversation later in his autobiography, my father noted, "This unusual exchange with my young son was another indication, to me, of the ability of certain psychic people to recall past incarnations."[1]

Today, about fifty years after this discussion, I would describe myself as open to the possibility of reincarnation. I cannot recall this exchange today or the past-life memories (which typically vanish when children turn six or so), but the comments I shared at that young age may have been the recounting of a previous existence or they could also be attributed to playfulness. That said, I was pretty straightforward as a child and did not have a particularly active imagination.

Dr. Ian Stevenson studied more than three thousand cases that strongly suggest the possibility of reincarnation. His research was primarily focused on interviews with children—many of whom were from indigenous communities—claiming to recall a prior life elsewhere. A good number of these children shared specific information about their prior life, including their previous name, names of friends and family members, as well as the names of their former tribes. Stevenson then traveled—sometimes hundreds of miles—to investigate these claims and often found that the information furnished was astonishingly accurate. In addition to dozens of published articles, Stevenson released a number of books on the topic including *Twenty Cases Suggestive of Reincarnation*, *Children Who Remember Previous Lives*, and several different volumes of *Cases of Reincarnation Type*, examining reincarnation accounts from a variety of geographies and cultures.

Professor Erlandur Haraldsson from Iceland worked with Dr. Stevenson and corroborated his findings. Further, Haraldsson published a 2008 article in the *Journal of Scientific Exploration* regarding the persistence of reincarnation memories over time.[2] The article focused on a follow-up study that he conducted which revealed that by adulthood only about 38 percent of those individuals interviewed as children retained memories of their prior life. These findings seem to indicate that Dr. Stevenson was wise to interview his subjects as children because their memories were fresh, and also to avoid contamination from cultural and social influences. More recently Drs. Brian Weiss and Michael Newton have used hypnotic regression to unveil compelling information from patients indicating past-life experiences. The cumulative evidence from these and other researchers provides a solid basis for a reincarnation hypothesis, so it seems there is good reason to give these ideas serious consideration.

Although I'm still on the fence to some degree, I must admit that reincarnation fits with my philosophical framework in many ways. First, I see life as a progressive, evolutionary process where the soul is refined through experience. It seems hard to envision a person moving from a state of being "unmolded clay" to that of a highly evolved, caring, compassionate, altruistic individual in a single lifetime. Is it possible that someone like Mahatma Gandhi became so loving and selfless because his soul had been honed over many lives on Earth? Perhaps Gandhi was experiencing his final earthly incarnation—having now attained the level of spiritual understanding and advancement necessary to exist in higher, non-physical realms forevermore. Or maybe he'd already reached that level before entering his last Earth life and came back out of a desire to give, teach, and show us the way.

If reincarnation exists, I imagine most of us would not return to Earth immediately after physical death. Rather, I suspect we would spend a relatively long period of what we perceive as *time* between physical lives in a pleasant spiritual realm. This time in-between would allow us to recuperate from the stress of Earth life while enjoying a blissful state of being with other friends and relatives who had passed—eventually reassessing where we are and where we want to go on our path of soul growth. Further, I surmise that we would have a choice about whether to come back, when to return, and under what circumstances. I expect that our advancement would continue in the spiritual realm, between physical lives, yet at a slower pace than here on Earth. The unique challenges posed by physical embodiment in this world seem highly conducive to accelerated learning when contrasted with a spiritual realm where there is presumably no need or conflict. In the physical world we are challenged in many ways. A person can become a slave to sensory desires, act selfishly, become greedy, and treat others in a callous manner. Conversely, a person can also yield to a higher calling, becoming self-effacing and compassionate.

This "time in-between" idea makes sense to me when considering communications I've received from mediums. During these sessions it was clear that my loved ones were communicating from a spiritual realm and they had not re-embodied, as evidenced by the meaningful and unique messages I received that fit them so precisely. (Some people suggest that our souls are multi-dimensional and therefore some aspect of us is always in the spiritual realm whether we are presently incarnate or not. I'm choosing not to delve that deeply here.)

Today the concept of reincarnation is a staple of Eastern religions and philosophies, including Hinduism and Buddhism, but it is not accepted within Christianity, the predominant faith in the West. However, it has been argued that evidence exists to suggest that reincarnation was a commonly held belief among early Christians for several hundred years. A key scriptural account that seems to point in this direction has Jesus speaking to a crowd about John the Baptist, in relation to the anticipated second coming of Elijah. "And if you are willing to accept it, he is Elijah who was to come." (Matthew 11:14) Further into this text the disciples specifically ask Jesus about the second coming of Elijah. To this query Jesus responds, "'Elijah has come already, and they did not know him but did to him whatever they wished. Likewise the Son of Man is also about to suffer at their hands.' Then the disciples understood that He spoke to them of John the Baptist." (Matthew 17:12–13).

Moving on from the topic of reincarnation to personal experiences involving psychic phenomena, I saw my father make accurate statements about events and circumstances throughout my childhood that he had no way of knowing via any conventional means. I remember wishing that he would be wrong—*just once!* One memorable occurrence took place when I was in the second grade, after my friend Raymond and I visited a small farm owned by his aunt and uncle. Among the animals cared for by Raymond's relatives were some cute baby rabbits, which they were giving away. Like most other children at such a young age, I was captivated by the bunnies and wanted to take one home as a pet. Raymond's uncle tentatively agreed—pending my parents' approval—but no one answered when I called home. So I promised to contact Raymond's uncle again after consulting my folks.

Early the next day I was horsing around with my father and suddenly remembered the baby rabbits. Excited and hoping for a "yes," I immediately asked for permission to bring a bunny home.

My father's expression suddenly turned somber and he replied, "Mark, they no longer have the rabbits."

Puzzled by his response, I asked, "What do you mean? Where are they?"

Straining to utter the words, my dad looked at me and said, "The rabbits are dead."

Stunned, I followed, "What happened to them?"

My dad hesitantly replied, "They killed the rabbits."

I responded angrily, "You're wrong—why would they have killed those rabbits?"

In an instant, I grabbed the phone and called the number given to me by Raymond's uncle. He answered after just a couple rings.

"Hello, this is Mark Ireland. I spoke to my parents and they said I could bring a bunny home."

Raymond's uncle came back, "I'm sorry but we don't have the rabbits; they are dead."

I was shaken and angry, and didn't even think to ask how the rabbits met their demise. I dropped the phone and broke into tears. My father tried to comfort me but his efforts were to no avail. The news of the rabbits' demise saddened me, and my father's unwavering accuracy frustrated me. I was sure that Raymond's uncle had not shared this information with my parents because of the way he delivered the message. It seemed to be the first time he had addressed the issue with anyone. Later, I asked Raymond why his uncle had killed the rabbits. He said that his aunt and uncle had given away some of the rabbits, but there were too many left and they couldn't care for them. It all seemed terribly cruel to me.

In fifth and sixth grade I remember friends and teachers who were truly intrigued by my father's unusual gifts. At times I'd be barraged with their array of questions, including gems like "Does your dad read minds?" and "Does he tell you about your future?"

In practice I rarely bothered my father for psychic information because everyone else was always after him for that. He traveled a great deal and his time was at a premium, so we enjoyed doing other things when we were together—like playing backgammon or other board games. I also wanted my father to understand that I was not seeking the things from him that others constantly sought. I just wanted him to be my dad.

While at my twenty-year high-school reunion, a former classmate named Geoff approached me. I remembered Geoff from as far back as fifth grade, although we had not really been close friends because we didn't have much in common. At the reunion, Geoff felt compelled to share a particularly interesting story about my father. He said: "Back in fifth grade, your dad really freaked me out. I stole a five-gallon gas can from your house when nobody was around. The next day I saw your father approach our house, walk into our garage, and go directly to the gas can. He picked it up and walked back to your house without saying a word."

Geoff added that he never again tried to pull a stunt on my family.

When I was growing up my father served as a minister and as an "entertainer," demonstrating his psychic abilities in showrooms and nightclubs. Some church members were upset that he worked in such venues, but my father saw things differently. He knew that television shows and nightclub appearances afforded him an opportunity to meet people who would never step foot in a church. My father believed that some individuals might be stirred after seeing his psychic gifts and possibly reassess their prior thinking. And indeed, he found that some people did open up their minds and reconsider their previous assumptions, especially in cases where he addressed their specific questions. He hoped that skeptics might say to themselves, "Perhaps there is something to this…. Maybe we are more than just flesh and bones."

Shifting to a more solemn matter, I suspect that my father may have had precognitive knowledge of my son Brandon's future passing at a young age. There were two occasions where I saw him speaking with Brandon in a unique manner. It was not so much what he said but rather my father's tone and how he looked at my son. It was as if two conversations were taking place simultaneously—one on the surface and another on a deeper, unspoken level. I'd come to recognize the times when my dad *knew something*, and these occasions fit the pattern. If my observation was on target, this would have been a huge burden for my father to bear—perhaps relieved to some degree by his awareness of a larger plan. The first of these instances took place when Brandon was about four years old and the second one occurred while my father was in the hospital, just months before he died, when Brandon was six. My father passed away twelve years before Brandon's accident.

During his life, my father Richard Ireland was acquainted with Glenn Ford, David Janssen, Amanda Blake, and other well-known actors and actresses. He was also friends with Darryl Zanuck, founder of Twentieth-Century Fox. My father appeared on shows hosted by Regis Philbin, Steve Allen, Alan Burke, Joe Pine, and other notable personalities. And while the term may seem a bit ostentatious, my father was widely recognized as "The Psychic to the Stars" in the 1970s.

Aside from his Hollywood connections, I possess something that suggests that my father had an even more intriguing relationship. Among the assorted documents left behind after his passing, I have a hand-written card from Mamie and President Dwight D. Eisenhower, sent to my father and mother in recognition of their marriage. What I am missing is *the rest of the story* about the nature of their relationship, but the possibilities are fascinating to consider.

My father's foray into celebrity circles was largely facilitated through his friendship with actress Mae West, whom he met through Reverend Jack Kelly in 1952. Mae West was a revolutionary figure in both film and on Broadway, particularly in the 1920s and 1930s. One could argue that she was the first Hollywood sex symbol whose groundbreaking work paved the way for Marilyn Monroe, Jayne Mansfield, and other stars who followed. It has been said that Miss West was endowed with clairvoyant abilities, spurring her fascination with psychic phenomena.

My father and Miss West forged a life-long friendship, and he became her personal consultant on psychic matters after the passing of Reverend Kelly. My father frequently performed psychic demonstrations at Mae's apartment in Beverly Hills, where she would invite large groups comprised of friends and celebrities. In her book, *Mae West on Sex, Health and ESP*, Miss West shares the following:

> Back in the fifties, when I was appearing in Washington, DC, in my nightclub act, I saw my friend Rev. Jack Kelly who was in town and he introduced me to Dr. Richard Ireland. Jack spoke very highly of Ireland and said he was an extraordinary psychic with headquarters in Phoenix, Arizona.
>
> I didn't see Dr. Ireland again until a few years ago when he was in Los Angeles for meetings at one of the large hotels. A few of my friends saw him and reported to me that Richard Ireland was "terrific." Before he went home to Phoenix, he came up to see me. He recalled our introduction by Jack Kelly in Washington. He was a youngish, good-looking man,

with a great personality and a fine sense of humor. Psychic since childhood, his extrasensory perception never fails to astonish people by revealing facts about themselves he could not possibly have known by any other means.[3]

In 1978 I had the privilege of meeting Miss West when my father, sister, and I were invited to attend a party that she hosted. Guests mingled for about an hour and then took seats for my father's psychic demonstration, which was a big hit. After the party, Miss West took us on a tour of her apartment. My initial impression was related to the décor, which gave me the eerie sense of being teleported back to the 1920s. I suppose Miss West's residence reflected a fondness for an era epitomizing the pinnacle of her career. I felt a bit sad to meet her at this stage in life when she was small and frail. But Miss West's inner beauty shone through unmistakably and she proved to be a kind, warm, and fun-loving individual.

My father's sense of humor was on task that night and he couldn't resist asking Miss West something facetiously risqué.

"Would you mind if my son sat on your bed? That way he can tell his friends that he's been in Mae West's bed."

She smiled back and said, "Certainly."

So I jumped up onto her large elevated bed, grinning, yet slightly embarrassed by my father's tongue-in-cheek request.

And because of my father's unabashed sense of humor on a special evening in 1978, today I can say with complete honesty that I have indeed been in (or at least on) Mae West's bed.

CHAPTER 7

Credibility and Trust

As I've been discussing in previous chapters, psychic phenomena and mediumship have long suffered from an image problem. Unfortunately, the world is littered with frauds and con artists of all varieties whose activities help to perpetuate this stigma.

In July 2005, my wife Susie and I were introduced to the Burgstahler family, who had lost their son Taylor in a tragic lake accident. When Taylor's mother Lori asked my wife how we were able to cope with such a loss, Susie pointed to faith and also talked about our experiences with credible mediums. Unbeknownst to us, after we met with Lori she decided to consult a "store-front" reader in hopes of connecting with her son. This proved to be a big mistake, as Lori was subjected to a horribly distressing and despicable experience.

The supposed "medium," who allegedly reads ruin stones, told Lori that Taylor had "not crossed to the other side" and that he was "not in the light." Adding to the insult, this charlatan told Lori that her deceased mother-in-law "had a dark side" and that she had "taken her son" after he passed. This statement made no sense to Lori, as she recalled her husband's mom being a very nice person during their one and only meeting, shortly before her mother-in-law's death.

The callous woman then proceeded to say that Lori had "a negative energy attached to her," resulting from a "curse" that someone had put upon her. For good measure, the hoaxer said that Lori's house was cursed as well.

These preliminary statements paved the way for the woman's punch line. Miraculously, this all-knowing mystic offered a way to correct this cosmic mayhem for modest sum of $750. In exchange for her nominal fee, the woman offered to eliminate all negative energy, thus clearing the way for Taylor to cross over.

Lori was emotionally distraught after this event and hurried home, where she broke down. Wisely, she never returned to see the con artist. Instead she picked up the phone and called Susie, asking if she might be able to recommend any "good" mediums. In turn, Susie offered the names of two trusted individuals.

Unfortunately, frauds like the woman referenced in this story fuel negative impressions associated with mediums, providing fodder for debunkers who assert that all psychics are of the same ilk. So with such cases in mind, one may wonder how to find a credible medium. How can a person "separate the wheat from the chaff"?

My first recommendation is to seek out a psychic-medium based on a referral from a trusted source—such as a relative, friend, or co-worker. Then before proceeding, ask the referring individual a few specific questions about their reading, which may reveal the true ability of the medium. (If this method won't work for you because there is no one you could ask or would want to ask, refer to page 108 of this chapter for other ways to locate a qualified medium.)

Ask the person whether the medium knew anything about them prior to the reading. To avoid what is known as "front loading" or "warm reading," it is best to attend such a session with the medium having little or no advance knowledge about the sitter.

In booking an appointment, people are typically expected to provide their name, which is understandable. That said, I have known several people who utilized a pseudo-name to avoid any chance for front loading, yet the medium still performed very well. As a result, I have great confidence in these mediums and gladly refer people to them—since they have proved their legitimacy beyond any reasonable doubt. Whether or not you choose to use your real name is up to you, but I don't recommend deception as a course of action. The medium may be willing to accept your first name alone if you can provide assurance that you won't "skip out" on the appointment, so you may wish to pursue that angle. Or if they come highly recommended from a trustworthy source don't worry too much about it.

I know a few reliable mediums who prefer some advance communication with the sitter, to facilitate a preliminary discussion about what the client wants from the session. I am okay with this if the medium's abilities have been proven, or if you have complete confidence in the source that referred the medium. As a rule of thumb, when it comes to obtaining a pure reading, the less information that is available to a medium, the better.

Back to questioning the person who gives you a referral in order to ascertain the aptitude of the medium: For one thing, the best psychic-mediums typically start by providing information on their own without asking a lot of questions. Lesser mediums tend to ask the sitter more questions, so they can focus their (sometimes-vague) answers in the same direction. It is fine for the medium to ask what the sitter wants out of the reading, but if the medium begins to probe—asking questions about marital status, children, or names of family members—it is typically not a good sign.

Conversely, the best mediums can often furnish names or at least the first letters of names that are meaningful to the sitter. Top-tier mediums are able to provide compelling and specific information as opposed to vague generalities. To me, the specificity of information given is every bit as important as the accuracy, so it is wise to ask a referring friend about the *quality* of the validations they received in their session. Being told that "an older man is trying to touch in" is not nearly as compelling as hearing "your father, Renaldo, wants to congratulate you on your recent promotion to a Director position."

Once you have selected a medium and scheduled an appointment, it is important to follow certain steps to avoid the possibility of "cold reading" (referring to a practice whereby the medium in question reads body language, interprets voice-tones and related emotion, asks general questions, and then modifies comments based on sensory input including sitter feedback). To guard against this risk, you should minimize eye contact with the medium, show minimal emotion when responding to questions or making statements, and be guarded when answering questions. You should only share general information when answering unless the medium has *earned the right* to receive specific feedback. For example, if a medium has correctly identified that you have a deceased brother named Greg who died of cancer, it is not detrimental to confirm the accuracy of their statement. But if the medium is "fishing" for information, generically asking if you have a brother, I suggest responding with a question of your own like, "Why do you ask if I have a brother?" Now keep in mind, it is important to avoid being too rigid or making the medium feel uncomfortable or they may not be able to do their best, so it is a fine line you must walk as a sitter. Be friendly and relaxed, just don't offer up too much—let the medium do most of the talking.

As a real-life example of an excellent reading with highly specific information, I had a phone session with Sally Owen in 2006 that included a number of remarkable validations. Sally entered the reading knowing very little about me, yet it didn't affect her ability to deliver solid, meaningful information. Among her hits, Sally stated, "You must have a son on the other side." She then referenced one of Brandon's toys: "You know those little jack-in-the-boxes that have the hand crank and then the jack-in-the-box jumps out?" Sally noted that Brandon showed her where other toys had been stuffed into the jack-in-the-box: "… put something in the clown in the box," she related.

This was a striking affirmation. As a young child, Brandon possessed such a jack-in-the-box toy and he inserted other small objects inside so he could watch them pop out after turning the crank. This activity never ceased to amuse him—Brandon would break into laughter every time the jack-in-the box emerged, accompanied by toy-shrapnel. What an obscure piece of information … and impossible to research.

General statements are typically less meaningful to a sitter and often cannot be substantiated. As a case in point, a medium is not required to go too far out on a limb to speculate that a forty-eight-year-old man may have lost a grandparent. Nor is it a stretch for the medium to say, "Grandma sends her love," even though the statement may be exactly what the grandparent is conveying to the medium. But if the medium is able to furnish the grandmother's name or share other precise information that can be validated, the statement will carry far more weight. Such information could be in reference to a name, a pet, a hobby, or a shared experience.

If you are meeting with a well-regarded medium, you shouldn't have to worry about the possibility of cold reading, but you may choose to take precautionary steps for your own sake—especially if you are naturally skeptical. This will lend an added sense of validity to the process when you reflect on it, keeping you from second-guessing things later on. It is important to remember that mediums are sensitive people, and if they feel threatened or excessively challenged, this could detract from the quality of your reading. If you choose to employ a guarded approach, please make a point of being friendly and positive when meeting the medium. This is easy to accomplish prior to the reading, as it allows you to set them at ease, explaining that you look forward to the process and that you are open-minded. You might even share your intention to be a bit guarded, letting them know not to take it the wrong way. You just want the best, most authentic reading possible.

Then again, if you truly trust the person or you have had other good sessions in the past, readings can be far more enjoyable without worrying about the risk of cold reading. But as a rule of thumb, I suggest waiting until you have a couple of readings under your belt before letting down your guard too much.

If you are fortunate enough to find an exceptional medium, the joy of the experience can sometimes extend beyond the quality of the information shared. On occasion, even the manner in which the communication is delivered can be startling … and uplifting.

In late 2007, I had a remarkable session with a medium named Tina Powers. Aside from the fact that she provided a multitude of specific hits, Tina actually took on my son's persona at one point—emulating his manner of speech to a tee, including Brandon's intonation and tone. This was completely unexpected and very touching. Besides a "dream visitation" I had experienced a couple of years earlier, this was the most intimate "connection" I had with Brandon since his passing. It really seemed as close to "talking to him" as I could get.

To ensure the best chance of contact with a deceased loved one during a mediumship reading, I encourage you to send out "thought invitations" in advance of your appointment. This can be something as simple as a prayerful thought request, or you may choose to think of it as a form of telepathic transmission. Why should we think that our lives are any busier than the lives of those who have passed on? Much of the feedback I've received during my various readings indicates that the lives of the deceased are quite active.

And if it is okay with the medium, I suggest that you record the session—preferably with a digital audio recorder, which provides higher-quality audio output than a magnetic tape device such as a cassette unit. If you cannot record the session, I recommend that you take copious notes. Recording is preferable to note-taking because it allows you to stay more engaged in the session and not worry about multi-tasking. The key point here is that most readings occur in rapid fashion, and you will likely have difficulty digesting all the information unless you log it in some way. With an audio recording or good notes at hand, you'll be able to reflect on the reading in greater detail later on.

To return to the circumstance of not knowing where to find a referral or a qualified medium, I want to acknowledge that this can be a challenging issue for the average person, especially those who find this topic new or foreign within the scope of their life experience.

You may initially assume that you have no sources for a reference, but you might be surprised to learn that someone you know has already consulted a psychic-medium. Because people sometimes worry about what others think, they may have participated in such an encounter but chose to remain silent about it. In the proper environment, engaged in dialog with a trusted other, the person may open up. I suggest broaching the subject in a calm and conversational way, mentioning a recent book on the subject or referencing a television appearance by a leading medium. This may lead to more discussion on the topic and possibly an opportunity to ask if the person has ever had a reading. If they have done so and are able to indicate satisfaction with the experience, you may wish to ask for a reference.

Some people simply won't have access to a credible reference, and I can recommend a few other suggestions that might help. I do not have personal experience with all the mediums mentioned here and therefore can rely only on the source that is furnishing the recommendation.

First, I co-founded an organization called "Helping Parents Heal" that is intended to assist people who have lost children. Our website www.helpingparentsheal.info has a link to a provider list that includes recommendations for a number of mediums who generated positive results for one or more of our founding members. Along with the name of each medium is a brief write-up from the person who experienced the reading.

A former skeptic turned researcher, Bob Olson, offers a list of mediums that he has personally tested on his website www.bestpsychicmediums.com. Bob has a second website, www.bestpsychicdirectory.com, with a far more extensive list of mediums who come with solid recommendations, but who have not been tested by Bob. One of the best features of Bob's psychic directory site is that it lists mediums from a wide range of geographic locations, so those who want an in-person reading can get one. Again, I've found that phone readings with a quality medium can be exceptionally good, but some people prefer the intimate feel of a face-to-face session. I know Bob and respect his work, but I have had a personal experience with only two of the mediums on his list. So again, these are Bob's recommendations and not mine.

In a similar vein, the Windbridge Institute and Forever Family Foundation both have certification processes to identify mediums who meet certain criteria, validating their ability and authenticity. To see their listing of certified mediums, consult their websites, www.windbridge.org and www.foreverfamilyfoundation.org. These lists don't provide references for psychic-mediums in all geographic areas, but they are a better alternative than stepping blindly into a session with someone who may be more interested in your wallet than your well-being.

It is my eventual goal to establish, or contribute to, a far-reaching network of certified psychic-mediums whom people can contact with total confidence. I am open to working with other like-minded individuals toward that end. My vision involves the utilization of test sitters who participate in blind readings. Results from these tests would be used to determine the abilities of the various mediums, via a stringent evaluation process. Controls would be set to prevent the possibility of front loading or cold reading, with standards focused on accuracy and specificity established to grade performance. Based on results achieved—as measured against pre-established standards—top mediums would be identified and a meaningful, "objective" reference list could be created.

Not all psychic-mediums would choose to participate in such a process, especially if they have an established clientele or if they don't care for limelight. But I suspect that there are many little-known psychic-mediums with tremendous ability who would like to share their gifts in order to help other people.

So my advice is to talk to people you know and trust, looking for solid recommendations, or utilize one of these other resources. Otherwise, if you choose to embark on your own without a recommendation, the rule is *buyer beware!*

CHAPTER 8

Psychic Phenomena and Mediumship in Religion and History

I saw value in writing a chapter to address the fear and apprehension that some people harbor toward psychic phenomena and spirit communication as a result of their religious upbringing. I live in a predominantly Christian culture where—within the modern church—these topics are shrouded in ambiguity yet suffused with an undertone that seems to imply "stay away from that stuff." Likewise, other monotheistic religions present a cautionary attitude when it comes to these topics.

In contrast, my father believed that his abilities, including psi and spirit communication, were a manifestation of the "gifts of the spirit" referenced in the New Testament. He saw his abilities as being supportive of many Biblical miracle stories, so this *other*, negative view puzzled him. He thought that some of this negativity was due to the infiltration into the modern church of a materialist mindset and its accompanying rigid skepticism. I agree with this while also seeing some of the reticence regarding the paranormal as a product of traditional views that have evolved over time without challenge. In practice, most members of the Christian clergy typically seem content to steer clear of discussions involving these topics because they're just too "sticky."

Regardless of church doctrine, people often come to their own conclusions about said phenomena by virtue of a deeply moving personal spiritual epiphany that outweighs traditional religious considerations. Such individuals may feel they have actually been touched by God or a divine benevolent spiritual energy, and who is to say they are wrong? These people know what they have experienced. They may have an inner sense—an arcane knowledge or awareness that transcends convention and tradition but reaches to the core of their soul.

In some cases people simply elect to think independently, asserting their right to participate in a church without accepting every ideological tenet associated with their chosen faith. I would surmise that this is a rather common occurrence, yet people's deeper opinions often likely reside below the surface of their persona or sometimes even their awareness.

In Western culture, the "miracles" referenced in scripture seem to have been relegated to the past as if to imply that they were reserved exclusively for certain historical periods. Some people consider them mere metaphors. But it is these miracle stories that resonate with paranormal phenomena—lending greater credence to scripture and providing support for the larger body of spiritual philosophy. This seems important at a time when Western society remains intensely focused on the "material realities" of our world, with less regard for the inner dimension of spiritual life. Such dismissals or disapprovals of psychically related phenomena also serve to aid some atheistic secular humanists who wage war against all things spiritual.

Speaking about how "miracles" are typically addressed within the modern Christian church, a friend recently offered the following tongue-in-cheek quip: "Something happened yesterday, and something will happen tomorrow, but nothing is happening today."

Addressing the issue of paranormal phenomena from a biblical perspective, the late Reverend Chancellor Garth Moore, one of the foremost Ecclesiastical lawyers of his era (1950s to '80s), stated:

> The theologian, too, has a duty to look at the evidence. Hitherto, all too often, he has either ignored the psychic altogether, or dismissed it as nonsense, or has acknowledged its

reality but shunned it as being of the devil. To ignore it is odd in those of whom the majority may be expected by profession to believe in a non-material dimension to Creation. For a Christian theologian to treat it as nonsense is to demonstrate how deeply he has been infected by the comparatively modern and now slightly outdated wave of secular materialism.[1]

Readers who are not particularly interested in how psychic phenomena and mediumship are viewed by various religions may choose to skip ahead to chapter 9.

When evaluating psychic phenomena and mediumship through the lens of various religious traditions, an interesting dichotomy is revealed. Views on the paranormal fluctuate significantly among different creeds and cultures.

In Eastern traditions such as Hinduism and Buddhism, psychic phenomena are viewed as a rather common thing. Faithful Hindus consider their scriptures, the Vedas, to be revealed knowledge. The word *Veda* actually means "knowledge" and comes from the term *Vid* in Sanskrit. Within the Vedas, specifically the Upanishads, it is acknowledged that psychic phenomena are often a natural byproduct of development in one's pursuit of enlightenment.

Scholars view the Vedas as the oldest surviving scriptures in the world, with the earliest portions dating to approximately 1500 BCE, likely preceded by a long oral tradition. In the Hindu faith, the word "Moksha" represents release from "Samsara"—the cycle of death and rebirth. This release leads to Nirvana—or oneness with the divine ground of being, known as "Brahman." (In some traditions, Moksha and Nirvana are interchangeable terms.)

In Buddhism, an offshoot of Hinduism, followers pursue enlightenment through diligent meditation and yogic practice, complemented by an altruistic lifestyle. Like their Hindu counterparts, Buddhists view Nirvana as the end goal—representing the cessation of Samsara and suffering. In the Buddhist tradition one attains enlightenment by recognizing the illusory and fleeting nature of the material world, known as "Maya," releasing from attachment to things (i.e., manifestations) of the physical realm.

In the Pali Canon, a key Buddhist scripture, the Buddha describes Nirvana (Nibbana) as,

> "... the subtle ... the un-aging, the stable, the un-disintegrating, the un-manifest, the un-proliferated, the peaceful, the deathless ... the un-ailing state ... the island ... the refuge...."
> (SN 43:14)

"Buddha" is a title meaning "Enlightened One" or "Awakened One," commonly used to describe a historical man by the given name of Siddhartha Gautama. Born a wealthy prince, Siddhartha felt great compassion for all people and living creatures. Because of the suffering he saw, Siddhartha was compelled to relinquish his lofty position and worldly possessions. Born in 560 BCE, he was a Hindu reformer known for his disdain of the caste system, which put people into hierarchical groups. Siddhartha believed in the equality of all people.

In his pursuit of illumination, the Buddha found extremes such as fasting and self-mortification to be ineffective, and he subsequently pursued the "Middle Path," which promotes moderation and balance in all aspects of life. Siddhartha's enlightenment occurred while sitting under a bodhi tree, in deep meditation. This process resulted in two great powers awakening within him: wisdom and universal compassion.

Because of his deep insights and paranormal abilities, people began to wonder about the true identity of the Buddha. First, they asked if he was a Celestial Being or a God.

To this query he replied, "No."

Next, they asked the Buddha if he was a magician or a wizard.

Again he responded, "No."

Then they asked if he was a man and once again he replied, "No."

The Buddha was then asked, "Well then, what are you?"

To this he replied, "I am awake."

In my father's unpublished writings I found an entry that reflects a view similar to the Buddha's. In this work he states, "… meditation has but one aim: to raise consciousness to the highest level … where the Divine is directly experienced." In these same writings I found an account of the spiritual perspective of indigenous peoples in North America—a viewpoint that he contrasts with contemporary Western society:

> Historically, Western man has always been more concerned with the visible than the invisible world. And by the invisible I am not referring to the colorless void of outer space … the mysterious domain of atomic and subatomic particles, or the imperceptible zones of the electromagnetic spectrum. Rather, I am alluding to the spiritual and psychical forces which have been known to Far Eastern initiates and North American Indian contemplatives for ages.
>
> The Sioux Indians were quick to recognize that the white man … was spiritually obtuse. Rather than appreciating the religious, symbolic dimension of a physical object, they noticed that he tended to disregard it altogether unless it had some obvious, practical use. Lame Deer, an Oglala Sioux Medicine Man, remarked that the "white man sees so little, he must see with only one eye."
>
> Exercising his intellect until he has become mentally muscle-bound and somewhat insensitive, he has erected an enviable civilization on the one hand and waged apocalyptic war on the other. But while his wars are wholly disgusting, his civilization, appearing as a glittering but sterile façade of glass and stainless steel, is not completely satisfying. Recognizing this [condition] is a step in the right direction, for it places him on the verge of realizing that the fulfillment he seeks in the world actually lies in the world within.

In some ways my father's depiction of modern Western civilization seems as relevant today as it did when he wrote these passages in the early 1970s. People continue to place undue focus on the accumulation of material possessions and incessantly strive to satiate their unquenchable desires for sensory gratification. Many of our doctors fail to treat us holistically—viewing people as "meat robots," mindlessly dispensing pills for every ailment. But it wasn't always so. Historically, Western culture finds many of its roots in ancient Greek thought, which offers a perspective far different than the materialistic worldview pervading people's outlook today.

In his "Allegory of the Cave," the Greek philosopher Plato depicts people mesmerized by shadows on a cave wall that they accept as truth and reality. Unfortunately, these individuals had fallen victim to delusion, failing to discover a deeper, underlying reality, imperceptible to the senses. In the story, people who have lived chained in a cave for their entire life are able to see nothing but a blank wall. When anything passes in front of a fire burning behind them, shadows are cast on the wall, which the captives see as forms that they consider reality.

In *The Republic*, Plato refers to a concept called "The Good," which he describes as "the light, which illuminates the world of the mind." When Plato states that from the perspective of The Good, "we can understand all things without sensory experience," he seems to imply that the term is synonymous with intuition or what we may think of today as psi.

Plato's teacher and mentor, Socrates, referenced a guiding force that appears to be synonymous with the "spirit guides" acknowledged by modern-day mediums. Socrates's intangible friend, known as a "daemon" or "daimon"—which we might think of as a spirit or guardian angel—provided guidance, especially in trying times. Speaking on how his daemon steered him clear of trouble when he was off course, yet left him alone when he was on track, Socrates reported, "The favor of the gods has given me a marvelous gift, which has never left me since my childhood. It is a voice which, when it makes itself heard, deters me from what I am about to do and never urges me on."[2]

To clarify a point of possible misunderstanding, Socrates's daemon should not be confused with the term "demon," which carries a different and negative connotation. As author Pamela Davidson reports, "The Greek term *daimon*, best translated as 'divinity' … was a being of intermediate nature between that of gods and men, sometimes identified with an individual's guiding force, whether for good or evil."[3] Another definition of the word "daemon" is "one replete with wisdom" or "knowledge." In later Greek tradition a more negative emphasis ensued and by the time early Christianity gained footing, the daemon morphed into something else entirely—the "demon," a malicious spiritual entity.[4] As Davidson notes, "With the advent of Christianity and the translation of the pagan gods into devils, this process was completed."[5]

Scholar and author Elaine Pagels notes that early orthodox Christians took an antagonistic approach in relating to other groups—demonizing those deemed to be a threat to their viability. It was implied that these other factions were under the deceptive control and manipulation of demonic forces.[6] Initially, salvos were fired at members of the Jewish tradition from which many Christians originated. It wasn't long, however, before this "us versus them" tactic was directed at Pagans and eventually other non-orthodox Christians. Followers we now call "Gnostic Christians" were considered heretics because they held a different view about the meaning and significance of Christianity.[7] Orthodox leaders of the day sought to diminish disruptions that could possibly threaten church control.

The Gnostic movement was a significant force in Christianity's formative period, during the first few centuries. Examination of documents discovered in the past century, including scriptures we now call "The Gnostic Gospels"—unearthed in Nag Hammadi, Egypt, in 1945—reveal that early Christianity was far more diverse than scholars had previously assumed.[8]

The term "Gnostic" is derived from "gnosis," meaning "knowledge" or "to know." Considered more "mystical" than its orthodox counterpart, Gnostic Christianity held that people could have a direct connection with God without an intermediary such as the church and its clergy. They focused on God's "Logos"—meaning the "word," or "logic"—revealed through Jesus's instruction, especially his private teachings. Jesus was said to have conveyed esoteric knowledge with initiates in private because most people could not understand the teachings. The initiates came to recognize their true nature as a soul temporarily trapped in a material world—a world they could escape by perceiving the deeper (or higher) reality.[9]

Given this backdrop, I suggest that gnosis implies an inner sort of knowing, likely facilitated through an intuitive or psychic capacity.

As mentioned earlier, numerous miracles are referenced in both the Old Testament and New Testament for which psychic-related phenomena seem a rational explanation. In the latter chapters of the Old Testament, extensive contributions are attributed to the "Prophets," from Amos to Daniel, each of whom prognosticates extensively.

Despite the biblical presence of such miracle references and prophecies, which essentially constitute "divination," mediums and seers still take a hit in some passages—yielding an apparent contradiction. Most negative biblical commentary on things construed as psychic or mediumistic are found in the Old Testament books of Exodus, Leviticus, and Deuteronomy. Within these texts are admonitions about activities described as "wizardry" and "divination" and also people described as "witches" and those "having familiar spirits." The latter is no doubt similar to the later Socratic idea of people accompanied by daemons.

But these Old Testament books also suggest that questionable practices such as slavery and murder of innocent people are acceptable, which doesn't seem to fit with the concept of a loving God—creator of all sentient beings:

> Your male and female slaves are to come from the nations around you; from them you may buy slaves. You may also buy some of the temporary residents living among you and members of their clans born in your country, and they will become your property. You can will them to your children as inherited property and can make them slaves for life...."
> —Leviticus 25:44–46

Today, it seems self-evident that such an edict would be immoral and barbaric. So I ask, is it possible that at least some portion of these texts reveal more about a specific set of ancient human norms and cultural mores rather than a series of divine insights?

In evaluating such references, one needs to consider that these books reflected the thinking of early Hebrew leaders. Biblical scholar Bishop John Shelby Spong refers to the authors of these Old Testament texts as "Priestly Scribes."[10] And the writings that these scribes produced were primarily intended to establish rules and guidelines for followers.

The aforementioned Rev. Chancellor Garth Moore provides a useful insight in regard to the censure of mediumship in the Old Testament:

> One need go back to the Hebrew [language] in order to understand what these passages mean, for the English translation is misleading. The prohibition … and the condemnation … are aimed at some practices, which were fraudulent, and others, which were sordid, and at any which were idolatrous. For example, the word which has been translated into English as "familiar spirit" is the Hebrew word, OB or OBH or OUV. This literally means an empty wine-skin or wine-bag, and became associated with the fraudulent practices of those who at a séance surreptitiously produced squeaks from it and indulged in ventriloquism for the deception of the sitter who had visited the "medium" to obtain information from the dead. The type of necromancy at which the prohibition was aimed was not simple communication with the dead but one which involved highly objectionable practices with corpses.[11]

This clarification seems to support some of my suggested precautions, detailed in chapter 7. Perhaps the biggest concern over mediumship was the same in biblical times as it is today—the possibility of fraud. Also, the undertone of most Old Testament warnings seems to point to God's desire for a direct relationship with us—something most of the psychic-mediums I know agree with and encourage people to seek. They will even limit how often a client is allowed to book a reading session.

In regard to this subject, a Christian Pastor I know and respect shared the following with me: The New Testament refers to this [a direct connection with God] as the priesthood of all believers. True, we shouldn't rely upon an intermediary, though they can be of great comfort when we are not at our strongest. Yet, human tendency is to seek out those who we perceive to having a stronger connection to the Divine and making leaders out of them. That's why mega churches are often more cults of personality rather than a force for bringing God's Kingdom *on earth as it is in heaven* (personal communication, 2013).

There are many other references in the Bible that offer a different perspective. Again, quoting Rev. Chancellor Moore:

> In the Old Testament, there are plenty of indications that psychic gifts are not to be condemned. The prophets, who had these gifts in great measure, are held in great honor on account of them. Joseph not only interpreted dreams but used a cup for the purpose of divination. Daniel, a 'man greatly beloved' by the Lord, received visions, interpreted dreams, and (as we should say today) was credited with the possession of ESP of a high order. So was Elisha, and by means of it he was able to warn the King of Israel of the movements of the army of the King of Syria.[12]

In seeking to understand these biblical inconsistencies, I examined the issue from several different angles. First, as one reviews the scriptures in any depth, a number of contradictions become apparent in many different areas, not just in regard to the paranormal. As an example, Jesus provides advice that runs contrary to the passage in Exodus 21:23–24 that says, "… take life for life, eye for eye, tooth for tooth." Rather, Jesus advises, "You have heard that it is said 'An eye for an eye and a tooth for a tooth.' But I say to you, do not resist an evildoer. But if anyone strikes you on the right check, turn the other also." (Matthew 5:38–39)

In another instance, Jesus was chastised by scribes for what they saw as a violation of one of the Ten Commandments, as Christ and his disciples plucked heads of grain while walking through a field on the Sabbath day. In response to the condemning remarks, Jesus retorts, "The Sabbath was made for man and not man for the Sabbath." (Mark 2:27)

To the point, I suggest that Jesus assumed the role of reformer by showing people the misstep of interpreting scripture in a literal manner (looking to the letter of the law rather than the spirit or intention of the law).

Next, one must consider the historical context in which these books were written and the related circumstances of the time, which surely influenced their message. The books of the Old Testament were written in a period when the Hebrew culture and religion were competing with other factions and philosophies for people's hearts and minds. Religious leaders and scribes of the day derogatorily referred to competing perspectives as "Pagan," while summarily denouncing their alternate belief sets and practices.

Interestingly, specifically relating to the subject of mediumship, the Old Testament tells of a corrupt leader named Saul who exiled mediums and wizards from the land, simultaneously outlawing practices of divination. As the story goes, fortune had turned against Saul—his adversaries, the Philistines, were assembling for battle, and God was no longer speaking to Saul in his dreams.

Desperate for answers about his destiny, Saul asked one of his servants to locate a medium. In pursuing this course, Saul defied his own decree that expelled "those who trafficked with ghosts and spirits," forbidding their practice on the penalty of death. The servant told him there was a medium in En'dor, so Saul went there in disguise—knowing the medium would likely fear for her life—but Saul's cloak did little to ease the woman's anxiety.

When he asked her to contact the spirit of Samuel (Saul's prede-
cessor and a faithful servant of God), the medium retorted, "Why
have you deceived me? You are Saul!" After assurances were made
that no harm would come to her, the woman proceeded in making
contact with Samuel's spirit. Unfortunately for Saul, the message that
was shared offered him no comfort. The spirit of Samuel told Saul
that he had become an adversary of God and his army was about
to be defeated: "... the Lord will give Israel along with you into the
hands of the Philistines; and tomorrow you and your sons shall be
with me...." (I Samuel 28:3–19)

An early numinous branch of Judaism also existed, which is under-
going a major revival today. Kabbalah (also Qabalah or Cabala) is an
ancient Hebraic system of mysticism that literally means "to receive."
My friend Cullen Dorn, a fellow author and student of Kabbalah,
indicated that the practice came into being thousands of years ago
when "The angels of heaven whispered into the ears of the early Rab-
bis, telling them of a celestial blueprint for the cosmos." This blueprint revealed the varied characteristics of the nature of God, as well
as the unconscious mind hidden deep within humans—all of which
are interrelated.[13]

Cullen was kind enough to share his insights on the topic with
me—the essence of which he described in the words "As above, so
below ... as below, so above," as well as "the macrocosm within the
microcosm." Cullen told me that the Old Testament contains the hidden keys necessary to understand the Kabbalah.[14]

Speaking to the manner in which non-conformity is sometimes
viewed from any traditional perspective, Cullen mentioned a story
that occurred during his stint as a postal carrier in New York City.
The setting was one of his delivery stops, a building where many
Hasidic Jews lived. Driven by curiosity, he once surveyed the occu-
pants, mostly men in their sixties, about whether they'd ever studied
the Kabbalah.

As Cullen explained, "The men uniformly replied, 'Our senior
Rabbi forbids it.' I surmised that this prohibition was tied to the fact

that the Kabbalah, providing a mystical connection, could lead these men to question traditional teachings."[15]

Cullen's feedback provides an interesting consideration when viewing mysticism and religion. Orthodox elements within any tradition can leverage fear to exert control over people. In such a framework the "truth" is sometimes regulated by the few, who determine the meaning of scripture. In this process, the value and relevance of one's inner guidance is often undermined or dismissed, while enhancing the value of intermediaries between oneself and God. Ironically, it is said that much of scripture is the product of inspiration—so we end up with what is effectively a case of collective cognitive dissonance, i.e., conflicting ideas held simultaneously.

Another major monotheistic religion yielded a unique and noteworthy spiritualistic sect to consider. Sufism is a mystical derivative of Islam, focused on the inner, or *esoteric*, spiritual aspects of the faith, as opposed to the outward or *exoteric*. Sufis pursue a direct discernment of God through mystical rituals based on divine love. In his book *Sufism: A Path for Today, The Sovereign Soul*, author Phillip Gowins notes that the objective of the fifteen-hundred-year-old spiritual tradition of Sufism is the "elimination of all veils between man and God."[16] As with Far Eastern traditions, Sufis seem to recognize psychic phenomena as a natural derivative of spiritual advancement.

Speaking about Sufi practices that nurture psychic development, author John Spencer Trimingham indicates:

> The deepest esoteric teachings did in fact find their expression on paper for all to read; but reading does not mean understanding; it still remains "secret" and "hidden" to the uninitiate and unilluminate…. The teaching is experienced by the *murid* [committed one] as he carries out his exercises in the *khalwa* [solitude]. In the ordinary way the stress is on the allocation of prayer-tasks, the times and modes of recitation, participation in other forms of devotion, pursuance of a course of ascetic discipline, fulfillment of the order's

material obligations, and acceptance of the spiritual experiences, supra-normal exploits, and continuing power of the saints.[17]

Trimingham further notes that "The *murshid* [teacher] measures the progress of the *murid* through some of the stages of attainment by interpreting the visions and dreams the murid experiences while carrying out his personal *dhikr* [invocation] exercises and prayers in khalwa."[18]

Returning to the Judeo-Christian tradition, I will illume some Bible passages that provide relevant examples of paranormal phenomena. On the whole I am not inclined to argue my points using a literal biblical interpretation—for the reasons stated earlier and others that follow. But I do see the importance of speaking to readers who come from a more traditional Christian orientation; therefore I will explore scripture from several angles to address their possible concerns.

While the Old Testament includes a few passages that disparage psychic phenomena and mediumship, the New Testament is filled with stories where such occurrences are held up as examples of divine presence. Miracles abounded as Jesus and his disciples displayed a wide array of paranormal phenomena. A clear example of clairvoyance occurs when Jesus speaks with a Samaritan woman who is drawing water from a well. In this dialog Jesus asks the woman, a complete stranger, to call her husband.

To this request the woman replies, "I have no husband."

Jesus responds, "You are right in saying, 'I have no husband': for you have had five husbands and the one you have now is not your husband."

Stunned by his insight, the woman confirms Jesus's accuracy, responding, "Sir, I see that you are a prophet." (John 4:1–19)

The story of "The Transfiguration," found in the Gospels of Mark, Matthew, and Luke, as well as 2nd Peter, reports on the ultimate form of mediumship. In plain view of the disciples, the spirits of Moses and Elijah are reported to have materialized and met with Jesus, who was glowing in white light. Interestingly, this description aligns with reports of spirit etherealizations and materializations, described by observers of such phenomena, said to be facilitated through rare and uniquely gifted mediums.

Some might argue that it was acceptable—perhaps even expected—for Jesus to facilitate such miracles and that he alone could accomplish them. Yet that line of reasoning ignores many other miracle stories found throughout the New Testament, carried out not just by Jesus but by his disciples as well. According to the Gospel of John, Jesus encouraged followers to develop and utilize these gifts, saying, "Truly, truly I say to you, he who believes in me will also do the works I do; and greater works than these he will do." (John 14:12) Along similar lines, the Gospel of Mark reports Jesus as saying, "And these signs shall follow them that believe: in my name they shall cast out devils; they shall speak with new tongues: they shall take up serpents and if they drink any deadly thing, it shall not hurt them; they shall lay hands on the sick and they shall recover." (Mark 16:17–18)

Some Christians argue that mediums can't communicate with the spirits of people who have passed because, according to their literal interpretation of certain biblical passages, the deceased enter a deep-sleep state and remain there until judgment day. The argument goes, *if deceased people are now in a state of suspended animation, then other sources (such as demons) must be responsible for providing mediums with accurate information.*

Among other things, this contention assumes that any such demons would be all-knowing beings, which seems a stretch. Also, as mentioned before, scripture is inconsistent, and many biblical passages suggest that the deceased proceed directly to the next realm without delay. A case in point is the aforementioned story of the transfiguration, where Jesus communes with the spirits of two deceased men, Moses and Elijah. Had these men been slumbering away, how could they have visited with Jesus? Rather, the story implies that the deceased go straight to the afterlife and do not wait in some sort of limbo-land for a judgment process that is supposed to occur at some future time.

A few years ago a well-meaning person pointed me to a scriptural reference that—according to their interpretation—implied that mediums cannot communicate with the deceased. The person mentioned a "chasm," referenced in a story known as "The Rich Man and Lazarus," that would purportedly prevent such communications. After hearing the argument, it was clear that I was dealing with an extremely literal interpretation of what many consider a statement on social justice from the "Lukan" perspective.

The passages in question are found in the Gospel of Luke, considered one of the "synoptic" gospels along with Mark and Matthew. This means that they are very similar in content, language, and structure, whereas the fourth gospel, John, is significantly different.

Modern biblical scholars have concluded that stories about Jesus, including his sayings, survived through an oral tradition for a period of twenty to thirty years after the crucifixion—prior to the creation of any written accounts. They consider Mark the oldest of the four canonical gospels, dating it to 70–80 CE—about forty to fifty years after the crucifixion—with Matthew and Luke following ten to fifteen years later, around 85–90 CE. As you see, this leaves a gap of roughly twenty years between the end of the oral tradition and the arrival of Mark.[18]

Researchers have deduced the existence of a lost gospel with the sayings of Jesus referred to as "Q" for *Quelle*, a German word meaning "source." They concluded that Matthew and Luke drew from Q, as well as Mark, implying that the early gospels provided a foundation for the later ones. Q is thought to pre-date Mark, likely originating between 55 and 60 CE.[19] This theory explains why many stories that appear in Mark are also found in Luke and Matthew—and stories not found in Mark but which are recorded in both Matthew and Luke are assumed to come from Q. The particular story referenced by the concerned individual has no parallel, however—appearing only in Luke.*

Specifically, the "Rich Man and Lazarus" passages come from Luke 16:19–31. This is a story attributed to Jesus regarding a rich man who "was dressed in purple and fine linen and who feasted sumptuously every day." The rich man's existence is contrasted with that of Lazarus, "a poor man covered with sores, who longed to satisfy his hunger with what fell from the rich man's table." (Luke 16:20–21) The moral of the story comes into play when both men die, and the rich man suffers in Hades while the poor man is "carried away by the angels to be with Abraham." (Luke 16:22)

It is then noted that the rich man "looked up and saw Abraham far away with Lazarus by his side" and so he asked Abraham for cool water to quench his thirst. (Luke 16:23) Abraham responded by telling the rich man that he and Lazarus were reaping the just rewards of their earthly lives. He then followed with "Besides all this, a great chasm has been fixed, so that those who might want to pass from here to you cannot do so and no one can cross from there to us." (Luke 16:26)

After realizing that he was destined to remain in Hades, the rich man asked Abraham to send Lazarus to warn his brothers, hoping they might avoid a similar fate. Abraham then retorted, "They have Moses and the prophets; they should listen to them." (Luke 16:29)

Undeterred, the rich man beseeched, "If someone goes to them from the dead, they will repent." (Luke 16:30)

---

* Of the four canonical gospels, it is thought that John was written last—around 95–100 CE. For the purposes of this discussion, however, John does not come into play. A fifth, non-canonical gospel named Thomas also exists. Some scholars believe that the Gospel of Thomas may pre-date all canonical gospels, and that early versions of Thomas may have served as source material for the other gospels—much like Q. (Funk, Hoover, and the Jesus Seminar, *The Five Gospels*, New York: HarperCollins, 1994.)

Abraham then steadfastly proclaims, "If they do not listen to Moses and the prophets, neither will they be convinced even if someone rises from the dead." (Luke 16:31)

Even if one chooses to read the previous passages literally (which I think is a mistake), there is nothing to suggest that communication between the living and the deceased is impossible. While the story implies that the rich man is restricted from moving from Hades to the "bosom of Abraham," he clearly communicates across the divide— seeing, hearing, and speaking with Abraham. So, while it is said that the chasm prevented the rich man from relocating from Hades to Abraham's domain, it had no bearing on their cross-dimensional dialog. Nor does it address the possibility of someone on Earth communicating with a deceased person.

At the end of the story, Abraham denies the rich man's request that Lazarus be sent to warn his surviving brothers so they might avoid a similar fate. Despite his rebuff, Abraham says nothing to indicate that the appeal is impossible. Rather, it seems a matter of principle— that people should live rightly without prodding—along with Abraham's apparent opinion that such an effort would be a waste of time because the brothers would not listen anyway.

This story uses allegory to illustrate a moral point—so I would suggest that it was intended to be read metaphorically rather than literally.

One must also consider the process by which the surviving gospels came to be—a topic I addressed earlier. They are essentially second-generation documents that leaned on earlier accounts that are no longer accessible. Also, those first-generation scriptures were preceded by a twenty- to thirty-year oral tradition, and we all know how the "telephone game" works. In addition, the Bible has been through many translations. So, we are left with questions that may never be answered. How can we know if certain passages were popularized stories that evolved within specific communities—taking on a life of their own—or if they were Jesus's actual words?

Scholars believe that the four gospels of canon developed within disparate groups, and that some of the differences among the texts may reflect the differing viewpoints of these various Christian communities. Even back then, it seems, Christianity was not unified.

One way of examining scripture in such cases is to look at the differences (or similarities) in stories appearing in multiple gospels. For example, in Mark 9:40 Jesus says, "Whoever is not against us is for us."

Similarly, in Luke 9:49 Jesus reports, "... whoever is not against you is for you."

Turning the story one hundred eighty degrees, Matthew 12:30 has Jesus saying, "Whoever is not with me is against me."

Given that Mark was the source for this story, the logical conclusion seems to be that the account portrayed in Mark and Luke is probably closer to the original story than the version found in Matthew. This is not "proof" but it is one way to look at the issue.

In the case of the story of the rich man and Lazarus, this method of comparison cannot be used because there is only one account—in Luke. It does not appear to originate in Q because it is not contained in Matthew, and it does not tie to Mark, thus weakening the argument that these words originated with Jesus.

Also running counter to the "chasm" argument is the previously mentioned case where the medium of En'dor successfully contacts the spirit of Samuel—not a demon—and facilitates communication between the deceased leader and his successor, Saul. How could this have happened if the chasm was a limiting factor? That would have prevented the medium from delivering Samuel's message to Saul.

I recall an incident that took place when I was six years old, when a friend told me that he was no longer allowed to visit our home. When I asked why, my friend said that his parents believed that my dad's abilities were "the work of the devil." After bearing the brunt of this painful statement I ran home, deeply upset, and told my parents what had been said. My father calmed me down and explained that some people fear what they don't understand. My dad also assured me that his gifts were from God, saying that even Jesus had once been accused of "having a demon" after performing a healing and exorcism.

Responding to his accusers, Jesus retorted, "How can Satan cast out Satan?" (Mark 3:24)

Jesus actually went a step further in Mark 3:29, warning his accusers that they should not make such *blasphemies against the Holy Spirit*. This is a key point, because anyone demonstrating similar gifts today may be the subject of similar accusations.

In his first letter to a fledgling church in Corinth, the Apostle Paul spoke extensively about these topics, providing these instructions to followers:

> Now concerning spiritual gifts ... I do not want you to be uninformed ... there are varieties of gifts, but the same Spirit; and there are varieties of service, but the same Lord ... it is the same God who inspires them all in every one. To each is given the manifestation of the Spirit.... To one is given through the Spirit the utterance of wisdom and another the utterance of knowledge ... to another gifts of healing ... to another the working of miracles, to another prophecy, to another the ability to distinguish between spirits, to another various kinds of tongues.... (I Corinthians 12:1, 4–11)

The New Testament contains other verses that validate the legitimacy of these gifts and spirit communication in general. One particular verse goes so far as to provide specific instructions for the process: "Beloved, do not believe every spirit but test the spirits to see they are of God." (I John 1:4) This passage supports the idea that mediumship is acceptable, for without spirit communication there is nothing to test.

Further, I do see validity in the suggestion that a medium should prepare in order to avoid the possibility of opening up to "lower energies." In other words, the medium must be on guard to ensure that only positive, enlightened, and truthful sources are allowed to communicate. To this end, my father would often recite the Lord's Prayer or use other mantras to heighten his level of consciousness prior to any reading or trance-state session. Addressing this issue, I wrote the following in the foreword to my father's book on psychic development:

> Psychic phenomena and mediumship are not a panacea—
> they carry a price. In assuming this path, you should not
> take the work lightly. There can be risks when the untutored
> dabble in the paranormal. Anxious to expand their psychic
> awareness, some individuals charge headfirst into this area
> without learning how to set proper boundaries for their
> work. They may open themselves to anything and every-
> thing—including less-than-desirable energies—which can
> result in a variety of problems. Not only are the proper pro-
> tocols important, but spiritual maturity and understanding
> are as well. These lessons are not easy; discipline and dili-
> gence are required, but rewards await the dedicated student.

Returning to the topic of Gnostic Christianity, I would like to address the scriptures discovered in Egypt in 1945 that we now refer to as "The Gnostic Gospels." Where were these scriptures during the formative years of the church? Why didn't this mystical variety of Christianity flourish? As Biblical scholar Elaine Pagels notes, "It is the winners who write history—their way."[20]

Failing to fit with the orthodox position, these scriptures were effectively banned and ordered destroyed by Archbishop Athanasius in 367 CE. If not for the foresight of some monks who hid secret copies of these texts more than a millennium ago, we may never have known about these unique Christian communities and their unortho-dox beliefs.[21]

What caused the early church leaders so much concern over these particular writings, leading them to seek their eradication? One answer to this question can be found in verses contained within the Gospel of Thomas (one of the relatively recently unearthed Gnostic Gospels), which suggest that individuals can enjoy a personal and direct connection with God, without the need for church or clergy.[22]

Today the Thomas Gospel is not without its critics, and certain passages have raised questions and eyebrows. For example, the final entry, verse 114, suggests that Mary, a female, must become male in order to become a "living spirit" and enter the Kingdom of Heaven. But some scholars and translators believe that this verse was added at a later date—not included in the original text. Other scholars see "male" and "female" as metaphors for the spiritual and physical dimensions of life, and the underlying meaning is lost when the passage is read literally.

According to some scholars—including Helmut Koester, Research Professor of Divinity and Ecclesiastical History at Harvard—early versions of Thomas date roughly to 50 CE, a full generation prior to the Gospels of Matthew, Luke, and John, and possibly Mark. As Koester notes,

> The authorship of this gospel is attributed to Didymos Judas Thomas, that is, Judas "the twin" (both the Aramaic Thomas and the Greek Didymos mean "twin"). In the Syrian church, (Judas) Thomas was known as the brother of Jesus who founded the churches of the East, particularly of Edessa (in a somewhat later tradition, he even travels to India).[23]

The Gospel of Thomas contains many sayings also found in the synoptic gospels (Mark, Matthew, and Luke) but regarding these parallels, Koester explains,

> If one considers the form and wording of the individual sayings in comparison with the form in which they are preserved in the New Testament, *The Gospel of Thomas* almost always appears to have preserved a more original form of the traditional saying.... In its literary genre, *The Gospel of Thomas* is more akin to one of the sources of the canonical gospels, namely the so-called Synoptic Sayings Source (often called "Q" from the German word Quelle, "source"), which was used by both Matthew and Luke.[24]

Regarding controversial passages contained within the Gospel of Thomas, Elaine Pagels states, "The 'Kingdom of God' is not an event expected to happen in history, nor is it a 'place.' The author of *Thomas* seems to ridicule such views: [Pagels continues with an extract quote]

> Jesus said, "If those who lead you say to you, 'Lord, the king-
> dom is in the sky,' then the birds of the sky will precede you.
> If they say to you, 'It is in the sea,' then the fish will precede
> you." (NHC II.32:19–24)

[Continues Pagels,] "Here the kingdom represents a state of self-discovery: 'Rather, the kingdom is inside of you, and it is outside of you. When you come to know yourselves, then you will become known, and when you realize that it is you who are the sons of the living Father.' (NHC II.32:23–33.5)."[25]

The Jesus speaking in Thomas offers people direct access to God, noting that this capacity is resident within them. In reading these passages today, one gains the sense that Jesus was encouraging a more introspective and meditative approach, yielding greater self-awareness and a direct, mystical connection to the divine.

Parables and aphorisms carrying a similar tone are found in the canonical gospels yet seem to have been ignored, downplayed, or spun in a different manner. One well-known example that closely mirrors the aforementioned passage from Thomas is Jesus's statement, "The Kingdom of God is within you." (Luke 17:21) Also, speaking of this inherent yet hidden capacity within people, Jesus says, "Whosoever shall say unto this mountain, Be thou taken up and cast into the sea; and shall not doubt in his heart, but shall believe that what he saith cometh to pass; he shall have it." (Mark 11:23) This particular verse seems to imply that mind can indeed affect matter, and that it is acceptable for one to exercise this capability, at least once a person has achieved a certain level of spiritual maturity.

The various religious traditions obviously provide a multitude of different perspectives on psychic phenomena and mediumship. Some of these reports are less than glowing, while others are very positive.

Ultimately it is up to you to consider the information and decide for yourself—perhaps leaning on your heart along with your head. Life is about direct experience and there is no good substitute. It may seem easier and more comfortable to follow the path of convention, but the truth you find there really won't be your truth.

From my perspective, psychic and mediumistic phenomena are tools to be used for the highest purposes and with the proper preparation. Just as a hammer may be utilized to build a house, it can also be used to tear one down. I would submit that the key factor is the motivation and makeup of the person involved. If you are seeking to develop psychic gifts, then spiritual growth and Christ-like service should be your primary goals. If you would like to have a reading, choose a spiritual medium who comes with solid recommendations from trusted sources. Finally, enter the process not from a perspective of fear, but rather joyfulness and love. As Jesus so aptly put it, "By their fruits you will know them. A good tree cannot bear bad fruit, nor can a bad tree bear good fruit." (Matthew 7:16, 18)

I know a number of mediums who bear very good fruit—operating from a place of love, as reflected in their deep sense of compassion and understanding for others. These mediums don't "conjure the dead." Instead they are sought out by the deceased as well as the living, both of whom desire to connect so that a necessary healing process can be facilitated.

CHAPTER 9

Unfoldment

W hile my father's psychic development book was a valuable resource, when I read it I was still trying to find greater balance in my life. Since I often found myself starved for time, I didn't fully commit to all the disciplines he recommends. For example, my father saw meditation as the bedrock of intuitive development and suggested that it be a regular part of daily life. I did try to meditate, but my efforts were inconsistent at best, both in terms of frequency and duration. Yet on a few occasions I experienced a spontaneous "knowing" without the benefit of any sensory input. For example, my wife Susie and I were recently out to dinner with our good friends Steve and Christina while visiting them in California. Christina normally orders beer with her meals, but on this occasion she indicated that she was going to have something else. The word *mojito* popped into my mind so I said it out loud. Christina looked at me with wide eyes and asked, "How did you know?" Other than seeing her order a whiskey on a single occasion, I'd never observed Christina ordering any alcoholic beverage other than beer or wine.

A while back, I experienced two impactful dreams involving Brandon in the same week. Each of these events occurred at the end of my sleep, while lying in what was likely a deep REM state. While these episodes were not as vivid as an "astral" experience I had in 2005 (detailed in my first book), which was as clear and tangible as waking reality—in which I believe I went "out of body"—they still bore the stamp of an authentic encounter with my son.

Brandon was younger in these dreams—about ten years old rather than eighteen as he was at the time of his passing. And while these particular experiences were not as lucid as the earlier event, my interaction with Brandon felt completely real and I could sense the love between us. Our talk was relaxed, and Brandon demonstrated the dry sense of humor I'd grown to love. We even hugged.

If the spiritual realm is an alternate dimension of reality, it seems reasonable to think that communication between such divergent spheres would be challenging. I also suspect that the type of manifestation may correlate to our emotional readiness for such a meeting. Further, the validity of the encounter should not be measured solely on the basis of the visual clarity, but equally or perhaps even more on the feeling of connection. Assuming that this sort of contact is telepathic in nature, perhaps the mind receives the equivalent of raw data and converts it into a meaningful message or experience, with consideration for our degree of understanding. When you think about it, such a premise is not so different from waking-state "reality" where our eyes and ears pass along information to our brain, which interprets the "sights" and "sounds" comprising a significant portion of a personal experience.

In the few days following these experiences with Brandon, I asked myself if they were real encounters or just comforting dreams. It wasn't until another dream a few days later that my question was answered for me.

Just before waking one morning, I dreamed that I was holding an open container of milk that smelled sour. This odor lingered even after I awoke. I wondered if the milk really had gone bad—the carton was less than a week old. I walked into the kitchen, reached into the refrigerator, and grabbed the carton. The milk was sour. It became clear that I should trust the information I received, whether dreaming or awake.

On the evening of September 8, 2006, my wife and I attended an intimate gathering with three other families, each having lost a son. Our host Sharon held the get-together on the one-year anniversary of her son Nathan's passing. Robin, another woman attending that evening, lost her son Eric on September 30, 2005—Brandon's birthday.

Before going to Sharon's house I had a gut feeling that I would receive an inspired message that evening but I didn't mention it to anyone. Robin had just returned from a reading with the prominent medium George Anderson in New York, which she found highly evidential and comforting. Robin related some of the most phenomenal aspects of her session to us, including the fact that Anderson accurately stated her son's first name, last name, and his rather unusual nickname. Additionally, the medium specified that Eric was greeted by his great-grandfather when he died. This was a key point of validation for Robin because both of Eric's grandfathers were still living.

Then something very interesting happened. Robin said that she was relieved to know that Eric was okay but was bothered by the fact that she would never see him again—in a physical sense. For some reason I felt compelled to tell Robin, "Don't think of it like he's gone—just out of sight. Think of it like he lives in Australia." When I said this, Robin looked at me with a puzzled expression and responded, "That is exactly what George Anderson said to me." Elaborating, she continued, "While sharing a message from my son, George said, 'Mom, if I hadn't died I would have moved away after graduating anyway, so think of it like I moved to Australia'."

It was pretty wild. I wondered if Eric had placed the thought in my mind. While strange things can happen, it seemed too meaningful to be just a coincidence.

In late fall of 2006, I reconnected with Lin Martin, a man my father had mentored in the early 1960s and '70s and who had served in my father's church for many years. I always admired Lin as someone who was spiritually motivated—a model of sincerity and compassion. Counter to those seeking psychic development for selfish reasons such as ego, Lin remained exclusively focused on spiritual growth, understanding, and helping others. Aside from a desire to develop a capacity for healing, Lin initially wanted nothing to do with the other spiritual gifts and was actually averse to honing his psychic abilities. Despite his original thoughts on the matter, Lin became quite psychic in a most natural and unplanned way.

At the time Lin and I re-established contact, he and his wife Torill were working in Norway conducting training classes and workshops focused on healing and "energy work." Initially we communicated by email but were able to meet face to face about a month later when the couple returned to the United States.

Lin outlined his plans to conduct healing and intuitive-development workshops in Arizona and invited me to attend an upcoming series. It was an easy decision to begin working with a man I respected and whose own development had been aided by my father. It seemed like everything was lining up as if it were meant to be. A number of intuitive persons had told me that I harbored some latent abilities that would be unfolding. Lin shared a similar message with me. I felt that whatever was supposed to happen would take place, at the proper time and in the correct manner.

During one of our discussions, Lin suggested that I might want to contemplate the type of gifts I would like to develop. This idea suddenly made me wonder about the significance of my intention toward the process; my focus on specific areas could play a role in determining the type of ability I might cultivate. Ultimately I didn't have a burning desire for any particular ability. I wanted to retain a singular focus on spiritual growth, anticipating that certain gifts could possibly develop as a by-product. I'd heard many stories about people who sought to develop their psychic capacity for the wrong reasons, mostly driven by ego. I'd also known humble and caring psychics who became a bit arrogant after fame came their way. I felt it was important for me to stay grounded and balanced in my approach, remaining true to my original intention of assisting others in a spirit of compassion.

After attending several introductory one-day seminars conducted by Lin and Torill, I committed to participate in a four-part course that required one full weekend of my time per month. It was a lot of time for me, but I knew that this process was worth a serious commitment. As the sessions ensued, a number of remarkable things took place.

In the second segment of the training I met a woman named Lyndsey Wagner with whom I was paired for an exercise. Lyndsey had offered a moving story earlier in the day about a request she had made of her husband, Larkin, prior to his death several years before.

"Honey, if you die first, will you please contact me when you get to wherever you go next?" Lyndsey explained that this question had ignited an animated discussion between the couple years earlier. During the chat they both shared their beliefs and vehemently disagreed on the topic of life after death and spirit communication in particular. Lyndsey explained that she'd served as a singer in Spiritualist Churches for many years and had seen numerous mediums share messages from departed loved ones. One of the mediums she visited indicated that she would later meet and marry a man who was described in great detail. Shortly thereafter, Lyndsey saw this man in a dream, so when she met Larkin six months later she *knew* that he was the one.

Despite Larkin's non-belief in an afterlife, he agreed to Lyndsey's request. She said to him, "Okay, when you die and find out I'm right, promise that you will find a medium and contact me." They also came to a mutual agreement about what would be communicated. There was a Pillsbury commercial with a jingle at the end that said "My heart to yours." She told me that Larkin used to sing it to her all the time. His glasses would be pushed down on his nose while his big sparkly blue eyes seemed to giggle at her. Lyndsey told him that's what the message would be when he found the medium.

During the next year Larkin's health began to fail as he struggled with heart disease, hypertension, diabetes, congestive heart failure, and other ailments brought on by a struggle with food addiction and obesity. Lyndsey stated, "After numerous hospitalizations, Larkin suddenly took a turn toward death and on May 25, 2002, I sat by his side and watched his spirit leave his body." Lyndsey held a wake and

memorial service, notifying people by email because there wasn't
time for the newspaper to print the information since it was Memorial Day. She noted that her email list was very large and included
many of her students and other contacts whom she didn't even know.
Here is what took place at Larkin's service, as described by Lyndsey:

> During the service many people shared their love and caring
> through songs, poetry, and letters. In the middle of the ser-
> vice, a man named Maha'al whom I had never met stood up
> and said he had a message that Larkin asked him to deliver
> to me. While I believe spirits can communicate, I was not
> sure I wanted this to happen in front of a large group of
> people, especially among Larkin's family, who I would char-
> acterize as highly skeptical. I asked the man to proceed
> anyway. Maha'al said that Larkin was standing next to him,
> and he began sharing some things Larkin asked him to say.
> Maha'al put his hand on his heart, swept it across the room
> in a grand gesture, and said, "Larkin now says 'my heart to
> yours'." Well, if my mouth didn't drop wide open, and at the
> same moment it felt like a flood of golden light entered me.
> I have never felt so much joy in my life.

Lyndsey then noted, "Later, Maha'al told me all about his experience that morning when Larkin told him to come. At the time,
Maha'al 'told' Larkin that he had the wrong guy, but Larkin insisted
that he was the right person since everyone at the service would be
certain that we didn't know him. Larkin also promised Maha'al that
if he was willing to do this for him, he would give him the gift of his
favorite song."

Lyndsey continued sharing, "After Maha'al gave me the message,
one of my students started singing 'Alleluia' to the tune of the Pach-
elbel Canon. The whole room spontaneously broke out in three-part
harmony. It sounded like a choir of angels. Maha'al immediately
began to weep uncontrollably. As it happens, this was his favorite
song, which he played in times of despair when he needed to connect

with God's love. The woman who started singing it later said that the song had been 'playing over and over' in her head all morning long. Larkin had been very busy that day!"

Returning to the developmental workshop, I was assigned to complete a "chakra balancing" exercise with Lyndsey. In this process, one person lies down while the other stands over them and administers healing. Through visualization and intuitive feel, the healer seeks to balance energy evenly among the body's seven chakras. (The concept of the chakra is tied to Eastern/Hindu philosophy and refers to seven energy centers where the physical body is said to be linked to the soul, spiritual body, or higher self, depending on your terminological preference.)

When I finished administering Lyndsey's healing, she started crying. I must have had a puzzled expression on my face because she looked up and was compelled to explain what had taken place. Lyndsey said that Larkin had visited her during the exercise. She sensed his presence very strongly *and felt his large face* next to hers but was frustrated that she couldn't hear him. Then, telepathically, she attempted to tell Larkin, "I can't hear you, try something else." A short time later, while my hands were above her second chakra, located near the lower abdomen, Lyndsey suddenly heard Larkin for the first time since his death. Later, in our group debrief, Lyndsey told everyone that this was the most compelling and exhilarating event she had experienced in the four years that had transpired since receiving the message from Maha'al at Larkin's service. Lyndsey divulged that her husband had apologized for an unresolved issue during the healing and also told her, "You are so precious." Lyndsey responded to Larkin with a sense of deep forgiveness and felt as if a major burden had been lifted.

Next it was my turn to experience a chakra balancing. I climbed onto the table, stretched out, and relaxed, hoping to achieve a meditative state. While lying there well into the exercise I started thinking, *this is nice but nothing much is happening.* The very next moment I received a mental impression that seemed to reflect my father's energy and sense of humor, conveying the message, "You're not done yet. We've got something else in store for you."

The next thing I knew, the Eastern meditation music being played seemed to morph into "How Great Thou Art," one of my dad's favorites and also a selection at Brandon's service. Moments later my body was flooded with what felt like a strong electrical current running from my head to my toes. This sensation was different from anything I'd ever experienced. I felt as if I were connected to two ends of a high-tension wire—one attached to my feet and the other attached to my head. Along with this electrical sensation, I felt a strong spiritual presence, which I assumed to be my father and possibly Brandon. It felt as if they had poured themselves into me for this brief period, which seemed to last about fifteen seconds.

Just as I was coming out of this state of consciousness, I felt someone touch my nose quite firmly. I initially suspected that Lyndsey did this to stir me, but when I opened my eyes I found her hands nowhere near my face. I then asked if she had touched my nose. She hadn't and there was no one else near us. This process impacted me deeply, and I surprised myself by breaking down when it concluded. What ran through me felt so loving, joyful, and lighthearted that I was brought to tears. It's very hard to capture the essence of these feelings in words, other than to say it was a hallowed experience.

In early December 2006, I received an email from the medium Jamie Clark, who shared the message, "Brandon says 'Merry Christmas.' He wants you to know that he is going to give you a present." Jamie then asked me to let him know when I received the gift. Christmas came and went and nothing unusual seemed to come my way that would fit the description of a gift from my deceased son. Then a few days after Christmas something rather remarkable happened that seemed to match up with Jamie's prediction.

I was attending one of Lin Martin's seminars on December 30, 2006, when another participant named Wendy Hill told me that she had a gift for me. When she handed me the present I noticed that the wrapping paper bore the word "Believe!" Wendy explained that she had been inspired to craft a hand-made wind chime for me, featuring a silver metal frame and stained-glass inserts. She noted that the gift was ready before Christmas and she planned to give it to me then, but she missed the prior session due to illness.

I thanked Wendy for the kind gesture but expressed my confusion over what had stirred her to do this. I couldn't see why I'd been singled out for such a gift when there were many other deserving people in our group. Wendy then told me that she'd been inspired and felt strongly compelled to craft this gift for me. She initially assumed that the inspiration was coming from my sister Robin, who had recently succumbed to cancer, but something else didn't seem to fit with that idea. Wendy explained that she had begun working on a specific piece when "a strong male energy" told her to try again with the design she had selected initially. Resistant to the unsolicited directive, Wendy continued to work with the piece she'd already picked, but the metal frame somehow broke in the process. She soldered the damaged spot but it immediately broke again. Resolute, Wendy soldered the spot one more time, yet it broke again! She had never experienced anything like this in many years of working with these materials. Submitting to the request she was feeling, Wendy said, "I give up—what is it that you want me to do?"

At this point, Wendy felt guided to start working on a different piece. She had been "told" that she must place a green bead in the center. This seemed to provide a clue as to who was doing the nudging; Brandon's favorite color was green, and the color had come to symbolize our son to us in many ways. Wendy also felt a sense of insistence that pushed her to wrap the item, although she initially intended to provide the gift unwrapped. Wendy's experience of being guided in this way sounded remarkably similar to the account provided by James Linton in relation to the composition and recording of the song "The Other Side."

As noted in my first book, James was with friends who were hiking behind Brandon and his group on the day my son died. When James reached Brandon they found him lying unconscious while his best friend Stu administered CPR in vain.

Shortly after Brandon's passing, Susie and I became friends with James. Just six months later James had an unusual experience while recording music in his home studio. During this session James noted feeling the presence of another person and he saw both shadow figures to his side and moving flashing lights in front of him—pushing him to modify the words and music of a recording. He later described this recording saying, "It is the best song I've ever written, but I didn't write it." James's encounter with the shadow figure was remarkably close to what Susie had experienced one day earlier—but James was unaware of this fact.

On Saturday, March 17, 2007, my son Steven and I attended another one of Lin Martin's workshops and both enjoyed some rather remarkable results. In the course of the day, we were each paired with another person who was a designated "Receiver." Steven and I were both assigned the role of "Giver" for two procedures—a chakra balancing followed by a clairvoyant reading.

I felt entirely at ease with the chakra balancing and healing process, but the clairvoyant reading was a bit out of my comfort zone. While I'd had a number of spontaneous psychic experiences in the past, the idea of giving a thirty-minute reading seemed a bit intimidating. I suddenly wondered what would happen if nothing came to mind and I was stuck sitting, twiddling my thumbs. Even worse, I was afraid I would say things that were entirely incorrect. At least I was among friends. I ended up working with someone who made me feel relaxed and comfortable.

From prior training, I knew that I must set my ego aside and not worry about results. My role was to sit quietly and simply relay whatever came into my mind without reservation, judgment, or modification.

During the healing portion of the process, I felt as if the woman I was partnered with for the exercise (we'll call her Dianne) had some pain or stress in her head and throat, correlating to the fifth and sixth chakras. After concluding my work, I shared these observations and she confirmed that her throat was irritated and that her head did indeed hurt. She also shared the fact that the chakra balancing/healing process seemed to have eased her pain somewhat.

I took my best stab at the clairvoyance portion of the exercise, sharing a few general impressions with Dianne that she said were on target. Dianne then asked about a possible promotion she was seeking at work. I relayed my sense that she had an outside chance for the position but was likely their second choice. I also told her that the post could fall to her, but she'd have to consider whether she was truly willing to take on some major changes that would require her to "stretch" significantly. In making these comments, I was relying totally on feelings. Based on her personal knowledge and views of the situation, Dianne felt that my assessment was accurate.

Things got interesting when Dianne told me that she was going to send me a question telepathically. Sitting there in a quiet contemplative state I began to visualize a few different things. First, I told her that I saw dominos, and that made her laugh. Apparently her co-workers had recently commented about the "dominos falling," referring to pending employee movements that were anticipated. I then noted seeing a heart, perhaps as a sign of romance, love, or friendship, but wasn't sure which one. I saw some flowers that looked like tulips, lilies, or roses. I then felt compelled to tell her that she was good enough, although I really didn't know if the words fit anything.

A while later, Dianne told me that her telepathic question had been "Will I ever have a romantic relationship?" Reviewing my responses, I'm not so sure that I answered her directly, but it seems I picked up on the essence of Dianne's query, given the heart and flowers.

I then told Dianne that I had a feeling that something very hurtful had taken place in the past, which was holding her back. I said that she needed to let go of the feelings associated with these painful prior events and move forward with her life. More specifically, I felt that there had been some sort of abuse or a bad relationship in Dianne's past, but I didn't share that information because it seemed inappropriate and I wasn't confident enough to say it. I didn't know if I was close and I wasn't trying to play Freud, just sharing my thoughts, but it felt very awkward speaking about something so sensitive, relying solely on vague mental impressions. She began to tear up as I told her these things but said nothing more back to me.

During the group debrief, Dianne spilled a dark secret from her past, telling us that she'd been abused earlier in life in a most heinous manner. As she shared these things with the group, Dianne seemed to purge old demons and take a first step toward recovery where she might regain a sense of empowerment and hope.

I also heard feedback about my son Steven's clairvoyant reading, and it seemed as if he'd done very well on several fronts. Not only did Steven impress his subject—an experienced psychic—with some specific information, he also received a personal confirmation that strengthened his own confidence. At the close of his session, Steven described a piece of luggage in great detail, including a red tag that he saw connected to the handle. The woman then retrieved her bag, which had been stowed away during the workshop, and it fit his description perfectly—down to the red tag.

The most touching part of Steven's reading occurred at a point when he visualized a Tibetan monk whom he assumed was the woman's guide. Steven felt an overwhelming sense of love and compassion coming from this man, who offered Steven a gift in the form of a vision. Initially the vision appeared as a cloudy or fuzzy apparition but soon crystallized into a vivid image of Brandon. Steven felt that the monk's gift was intended to indicate that his brother was here and doing well.

Through these intuitive development courses I began to see a few things clearly. First, it requires a huge amount of trust to share whatever comes into your mind without hesitation, especially when there is no immediate confirmation of the accuracy of what you're saying. To paraphrase Lin Martin, "It's like diving off the high board at midnight into a pool shrouded in fog. You have to trust that there is water below you, which is tough to do."

I also questioned myself after the reading, wanting to make sure that what seemed an exercise with a reasonable degree of accuracy was not a product of cues I'd picked up on. It was important to be honest with myself, acknowledging that I had observed Dianne's behavior in prior workshops—albeit from a distance. I had to consider the possibility that I had made some observations that might have led to assumptions at the subconscious level. I then pondered how much of what I'd said was intuitive and which things may have been the product of my logical mind—perhaps it was a blend of the two. How do you know for sure?

I knew for certain that my impressions about the "dominos," "hearts," and "flowers" were not the product of logic. These thoughts flowed into my consciousness softly and were not associated with anything I had observed. When I told Dianne that she was "good enough," I felt as if the words came to me from an external source and I was pushed to say them.

It was very helpful for me to participate in such an exercise with a group of supportive people in an environment of heightened energy. I don't know that the results in my session would have been as positive if I had completed the exercise elsewhere. These experiences also brought to mind some thoughts about charlatans (per earlier comments I made in chapter 6). I started reflecting about how in their desire to reach out and exercise their newfound skills, beginners could stumble. I envisioned scenarios where a neophyte could be viewed as a con artist simply because he or she lacked experience and development, or—despite their best intentions—simply didn't have the aptitude. The aspiring intuitive should be mindful of these things when seeking opportunities to exercise their psychic faculties, as should volunteer sitters. Psychics in training must remain grounded and honest with themselves about results, not trying to make things fit.

Well-intentioned individuals who are sincerely committed to developing their abilities need practice partners, so I suggest that they seek out friends and like-minded people with whom they can work. This means giving free readings to sitters who would need to understand that this is a learning process and that compelling results are not a given. Simply put, the student needs a nurturing environment or safe haven in which to develop.

Reflecting on my session with Dianne, I recognized that I'd enjoyed some success but probably wouldn't have been completely satisfied had the tables been turned, especially if I had paid money for such a reading. There just wasn't enough depth and breadth to the session for my satisfaction. Developing my psychic capacity was far different than any other endeavor I'd ever tackled. It was both the hardest and the easiest thing, requiring complete trust in subtle thoughts and feelings and a willingness to verbalize them to others.

In the first few years after my participation in the workshop, I found that I didn't have the driving commitment necessary for a full-fledged psychic developmental effort. For one thing, I felt my calling was a bit different than my father's and that I was settling into what I was best suited to do, this being forthright, inspirational sharing of my personal experiences and ideas with other open-minded people, not being a medium for them. My livelihood was provided via other full-time employment, managing a sales force in the field of advertising, print, and promotions, so I couldn't dedicate all my time to these mystical endeavors. I remained committed to working in the arena of psychic communications, especially to help the bereaved, just not in the same manner as my father before me. I would embrace intuitive insights whenever they might come and let them serve appropriately, but I no longer focused on being a psychic in the way that my father had been. After all, who could measure up to those standards? That said, I had progressed enough to recognize instances when intuition was at work and needed my attention.

In the spring of 2008, I was in Tucson conducting employment interviews for the advertising company where I worked at the time, looking to hire new sales associates, with assistance of an associate named Leah. We wrapped up our sessions late one afternoon, setting plans to reconvene at 9:15 the following morning. Leah offered to pick up Starbucks coffee on her way back to work. At 9:05 the next morning my cell phone rang and I could see that it was Leah calling. After answering I spontaneously blurted out, "What's wrong, did Starbucks run out of coffee?" Leah replied, "No, I'm running a little late and haven't made it to Starbucks yet. Do you still want me to stop there?" I did. (Without my morning jolt of caffeine, delivered via a robust cup of coffee, I can get a bit grumpy and operate rather slowly.) About ten minutes later Leah called back again and said, "You're not going to believe this, but Starbucks actually did run out of coffee." Leah explained that she had ordered two cups but there was only enough coffee left to fill the first one so they substituted a Café Americano—an espresso drink—for the second cup. We both chuckled over long odds of a Starbucks store actually running out of coffee and what had compelled me to suggest that in the first place.

Leah and I met with a client early the following week, and the Starbucks story came up during our conversation. I noted how odd that situation had seemed, tossing out the analogy, "It's like Shamrock Dairy running out of milk." The client then gave me a funny look and said, "Mark, I was watching the news earlier today and saw that a Shamrock Dairy truck had overturned on the freeway this morning." Unlike the client, I had not watched the news nor had I heard about this event. It seemed pretty odd but also humorous.

In mid 2012, a woman named Elizabeth Boisson and I cofounded an organization called "Helping Parents Heal" to assist bereaved parents. At the conclusion of a recent meeting of the Scottsdale chapter, I was asked to conduct a prize drawing. Roughly twenty-five people were in attendance, and I was asked to pull a name from a vase containing about the same number of folded papers, bearing attendee names. In the interest of fairness I turned the vase so that the neck was pointed in a slightly downward angle, hoping that one paper might find its way out—rather than reaching my hand into the vase to pull one out. Sure enough, one paper edged its way into the neck and I picked it from the vase. At the moment I touched the paper I *knew* it belonged to my friend Lynn Hollahan. I then unfolded the paper and saw the name *Lynn Hollahan* written on it and announced her as the winner.

I did not see an image of her name, nor did I hear it, I simply had an inner knowing that told me the paper belonged to Lynn.

On the heels of the drawing, about a week later, I had a dream in which Lynn's mother was having trouble with her arm and suffering pain. I popped off an email to Lynn to share this information, although I told her that it might have been nothing more than a run-of-the-mill dream. She responded with the information that her mother was traveling and wouldn't return for a few more days. Later that week, Lynn picked up her mother at the airport and inquired about her arm, finding out that her mother had indeed been having pain in her arm. Further, Lynn told me that she herself had also been having arm pain.

So while I wasn't ever going to be my father, I had grown and changed by virtue of these experiences. What I found most fitting and rewarding was to speak to people from my heart, allowing my rational mind and intuitive insights to work in unison. I didn't have to worry about what to say because the information would just flow in a natural way and I'd convey the right things more times than not. I could see that my words helped grieving people heal, whether I was talking to one person or a gathering of two hundred. I'd also been able to nudge people to think more deeply about the possibility of a spiritual side to life—people who were previously strict materialists. I felt that inspirational sharing was my primary calling.

The one area where I felt that I had connected a bit more to my "psychic side" was writing. One example involves a call I received from medium Debra Martin regarding my father's previously unpublished manuscript, *Your Psychic Potential: A Guide to Psychic Development*, which was soon to be released. She told me that my father had touched in with her and wanted to share a message. With a sense of urgency Debra then said that *this was a sacred book*. Debra also said she'd asked my father why he hadn't published the book before now since it had been completed in 1973. She said that my father told her this book couldn't be published before his passing. "It wasn't time, in a world sense—the world was not ready for it until now."

At the time of Debra's call I'd been working on the foreword to my father's book and was pretty far along. Startled by the congruence between her message and what I'd already written, I read the following passage to her from my work:

> And on reflection, there seemed good reason for the delay. Because the book was so far ahead of its time, it actually seems better suited to the world now than to the one my father knew in the early 1970s. For all of the newfound interest in alternative spiritual paths back then, such exploration had yet to become widespread. People today seem more open-minded and interested in diverse forms of spirituality and less accepting of the dogmatic approach of traditional religion.

My next clue that my father may have inspired some of my writing came in the form of a one-page document that I discovered a couple of weeks after my conversation with Debra. It was in a manila envelope inside a box where it had been stored for decades. The document, entitled "To the Would-Be Medium," was my father's writing, and its contents were closely aligned with Debra's statements as well as things I had written in the foreword. Now recall that Debra shared the phrase, "This is a sacred book," in regard to my father's psychic development manuscript. Within the newly discovered document I found the following passage: "Finally, remember that mediumship is a sacred office, the one original priesthood of God. Regard it as such and by daily prayers and meditation seek to become a channel for the highest."

Following are some additional excerpts from the writing I'd done for the foreword in my father's forthcoming book, also completed before I ever saw the aforesaid document. I wrote:

> He intended the book for individuals who have a sincere desire to grow spiritually and to expand their psychic abilities as a natural by-product of that process....

This book is not recommended for individuals who want to develop psychic abilities as a novelty, to serve as a showpiece....

Psychic phenomena and mediumship are not a panacea—they carry a price. In assuming this path, you should not take the work lightly. There can be risks when the untutored dabble in the paranormal. Anxious to expand their psychic awareness, some individuals charge headfirst into this area without learning how to set proper boundaries for their work. They may open themselves to anything and every-thing—including less-than-desirable energies—which can result in a variety of problems. Not only are the proper pro-tocols important, but spiritual maturity and understanding are as well.

Now, consider the following passages from my father's document, "To the Would-Be Medium." You can draw your own conclusions about similarities between this material and my writing, as well as the information shared by Debra. My father's words were:

Do not seek the development of psychic powers out of mere curiosity; it is a serious study only to be undertaken with pure motives and a desire for the highest.

Do not mistake motives of vanity for altruism. Be sure that it is the desire to serve that actuates you and not the desire to wield unusual powers. Many people's vanity mas-querades as altruism. By and by the cloven hoof appears and the sensitive goes down at the first temptation.

Always live rationally. Do not seek to exercise your pow-ers at any and every time of day. Be as regular in the exercise of your mediumship as in performance of other duties.

"Try the Spirits": do not accept any control who may wish to use you. A medium is known by the company he or she keeps on the psychic plane as well as on the physical plane.

Do not think the development of mediumship means that the necessity for study and self-improvement has come to an end, often it has just begun.

Remember that an ignorant medium can be a danger. "If the blind lead the blind they will fall into the ditch together." The wider the sensitive's knowledge and the better trained his or her mind, the more effective will be his or her work.

Keep the mind calm and poised. Cast out fear and cultivate a loving heart.

Before either of us had seen "To the Would-Be Medium," Debra felt so strongly compelled by what she'd received that she suggested we draft a pledge for my father's book. I agreed with her sentiment and we refined the document until it felt right to both of us. Following is our finished pledge, which is now part of my father's book:

I will use this manual to seek guidance in growing my spiritual abilities and sense of inner knowing. In assuming this path I choose to pursue a new and heightened level of connection with the Divine Source and Spirit, from which assistance will be furnished. Using my abilities I will strive to help others—and in doing so honor those I assist, my spiritual hosts, and myself. I will always carry the highest and best intentions for all—everything I do will emanate from positive energy and pure love. If I use these abilities in the wrong way, my gifts will be taken away from me.

In sharing these passages from my father's psychic development book, the congruent writings that came to me, and Debra's message about the sacred nature of psychic work, I want to state that the path I have chosen feels right for me and I recognize that it is not for everyone. Some will commit to a developmental process and notice a significant expansion of their psychic abilities, while others may see modest gains or perhaps none at all. Whether you choose to tackle such an endeavor is your decision. No one else can say what is right for you. Whatever you decide to pursue must resonate within your heart. Each of us has a unique gift that I would suggest we need to uncover and utilize, whether it's related to healing, music, writing, counseling, teaching, molding pottery, psychic abilities, or anything else. It's not about notoriety and fame but doing what makes you happy and brings fulfillment to your life. And ideally it is something that helps others too.

In closing this chapter I wanted to share that I took a step forward in developing my intuitive abilities in 2012, conducting a number of test readings for people that largely generated encouraging results. In the early sessions I seemed to have a knack for remote viewing, as I was able to identify physical objects that were relevant to the sitters. (In some cases the sitters retrieved the objects from other locations and showed them to me.) In addition, I had success in providing specific validations related to deceased loved ones, especially in the later sessions. I have captured these experiences in a journal and plan to share more about them in the future, suspecting that this information may be helpful to others on a similar path. This is still difficult for me, because I receive the information in the form of feelings and mental imagery that is often vague and easily mistaken for my imagination. Perhaps I'll gain confidence and trust in this capacity more as time progresses, but I still have a pragmatic side and I don't think it's going away anytime soon.

CHAPTER 10

Robin's Flight

In the fall of 2005, my sister Robin, who is two years younger than me, was diagnosed with a rare form of pancreatic cancer that could not be treated with chemotherapy or radiation. However, her strain was slower to progress than most other forms of the disease. In the course of receiving this news we learned that the culprit—a tumor around the head of her pancreas—could not be removed surgically. Robin was told that no cure was available but that she was likely to survive longer than most "pan-can" patients because of the unusual nature of her cancer strain. The doctors couldn't tell us whether Robin would live one year or ten. For my sister, this probably seemed like she was riding on a plane that she knew would eventually crash, but which remained temporarily aloft by virtue of a single sputtering engine.

As kids, Robin and I were close but still clashed on occasion. She was a cute little girl with a bit of an ornery streak; she just couldn't resist getting under my skin. I'm sure that I pushed many of her buttons as well.

From an early age we both shared a strong interest in music. When I was about nine and Robin seven, we would set up toy instruments and play along with favorite records, pretending that we generated the tunes. As Robin developed an amazing voice and I learned to play guitar, this love of music continued. Robin's musical prowess grew, both in the quality of her voice and her skills as a songwriter, but my sister never achieved the level of success that she'd dreamed about.

In September 2006, Robin began to experience a great deal of abdominal pain and started passing blood. She immediately checked into the hospital. After about six weeks of inpatient care, including various tests and monitoring, she learned that her pancreatic cancer had worsened and that it had metastasized to her liver. Robin was advised that her condition was terminal and she would be moved to a hospice for the duration of her physical life. Robin showed tremendous composure and grace, never once becoming angry or curt. Rather, my sister demonstrated a calm acceptance of what was to transpire, finding hope and comfort in her spiritual faith. Once again my family and I were facing the loss of a loved one, yet we felt prepared because we understood the unending nature of life.

During the course of Robin's hospice stay, some remarkable things began to transpire. I'd previously read about "deathbed visions" (DBVs) and "near-death experiences" (NDEs), where dying patients describe extraordinary events such as separation from their physical body and communication with deceased loved ones. I was fascinated by these accounts and curious to see if Robin might experience anything similar.

Less than two weeks before my sister's passing, I visited her and administered a healing. I accomplished this by laying my hands on her and also through another non-touch healing energy exercise that I'd recently learned. During this healing process Robin was lying down with her eyes closed, seemingly unaware of my actions. Later that day my sister was occasionally lucid, yet faded off intermittently between brief stretches of dialog.

After a while Robin sat up on the side of her bed, mumbled a few inaudible words, and then clearly stated, "They said that what you did helped."

Surprised by her comments, I moved closer to my sister and asked, "Who are they?"

Robin looked at me blankly for several moments and then exhaustedly said, "Never mind."

It could be argued that she was hallucinating, but I considered the possibility that my sister may have had one foot in this world and another one in the next. She had seemed incognizant of the healing I'd administered, and there was a unique nature to her comments that made them seem a gesture of appreciation from other unseen parties.

An episode of this type is considered a deathbed vision, which shares certain characteristics with NDE phenomena. A common theme attributed to both is the perception of contact with deceased loved ones. But while many DBV accounts are compelling, NDEs make for better case studies because they uniquely offer evidence that perception and consciousness can occur outside the brain. Certain skeptics have tried to dismiss NDEs as brain-induced phenomena, yet many highly credible researchers have drawn significantly different conclusions.

Pim van Lommel, a prominent Dutch cardiologist and researcher, has studied NDE phenomena extensively and published some remarkable findings—for example, the fact that people with flat-lined brain activity, *clinically dead*, could later accurately describe events in the area surrounding their body. The term "cardiac arrest" refers to the loss of heart function and implies that blood flow has stopped. A person could suffer cardiac arrest while still maintaining brain function for a certain period of time, but the patients involved in these studies had also experienced a cessation of measurable brain activity.

In his article "Life Goes On," Tijn Touber reports:

> The most remarkable thing, van Lommel says, is that his patients have such consciousness-expanding experiences while their brains register no activity. But that's impossible, according to the current level of medical knowledge. Because most scientists believe that consciousness occurs in

the brain, this creates a mystery: How can people experience consciousness while they are unconscious during a cardiac arrest (a clinical death)? "At the very moment these people are not only conscious; their consciousness is even more expansive than ever and yet the brain shows no activity at all" [says van Lommel]. ...

[The article continues:] The majority of people who have had a near-death experience describe it as magnificent and say it enriched their lives. The most important thing people are left with is that they are no longer afraid of death. This is because they have experienced that their consciousness lives on, that there is continuity.[1]

Pim van Lommel's excellent work and grounded approach yielded a comprehensive article in *The Lancet* (a British-based leading journal of medical research) that established him as one of the world's pre-eminent authorities on near-death experiences (Vol. 358, December 15, 2001).

Reading about Pim van Lommel's work made me think of my uncle Robert Ireland, who shared an account of his NDE experiences with me a few years ago. In the late 1990s, my uncle was admitted into Tucson Medical Center after suffering a major heart attack. While lying on an examination table surrounded by medical personnel, his heart activity suddenly flat-lined. During this period, my uncle recalled hovering over his body while doctors worked feverishly to resuscitate him. He noted seeing deceased relatives nearby who were there to provide comfort and support, but they did not try to influence his decision to stay or to go. My uncle also saw his wife and daughter crying next to his body, pleading for his recovery. He felt a deep sense of peace and serenity and had a strong desire to leave this world. He knew the choice was his and ultimately chose to stay in the physical world because of a sense of love and obligation for his wife and family. After regaining consciousness in a physical sense, my uncle spoke to the doctor and shared precise observations about the positioning of electrodes used to revive him. When asked how he was aware of these specifics my uncle replied, "I saw the whole thing," which both astounded and befuddled the attending surgeon.

To return to the report above, the details of what constitutes physical death are not a mystery:

> When the heart stops beating, blood flow stops within a second. Then, 6.5 seconds later, EEG activity starts to change due to the shortage of oxygen. After 15 seconds there is a straight, flat line and the electrical activity in the cerebral cortex has disappeared completely. We cannot measure the brain stem but testing on animals has demonstrated that activity has ceased there as well. Moreover, you can prove that the brain stem is no longer functioning because it regulates our basic reflexes, such as the pupil response and swallowing reflex, which no longer respond.[2]

Some skeptics have continued to assert that such experiences must take place when there is still some brain function. Pim van Lommel addresses this contention directly in his 2010 book *Consciousness Beyond Life: The Science of the Near-Death Experience.* He also brings in the emotional and spiritual side of an NDE—for example, sharing the following commentary from a patient who went out of body: "I'm no longer afraid of death. I see the experience as a gift. Now I know there's more after death. I'm grateful. I feel that I have to talk about it to help others, to reassure them if they're afraid of death. I feel privileged."[3]

One of the most compelling documented cases of NDE phenomena involves a woman named Pam Reynolds. Due to a large aneurysm in her brain deemed too risky to treat through normal surgical procedures, doctors employed a highly unusual method called "hypothermic cardiac arrest." In this process, all the blood was drained from Pam's brain to relieve pressure from the aneurysm so they could safely operate.

In his book *Light and Death*, Dr. Michael Sabom offers a detailed analysis of the Pam Reynolds case. "She underwent a rare operation to remove a giant basilar artery aneurysm in her brain that threatened her life. The size and location of the aneurysm, however, precluded its safe removal using the standard neuro-surgical techniques." Continues Dr. Sabom:

> ... the operation, nicknamed "standstill" by the doctors who performed it, required that Pam's body temperature be lowered to sixty degrees, her heartbeat and breathing stopped, her brain waves flattened, and the blood drained from her head. In everyday terms, she was put to death. After removing the aneurysm, she was restored to life. During the time that Pam was in standstill, she experienced a NDE. Her remarkably detailed veridical out-of-body observations during her surgery were later verified to be very accurate. This is considered to be one of the strongest cases of veridical evidence in NDE research because of her ability to describe the unique surgical instruments and procedures used and her ability to describe in detail these events while she was clinically brain-dead.

Elaborating on the case, Dr. Sabom continues:

> When all of her vital signs were stopped, the doctor turned on a surgical saw and began to cut through Pam's skull. While this was going on, Pam reported that she felt herself "pop" outside her body and hover above the operating table. Then she watched the doctors working on her lifeless body. From her out-of-body position, she observed the doctor sawing into her skull with what looked to her like an electric toothbrush. Pam heard and reported later what the nurses in the operating room had said and exactly what was happening during the operation. At this time, every monitor attached to Pam's body registered no life whatsoever. At some point, Pam's consciousness floated out of the operating room and traveled down a tunnel which had a light at the

end of it where her deceased relatives and friends were waiting including her long-dead grandmother. Pam's NDE ended
when her deceased uncle led her back to her body.

Detailing the clinical processes used to assess brain function, Dr.
Sabom writes:

> For practical purposes outside the world of academic debate,
> three clinical tests commonly determine brain death. First,
> a standard EEG measures brain-wave activity. A "flat" EEG
> denotes non-function of the cerebral cortex—the outer shell
> of the cerebrum. Second, auditory evoked potentials, similar
> to those [clicks] elicited by the ear speakers in Pam's sur-
> gery, measure brain-stem viability. Absence of these poten-
> tials indicates non-function of the brain stem. And third,
> documentation of no blood flow to the brain is a marker for
> a generalized absence of brain function. During "standstill,"
> Pam's brain was found "dead" by all three clinical tests—her
> electroencephalogram was silent, her brain-stem response
> was absent, and no blood flowed through her brain.[4]

Acutely aware of such cases, I was on alert for signs from Robin.
As I spoke to my sister later that day during a period of reasonable
coherence, I asked for details about her experiences. Robin told me
that she sensed the presence of others, yet seemed unable to focus in
on them. She said, "It's like I hear and see people to my side but when
I turn to look, no one is there."

I wondered if my sister's consciousness might be drifting between
two worlds in preparation for her transition. In some ways Robin's
account reminded me of my wife Susie's experience when she saw
Brandon appear as a shadow figure to her right. During this incident,
which occurred in July 2004, Susie intentionally avoided turning to
look directly at Brandon, intuitively sensing that she would lose the
connection that enabled her to perceive him. Interestingly, she *felt*
Brandon's presence prior to seeing him. In the world of paranormal

acronyms, Susie's experience would be considered an "ADC," or an "after-death communication."

On Sunday, November 19, I was visiting my sister in the hospice, accompanied by my mother Shirley Christie, my cousin Beverly Klinger, and our musician friend James Linton, who played songs for Robin. At this point my sister no longer seemed coherent. Sadly, Robin was moaning, turning from side to side in bed, with her eyes rolling back in her head, eyelids half open.

Thirty minutes into our visit, my mother was overcome by sorrow and rolled her wheelchair away from my sister, sobbing uncontrollably. At that moment, I started walking toward my mother to provide comfort when a strong, inexplicable feeling came over me. I suddenly felt that my father was around us and I sensed his energy as very happy, uplifting, and upbeat, contrary to the sorrowful tones present in the room. That feeling actually filled me with joy in the midst of everyone's distress. I also sensed that my father wanted to let me know that *they* were planning a party for my sister, which was to occur after her passing. I proceeded to share this with my mother even though I found myself questioning whether the inspirational thought was "real." I didn't hear or see this, *I just felt it*. My typical internal dialog after such an experience questions whether I should share the information, but I did not hesitate in this instance.

Two days later I received a startling email message that touched on this very issue. The note came from Linda Williamson, a prominent English medium whom I had come to know over the past couple of years. She was responding to an earlier message that I'd sent to advise friends of my sister's condition and to share information about her apparent deathbed vision. Linda's comments were quite astonishing, especially the last sentence.

Dear Mark, Thank you for the news of your sister—she is in my prayers. No doubt all the healing she is receiving will be directed in the way that is best for her. As you know, even if it is not meant for a person to make a physical recovery because it is their time to return home, the healing helps to make the transition easier. As I type this, I am aware of someone connected with you—possibly your father—saying to tell you that *we have a great big party waiting for her.*

Needless to say, I was astounded by the confirmation, and my mother was greatly comforted. I saw it as a personal message from the universe telling me to trust my intuition.

Robin passed on the night after Thanksgiving 2006, surrendering to the devastating effects of cancer at 2:45 AM. Services were held the following Friday.

Remarkably, we started receiving after-death communications almost immediately after Robin's passing. The first incident involved my sister's friend Denise Huber roughly fifteen hours later. Denise was home, visiting with her cousin Jodi, who noticed a wristwatch lying on a table in the living room. After taking a brief glance, Jodi noticed something unusual and asked Denise, "Did you happen to see what time is showing on this watch?" Jodi then handed the watch to Denise and she saw that it was frozen on 2:45, which was the exact time of Robin's passing.

The next episode involves a Phoenix, Arizona-based medium, Melinda Vail, with whom I'd had two prior readings. My last meeting with Melinda occurred nearly a year earlier. I found her to be very precise—capable of providing names and many other specifics including uncannily accurate descriptions of the deceased person's personality traits. In this regard I recall a rather funny incident during our second reading when my father apparently tossed a risqué innuendo in Melinda's direction, causing her to stammer and blush. I found this episode quite amusing, as it fit perfectly with my dad's fun-loving, flirtatious personality.

Less than two weeks after Robin's passing, my friend Joe Colucci received an unexpected call from Melinda, who asked him how I was doing. Not wanting to tip his hand, Joe replied, "He's doing fine, why?"

Melinda followed, "Someone by the name of Roberta or Robin came to me and asked that I let Mark know that she is safe." Joe then told Melinda that I'd just lost my sister, Robin.

While it is theoretically possible that Melinda could have seen my sister's obituary, I don't believe that is what happened. The column appeared only once, eight days earlier, and there didn't seem to be a compelling reason for such a delayed response. Also, if this were Melinda's method of operation, it would require that she scan the newspaper on a daily basis year-round. If she had known the correct information from the start, there would have been no need for her to share the incorrect name "Roberta."

The hits kept coming. On Sunday, December 9, a young woman named Darinka, who works as a med-tech at my mom's assisted-living center, was driving to work. During her commute Darinka heard a voice say, "Buy some apples." Although she felt a strong urge to visit the grocery store, Darinka didn't have time to stop without being late for work so she continued on. After arriving at the center she spent the entire day consumed by a strong desire to leave for the store because her impulse to buy apples was almost overwhelming.

Darinka later told me that she rarely shares her "inspirations" with people because they don't understand, but she felt compelled to tell my mom about this particular episode. While the voice didn't tell her that the apples were for my mom, Darinka knew it intuitively. Her decision to share this insight with my mother turned out to be a positive, because unbeknownst to Darinka, my sister always made a point of bringing apples to my mother.

Amazingly, my sister's friend Denise Huber brought groceries to my mom later that same day but forgot to include the apples that she'd purchased for her. After hearing these two stories, which appeared interrelated, I spoke to Denise and asked if she had told anyone about the apples that she'd forgotten. After chuckling at her oversight, Denise confirmed that she had not spoken to a soul and was quite surprised to hear the rest of the story. I then spoke to Darinka and she was also stunned to learn that Denise was planning to bring my mother apples but that she'd forgotten them. It seemed my sister knew in advance that Denise would drop the ball—so to speak—resulting in her request for assistance from another party.

I personally spoke with Darinka (who came to the United States from the former Yugoslavia). During our chat, it became clear that she had strong psychic-mediumistic abilities but did not know what to do with them, having no one with whom she could talk. Afterward I pulled together some books for her to read and steered her to a group designed to nurture people with such gifts.

About two weeks after Robin's passing, I had to travel to Connecticut on business. On both Monday and Tuesday that week, my wife heard people walking about our home in the middle of the night, yet she wasn't frightened. Despite the unusual sounds, Susie seemed to know, through some intuitive faculty, that the activity originated from benevolent sources. *Perhaps the party was still going on....*

Other notable events occurred at our home while I was in Connecticut. On Monday night that week, my wife turned a light switch in our pantry to the "on" position before going to bed. Oddly, she awoke the following morning and found the light off. At first Susie assumed that the light bulb had burned out but soon discovered the switch was actually in the "off" position. Susie was certain that she'd turned the pantry light on during the prior evening because she needed it to make her way back to our bedroom from the kitchen. Our stovetop bulb, her normal light source, was burned out—leaving the pantry light as her only other option. This event, which could be described as physical phenomena, seemed tied into the aforementioned encounter.

Roughly six weeks after Robin's passing, I received an interesting email from a friend named Tim Baldy, who had lost his mother a few months earlier. Tim's note didn't refer to contact with my sister but it did include a notable affirmation, ostensibly originating from his mother, whom I knew well. With a sense of curiosity, I read Tim's words:

> Mark, I hope you're sitting down. I had a reading today with a psychic from Brooklyn, New York, named Christina Ambrosino. I wanted to talk to my mom and she came right through, very clearly. While my mom and I "talked" about a variety of things—and she validated several things with particular comments—I had no plans of talking about you; however, it seems that my mom did. While conversing, the medium asked if I knew someone named Mark and I immediately said yes. Christina then asked if Mark is someone my mother would have known. Again, I said yes. Christina then said she felt like Mark had experienced the passing of someone close very recently. In response, I said yes. Christina then said, "Your mother wishes for you to pass along her condolences to Mark, as she is aware of everything he has been going through."

A few weeks prior to Robin's passing I spoke to her about an idea that came to me regarding an unusual experiment. I thought that if this test were successful it could provide uniquely compelling evidence of an afterlife.

I am not a scientist and I did not allow myself to think this test would be viewed as a serious, controlled experiment by mainstream science. Rather, my goal was to facilitate a process that if successful would help my mother, family, and friends cope. Further, given positive results, I thought that other people might find healing in the story. In proceeding with this initiative, I wanted people to know that I was absolutely honest about everything that took place and that my motives were sincere.

After hearing the concept, Robin also thought it could help other people and agreed to participate. This design came about as I was thinking about the old "Houdini code," wondering how to improve upon the early-twentieth-century magician's model.

In 1929, celebrated medium Arthur Ford received considerable notoriety for his apparent solution of Houdini's secret code, "Rosabelle, believe," although two divergent perspectives emerged in the aftermath of this event. As author Allen Spraggett notes, "... Ford cracked the posthumous coded message from Houdini, thereby convincing his widow Beatrice—at least temporarily—that the famous magician, escapologist, and debunker of phony mediums (and some genuine ones, too, according to his detractors) had kept his deathbed promise to contact her from the beyond. The Houdini affair generated enormous controversy that continues to crackle even today...."[5]

Skeptics attacked Ford from a number of angles, suggesting that the code may have already been known to other parties or, worse yet, that Houdini's wife was Ford's partner in an elaborate hoax. Beatrice Houdini denied such allegations. She said, "Others say the message has been common property for some time. Why do they tell me this now when they know my heart was hungry for the true words from my husband? I have gotten the message I have been waiting for from my beloved, how, if not by spiritual aid, I do not know...."[6]

Although he was a staunch skeptic, Harry Houdini (born Erich Weiss) predicted that if there were an afterlife, it might be proven through the conveyance of a secret code after his passing. On his deathbed Houdini told his wife, "Remember the message, 'Rosabelle, believe' ... When you hear these words, know it is Houdini speaking."[7]

According to Spraggett, "Houdini was a skeptic who had a good deal of believer in him, as attested by the covenants he was in the habit of making with people to contact them—or if they died first, for them to contact him—from the grave. Ford, on the other hand, was a believer in Spiritualism who had a good deal of the skeptic in him, as indicated by his scarcely veiled contempt for many of his fellow mediums, and his constant advice to people, when confronted with a so-called spirit message, to *check it out*."[8]

Today, roughly eighty years after this controversy began, there is still no definitive answer regarding the outcome of the case of the Houdini code. Because of the allegations of fraud, which seem hard to prove or disprove, the subject remains a mystery. Despite the clamor and lack of resolution surrounding this case, I believed that Houdini's idea provided a good basic premise for an experiment involving my sister. However, I wanted to address some of the weaknesses in his methodology that led to the later assertions of fraud. I asked myself, *What were the shortcomings of his experiment?*

It came to me quickly: the primary flaw in Houdini's experiment was that a living person actually knew the code. The crux of the fraud allegation hinged on the idea that someone knew the secret words and could have spilled them. I also realized that there was a second matter to consider. Some scientists acknowledge the reality of psychic telepathy, yet argue that there is no proof that such communications originate with the deceased. Even in Houdini's day such assertions were made. Joseph Dunninger, a Houdini contemporary, stated, "In as much as Bessie knew the code words which Ford uttered, they were known to a living person. Therefore, since telepathy cannot be ruled out, Ford's demonstrations gave no proof whatsoever that the words came from Houdini's spirit."[9]

On the very last day that my sister was lucid, I gave her a piece of paper, a pen, and an envelope and asked her to write down a secret phrase of her choosing. I then requested that she fold the paper, place it in the envelope, and seal it. I turned away as Robin executed the process, with Susie and friend Tony Deprima standing nearby, just outside the open doorway to the room. After she completed the task, I asked Robin to initial the outside of the sealed envelope. She then handed it to me. No one saw what she wrote and therefore no one knew the phrase except Robin.

In devising this experiment, I wanted to address the aforementioned contention that mediumship may involve telepathy between the medium and sitter, rather than communication with a discarnate personality. In this case, given that no person other than my sister knew what was written on the paper, it would not have been feasible for any medium to pull the secret phrase from a sitter's mind via telepathy.

After taking the preliminary steps described above, I consulted Dr. Don Watson, a researcher in this field of exploration. My hope was to execute the experiment with the highest degree of integrity using the best possible protocols, given the circumstances at hand. Dr. Watson responded in an accommodating manner and agreed to assist me with the test.

I recognized that certain aspects of the experiment were not perfect. For example, it was probably not optimal for me to have been the recipient of the envelope. Given the reality of the situation, however, I didn't have sufficient time or resources to incorporate every desired control. Looking back to my sister's last day of clarity, it was apparent that she was fading fast. If I wanted to carry out the experiment I knew it was "now or never."

After our initial communication, Dr. Watson recommended that I mail Robin's envelope to him as an added control. Following his instructions, I sent the package less than a week after my sister's passing and he acknowledged receipt within three days. Dr. Watson then suggested that we contact a few mediums who might be willing to share insights about what Robin may have written. For an additional level of control he initially recommended that we use a third person, unbeknownst to me, who would open Robin's envelope and compare her phrase with the medium's responses.

Digressing for a moment, I feel it is appropriate to share some information about Dr. Watson that is pertinent to this discussion. Dr. Don Watson is noted for his authorship of "TES," or "Theory of Enformed Systems." TES asserts that consciousness precedes matter and is essentially responsible for the manifestation of the material world.

Unresolved questions about the true nature of consciousness drove Dr. Watson and his colleague, Dr. Bernard O. Williams, as they sought to develop a comprehensive hypothesis to challenge prevailing models, virtually all of which are materialistic. In a compelling essay on the subject of consciousness, Dr. Watson shared some interesting questions that shed light on his thinking:

> So, what do we know about consciousness? Can it be studied scientifically at all? Or must we surrender to extant ethnic beliefs, and continue to exclude the sine qua non of both religion and science from scientific exploration? I think not. Nor must we continue to dodge the question posed in 1944 by Schrödinger, What is Life?
>
> Today, it is ethnically [sic] correct to equate life with DNA, to attribute the phenomenon of life to a "pack of molecules." Schrödinger was dissatisfied with this reductionist idea, noting that there is no justification for assuming that the known laws of physics comprise the complete set of nature's laws.[10]

Reductionism argues that we can learn what "makes things tick" by looking more closely at matter, examining the underlying units. There are at least two problems with this approach. First, reductionism assumes that only observable, material items are "real," even though the vacuum of space is known to contain vast amount of inaccessible, "invisible" energy. Subatomic particles go in and out of observable "existence," and science does not know "where" they go when they are not manifesting here. Second, this path of reasoning ignores a major quandary encountered in the realm of quantum physics. When examining matter more closely—diving down from the molecular level to the subatomic—a point is soon reached where there is virtually nothing present, at least not an obvious "material something." (As noted in chapter 3, an atom is 99.99999 percent empty space.)

In an essay on TES, Dr. Watson uses a novel metaphor to describe a more holistic approach to the problem:

> According to the mythology of science, we will eventually understand living systems if we divide them into increasingly simpler parts—organs, cells, molecules, and finally the fundamental particles and forces studied in physics. This is

absurd because neutrons, protons, electrons, and the rudimentary parts of, say, possums are also the rudimentary parts of every other material system. They don't entail *possumness*.

The only justification for reductionism is the tacit assumption that it is reversible. To see the fallacy of "reversible reductionism," consider this Possum Principle: Two half-possums do not equal one whole possum. The possum principle applies to reductionism because dividing a possum into two parts irreversibly annihilates the essential quality of the whole possum: its organization, i.e., the "map" of the relationships among its parts in space and time.

This annihilation is accompanied by examining two pivotal losses: The possum loses its life, of course, and scientists lose the opportunity to study the map of its organization. In other words, after reducing it, the ostensible object of study no longer exists, either in reality (the living possum) or in concept (the possum's map).

Despite the absurdity of applying nonexistent concepts to nonexistent possums, the lore of science promises that, if we believe strongly enough, and if we work hard and long enough, we'll eventually find our reward in watching the possum reintegrate itself from the "building blocks" to which we've reduced it. Today this futile hope is often expressed as "self-organization"—a chimerical bootstrap operation that would somehow occur without boots or straps.[11]

Shifting to the topic of self-awareness, Dr. Watson provides a brief synopsis of his theory:

So, what is consciousness—the entity that is aware of its own existence? This is my driving question. Because organization per se cannot be described by any existing theory of physics or biology, I have posited the existence of a basic principle of organization—enformy—to account for life and mentality. As energy is the capacity to perform work, enformy is the capacity to organize. Two aspects of enformy are information and complexity. As a fundamental quantity, enformy cannot be described in terms of energy and mass. Perhaps enformy is consciousness. Perhaps we—the entities that are aware of our own existence—are collections of enformy existing in a region of space-time, enforming the physico-chemical structures we call our bodies. This is the tantalizing idea I am currently exploring.[12]

Returning to Robin's experiment, it was December 23, 2006, about a month after her passing, when requests were sent out to ten mediums. Our goal was to gain feedback from at least five individuals, and we didn't know what kind of response to anticipate. In our communiqué, we furnished a brief explanation of the experimental protocol and asked for their help in trying to "receive" the contents of Robin's message.

Within days, I began receiving responses from several interested individuals. Some of the mediums offered a short telephone reading, while others preferred to send notes via email. A few mediums offered to do both.

I then felt like I'd stumbled upon a gold mine after becoming acquainted with Tricia Robertson, Honorary Secretary and Immediate Past President of the Scottish Society for Psychical Research, a person introduced earlier in this book. Upon hearing of my experimental design, Tricia offered to contact some mediums in the United Kingdom and would later relay their responses to Dr. Watson and me.

Except for one instance where she forwarded my query to a medium, Tricia kept her participants at arm's length. She told them only that a young woman named Robin had recently died and left a secret message in an envelope. The mediums knew nothing else about Robin, or me, the author of the experiment. In two of four cases, Tricia played intermediary by passing along the medium comments herself, thereby adding another buffer to the process. In the other two cases, Tricia had the mediums respond directly to Dr. Watson and he then shared the responses with me.

As the medium responses began coming in, Dr. Watson and I were anxious to see what kinds of messages would be relayed. As it happened, two things immediately garnered my attention. First, some of the mediums provided information about Robin that I knew was accurate—so I started to wonder if these people might also be on the right track in regard to her secret message. Second, I found some parallels between medium responses and wondered if those similarities might point the way to the message.

In terms of "hits," or statements that I saw as being relevant, English medium Melanie Polley delivered the phrase "Little House on the Prairie." This clicked with me, as it referenced one of Robin's all-time favorite television programs. Melanie also indicated, "She made it to Thanksgiving but not Christmas." This made sense, because Robin passed the night following Thanksgiving.

Scottish medium Jacqui McGleish noted a problem with Robin's throat, "Like she could not swallow." Fellow Scotsman Tom Johnston spoke about a pain in Robin's throat, "as if she were choking." Both of the Scottish mediums were on target, as Robin had great difficulty swallowing during her last few days. This proved to be quite problematic because she was in great pain but unable to take her medication orally. Worse yet, the hospice attendants were not equipped to administer drugs intravenously.

Tom Johnston stated the term "Arizona," which I found quite unusual, seeing that he lived in Scotland and had no means of knowing that Robin was from Arizona. He also shared "Wednesday, Thursday," which were in fact Robin's final two days as she spiraled down physically.

Linda Williamson said, "There were two people who knew her or that you contacted on behalf of her. I just got, 'Both of them.' She thanks you for doing that for her."

I had in fact recently made contact with two of Robin's old friends, Susan Murray and Craig Cedarstrom. Neither person had seen Robin for many years—thirty-five in Craig's case. I told them both about her illness, and Susan was actually able visit Robin while she was still lucid.

Linda also said, "She's aware of you writing it all down. You know, she's very interested in this experiment. And I'm seeing pages and pages being filled up, so I'm feeling that there's a lot to come through but that you need to give it a little bit of time. Don't set too short a cutoff point because she'll get more through to you if you give it a little bit of time."

Indeed, I had been keeping detailed notes on the entire process including the aforementioned ADCs. It was my intention to document everything that took place. I had a nagging feeling about Linda's comments telling me to allow enough time for this process. I was concerned that my impatience could lead to the omission of additional medium responses—possibly to include the best ones.

I booked a private reading with a medium from the Midwest United States, whose name I choose not to disclose. I did not tell this person about the experiment in advance, which seemed to put him at a disadvantage compared to the other mediums. During the reading, I did share the fact that my sister had left behind a secret message and asked if he could deliver it. Early on, he correctly stated my deceased aunt's first name, "Gloria." Later in the reading, he correctly delivered my aunt's last name, "Banks," and indicated that she was somehow involved in the process of bringing through my sister's message.

Relaying a communication said to be coming from Aunt Gloria, he shared, "You will have that code—that message."

Then posing what seemed a follow-up question to my aunt, he asked, "And when? Well, I know it will be before the scientists finish, but when?"

He then uttered, "She says, *we will give it to him … I know exactly what he's talking about.*"

This was completely out of left field, as he knew only that my sister had left behind a secret message, based on what I'd told him moments earlier. He was completely unaware that this was an actual experiment and that any scientists were involved in the process.

Looking back on my reading with Melanie Polley, I realized that she had also referenced an aunt. Melanie said, "I feel this strong character, so gentle, a very kind woman, very caring. Oh, is this the aunt? Because she's showing me an envelope." Her description of my Aunt Gloria was right on the money.

Melanie was aware of the experiment, yet her mention of my aunt made me wonder about the possibility of a unique communication method I'd not considered. Could it be that my sister's transition was so recent that she did not yet have the ability or understanding of how to relay her message? Maybe she needed assistance. It also made me wonder why my aunt couldn't simply relay the message if she were *there* with my sister.

Where was this mysterious *there* anyway? I pondered the potential complexities of our "being" in the next realm, wondering if some aspects of existence *there* may be very different. Who knows, perhaps my aunt and sister were not yet "together" in the same exact *place*. Maybe there were many *places*, and I had much more to consider. I also wondered about a possible correlation with the statement attributed to Jesus, "In my father's house are many mansions." (John 14:2)

It was always my father's contention that there are different "planes," or dimensional realities, where our consciousness shifts after physical death. Where we end up is a matter of resonance, meaning that we automatically "go" where we belong. It has also been asserted that after our passing each of us must go through an adjustment period before moving on to our "destination." This "in-between" realm where the adjustment is said to take place is usually referred to as the "ethereal plane."

Lastly, I wondered if my sister may have experienced difficulty in recalling her message after her passing, since she was heavily medicated at the time she wrote it. This led to another question. Where are memories stored? Materialists suggest that they are retained in the brain, yet evidence gleaned from medium communications would suggest that memory must reside elsewhere. Perhaps memory is something entirely different from any of our conceptions about it.

In regard to the subject of memory, my father referenced a concept that he called the "level of A-ONE-NESS," which he described as the "Cosmic Consciousness." Elaborating on his hypothesis he wrote, "Such familiar concepts as space, time, and the apparent diversity of the universe are useless when attempting to explain the operation of A-ONE-NESS, because its nature is primarily mystical."

My father's model is similar to what Eastern traditions refer to as the "Akashic Record"—a sort of universal database, capturing every event and thought throughout all history and existing outside space and time.

I suspect that there is an individualized component to memory as well. If one accepts the concept of a holistic self (body, mind, and spirit), perhaps memories are retained by the non-physical self. Alternately, the non-physical self could retrieve relevant memories via Akasha—the centralized memory mind—accessing those records matching with the personalized energy signature of the individual.

Continuing with medium feedback, speaking to the general proximity of Robin's cancer, medium Jamie Clark noted, "I have a real twisting in my lower abdominal [area]. I feel like it was a tag."* As mentioned earlier, Robin suffered from pancreatitis, which caused her to experience extreme pain in the abdominal area.

Speaking to apparent "deathbed visions" prior to her passing, Jamie said, "Robin makes me feel like she was already getting visits from the other side prior to her passing. She wasn't crazy and she wasn't making stuff up. I literally feel like she expressed this to somebody."

I immediately recalled my sister's interesting behavior and comments, made to me shortly before her passing, indicating her perception of "unseen" people. Jamie's comments seemed a confirmation that the experiences Robin had mentioned were an actual form of contact—perhaps intended to prepare her for the transition we call death.

---

* Mediums use the term "tag" to signify a person's cause of death, allowing them to confirm that they have connected with the right personality.

Jamie then asked, "Do you know if she had been working on a book or poetry? I get a very creative writing energy prior to her passing. I feel like there are either multiple written paragraphs or like multiple things. Not just one thing—I get multiple aspects."

After Robin's passing we did find a number of poems and songs that she'd left behind, and no one was aware of these works prior to her death. Also, she had just started writing a book about her experiences in overcoming alcohol dependency.

Jamie had added, "I feel like you'll see at least five different things; like paragraphs or lines or words...."

At the time, all I could do was wonder if Robin's phrase might be five words or five sentences but I wouldn't know until the envelope was opened.

Jamie then said, "She draws my attention to a painting. She says *the painting*."

This seemed clear to me. I'd just left Robin's former residence and took home a painting that carried sentimental value. It had been with our family since the 1960s and reminded me of happy times in childhood.

Medium Pam McKeown reported, "Your sister had a disease of the blood." This seemed true, as Robin's liver failure led to heightened toxicity in her blood. Additionally, she said, "I am also hearing the number *forty-seven*. Is someone's birthday coming up?" Unbeknownst to Pam, Robin would have turned forty-seven had she survived until her next birthday.

Apparently passing along a message of gratitude from Robin, George Dalzell shared, *"I have my teeth back."* This was relevant because Robin had several teeth pulled over the preceding few years.

George also said, *"I finished my degree."*

Our father Richard Ireland always spoke of death as a positive thing. When someone died, he would say that they had "graduated."

I could continue with these responses, but the ultimate question was whether any of these mediums had delivered the secret phrase. My analytical side took over and I started looking for consistencies from medium to medium.

Both Linda Williamson and remote viewer Craig Hogan noted an image of a "bird in flight." Linda said, "The only impression that came to me—and it was a fleeting impression and may well be wrong—was of a bird in flight. I know your sister's name is Robin but this didn't look 'robin-shaped' … more like a dove—perhaps an obvious symbol of the soul flying free."

Three mediums, Clark, McGleish, and Johnston, referenced the "sun," "sunshine," or "stars." Further, McGleish noted that the word "sun" was likely used in a poem or song. Jamie Clark mentioned something about a "good day" or "great day" in conjunction with the sun imagery. Pam McKeown offered the phrase "carpe diem," a Latin term meaning "seize the day." Based on this feedback, I started to think that the secret message might be the Beatles song, "Good Day Sunshine." The mediums' comments seemed to incorporate the words from the song title, but it was more than that. I recalled an instance when Robin and I were young, where we took my father's cassette recorder—without his permission—and taped ourselves singing this very song. Additionally, for fun, we also sang an inverted version that we called "Bad Day Raindrop." No one else was home that day and we were bored, so we started looking for something fun to do. When Robin found the recorder, we placed it on the family room floor and sat down—one on each side of the device. After agreeing on the song, we belted out the tune and then followed with our "alternate version" for amusement. It was silly; we were just kids. When my father needed to use the recorder with a client, he heard our singing and broke into laughter. Later, I remember him joking about our song-making exploits. He was not angry; rather, my father seemed to relish our creativity and fun-loving spirit.

I considered a second possibility based on another set of messages that appeared to coincide. Jamie Clark had mentioned something about "rainbows," and Melinda Vail referenced *The Wizard of Oz* and "Follow the Yellow Brick Road." I came to see that, taken together, "Somewhere Over the Rainbow" was a viable alternative—my second choice. And since *The Wizard of Oz* was one of Robin's favorite movies, this seemed to make sense on several levels.

Well before the envelope was ever opened, Dr. Watson recruited two more people to assist with the experiment: the aforementioned Dr. Bernard Williams and paranormal researcher Bill Walker. Dr. Watson asked each of us to peruse all the medium feedback and come up with our best guess as to the content of Robin's secret message. Naturally, the others didn't have the luxury of recognizing which statements were accurate because they didn't know Robin. Nevertheless, Dr. Watson asked me to remain silent about this and allow each person to draw their own conclusions—solely on the basis of information they had been given.

For this purpose, Dr. Watson developed a questionnaire that each of us completed. The form included the following guidance: "Reports by mediums are often ambiguous. For that reason, we don't expect that Robin's message will be provided verbatim. Instead, we can expect a range of impressions that pertain to the message, including words, phrases, feelings, colors, and other associations."

It seemed the reason for this exercise was to allow us an opportunity to try to decipher a possible phrase since medium feedback might be highly symbolic in nature. Apparently Dr. Watson thought that the experiment would be viewed in a more credible light if we had arrived at our consensus "best guess" prior to opening the envelope. We didn't want to find ourselves having to search for a relevant phrase after opening the envelope, as if we were trying to make something fit.

At the end of this process Dr. Williams took a stab, guessing that the phrase would be "Somewhere over the rainbow." Bill Walker's guess was similar: "Something related to *The Wizard of Oz*, or *The Wiz*, like 'Somewhere over the Rainbow,' or 'Follow the Yellow Brick Road,' or 'Brand New Day'." Serving as a moderator, Dr. Watson did not offer a guess.

Before the envelope was to be opened, I was in store for a few last-minute surprises. First, Dr. Watson explained that he had gone back to one of the mediums, Pam McKeown, to solicit an additional reading. In that session, Pam felt she was able to connect with Susy Smith, a former colleague of Dr. Watson's. Prior to her death, Susy

Smith had been a medium, author, and researcher. In life, Susy Smith had designed an experiment much like this one, so it seemed a synchronous link. I wasn't sure why Dr. Watson had contacted Pam but assumed that he sensed some stones left unturned.

We then addressed Dr. Watson's transcription of his reading with Pam McKeown, which took place one week prior to the envelope opening. During the reading, Pam relayed information that she felt came from Susy Smith.

Her early Q&A with Dr. Watson seemed directed primarily at the experimental protocols. Along these lines, Pam asked, "Have you contemplated adding another view to this experiment?"

Dr. Watson replied, "You're too good."

In answering in this way, Dr. Watson seemed to be acknowledging his consideration of a wide variety of approaches to garner the right information, including his reason for coming back to Pam for this extra session.

Pam resumed, "It's like you want to open it but are hesitating for some reason. You feel so close and then not. It's like you are missing or forgetting a piece, like you haven't covered all the angles."

Without elaborating, he responded, "That's right."

Dr. Watson then asked Pam if her earlier message, "Carpe diem," originated with Susy, because it sounded like something she would have said.

Pam replied, "Yes, the message came from Susy," adding, "It was a message to all ... 'All' being life, love, compassion." Pam then said, "I feel as if I'm channeling this information now. That wasn't me."

She reiterated, "Tell everyone to live, love, and have compassion for one another. Seize the day."

Dr. Watson came back, "That sounds like Susy."

Pam continued, "This place of existence [the physical world] is truly the only one where we can make a difference, to learn, and to grow. The spiritual plane sees all—past, present, and future—but the differences are to be made here [in the physical realm]. It is up to us to make up for our differences, to become one again, back to the source. When we become enlightened here [on Earth] we begin at a place that is closer to the source when we cross over. Susy wants us all to start at a closer place [when we cross over]. Right now everyone is scattered about. When the understanding of the existence of the other side comes, then everyone will come closer together. That is the true meaning. We have to do it on this side—clean people."

Pam then, seemingly unsure of the meaning of her last utterance, remarked, "Clean people—what's that?"

Dr. Watson responded, "Maybe 'clean people' are those not contaminated by material stuff."

This spurred a memory for me regarding a possible definition for "clean people." I thought of a reading that I'd had with Linda Williamson nearly three years earlier, in which she made a reference about people who had passed "that were working to bring a heightened understanding about the afterlife into the world today."

She said, "People like you have been drawn into this Network— those with a sincere interest in the subject. This would include mediums and researchers but they always choose people of integrity."

So perhaps, along the lines of Dr. Watson's observations, "clean people" meant individuals involved for the right reasons.

Dr. Watson continued, "Through her books and experiments, Susy always tried to spread the message [of an afterlife] to everyone. That was her life work while she was here."

Pam responded, "She is still trying to do this, through you, and apparently via me. This experiment may not work the first time but it will bring huge attention and that is also important to your work.… Don't lose sight of the prize without learning the lesson along the way (she says). Either way, it will be a success."

As an added twist to the experiment, a few days prior to the envelope opening, Dr. Watson suggested that I send a final request to the mediums who had participated. Based on his suggestion, I posed the following question in this communication: "If you were the one dying, rather than Robin, what message would you have written?" When I sent out the email I didn't really expect much back, but a few responses later proved to be significant. Also, because of the short time-window, several of the mediums' responses came to us after the envelope had been opened, but before they had been informed of Robin's message.

The next surprise came from Dr. Williams, who indicated that he had recently discussed the experiment with another person named Alison Roepe, who was not initially involved. As he explained it, "Two of the submissions we will receive on Monday were completely unexpected and it all started with an intuitive response from a woman named Alison Roepe. I was describing the experiment to Alison, sharing with her the conclusion Bill and I had drawn from the medium responses. I did not consider that I would be interacting with this process in this way, so I openly stated our guess to her—the song title, 'Somewhere Over the Rainbow.' When Alison heard that, she got a strong intuitive *NO* and that response led her to ask for a session with a medium to see if she could get closer."

As Dr. Williams explained to me in an email,

> Alison subsequently booked a reading with a medium named Gail Larmer but also sought information through her own private meditation. In her session with Gail, she was hoping to receive some information from Robin, but most of the contact seemed to originate with Alison's ancestors. A few days later—about one week before we opened the envelope—Alison took time for a morning meditation and received the information that she submitted to us. In the end, we received two independent messages: one from Alison and one from Gail. Both were written and sealed prior to September 8, but neither was available to us at the time of the envelope opening. As Dr. Williams noted, "Both of these messages were obtained [by the mediums] before we opened Robin's envelope on September 8. Gail's is postmarked September 7, but the other one does not have a postmark because it was hand-delivered by Alison. It was, however,

sealed in the envelope before the other [postmarked] message was mailed."

One day before we opened Robin's envelope, Alison called Dr. Williams to share her intuitive message verbally before mailing it off. On the following day, just before we opened the envelope, Dr. Williams shared this information with us—his colleagues. While he didn't remember Alison's exact words, Dr. Williams did recall that "it was about love."

It was almost ten months after Robin's death when we opened the envelope, since that was the first time frame that worked for everyone involved. Dr. Watson and Dr. Williams were together in Kansas, while Bill and I communicated via instant messenger from our respective homes. Dr. Watson was in charge of opening the envelope and manning the computer—keeping Bill and me apprised of developments—while Dr. Williams videotaped everything. The impending nature of this event caused me to feel a sense of nervous tension.

The wheels were now turning. Dr. Watson and Dr. Williams both inspected the outer mailing envelope and agreed that it had not been tampered with. They then removed and inspected the inner envelope containing her message. After noting that Robin's initials had been written on the outside of the envelope and that it had not been corrupted, Dr. Watson opened it with a knife. After pulling out the note, he unfolded it to reveal Robin's secret message, which read, "LOVE is ALround US."

At first I felt a bit of disappointment because our educated guesses had proven wrong, and the initial medium responses also seemed to be off. But I did see Pam McKeown's last-minute entry as a reasonably good hit. While her submission did not match Robin's phrase in verbatim fashion, it did seem to convey the essence of her theme: "It was a message to all … 'All' being life, love, compassion … Tell everyone to live, love, and have compassion for one another. Seize the day."

I also felt a sense of hope from Alison Roepe's late submission, which Dr. Williams said "was about love." Her comments seemed to point to the possibility of at least a partial victory, if not a clear-cut one. Maybe the pieces were starting to come together in the eleventh hour. I wondered about the rest of Alison's message, and the response from Gail Larmer, but those would have to wait....

While debriefing with the others, I suggested that we collectively consider the possibility that Robin's message, "LOVE is ALround US" might have been an allusion to the Troggs song, "Love is All Around Us." We even looked up the lyrics online but found nothing too startling. We also weighed the likelihood that Robin's message may have revealed more about her state of awareness at the time, including the possibility that she was experiencing deathbed visions. If that had been the case, it was a comforting thought. At a time when Robin knew she was about to die, the foremost thing in her mind was a sense of love that she felt all around.

I then recalled something Linda Williamson said earlier, which now seemed pertinent:

> I feel like you've set a puzzle for your mediums. I'm also feeling your father around and you're putting a lot of pressure on yourself in some way. I get this feeling from your father of *don't overdo it, or don't do too much.* It will come more easily if you don't work so hard at it. You like to have everything cut and dried. It's as though you set yourself certain targets or things that you want to achieve.
>
> Where the communication from your sister is concerned, as well as other things you are doing on the psychic level, just ease up a bit. It's more a case of waiting for spirit, rather than setting objectives and saying, "This is what I want." You need to wait for them more, because I do feel that you will get this from your sister, *but it may come in from unexpected quarters, or in unexpected ways.* Conducting an experiment like this—there's nothing wrong with that, but as you probably know the evidence tends to come in different ways and not always in the particular way that you're hoping to

achieve it. So maybe they're saying in a roundabout kind of way that you'll get something that you can present to other people and say, "look, this is good evidence," to give other people encouragement. And they are aware that you want this and they are working on various ways that they can bring it to you. Experiments like the one set up with your sister are not often successful. I think it is hard for spirit to transmit an isolated word or phrase. It is easier for them to convey a picture, an idea, or an emotion. If I was to arrange such a code with someone I think I might try to convey an image or a memory that has a happy emotion with it. If the code was for the benefit of one particular person, it might be a memory of a shared experience with that person, such as a holiday, a wedding, or a much-loved house.

With Linda's comments in mind, I considered the late entries from Pam McKeown and Alison Roepe. While I didn't yet know the full content of Alison's message, it seemed clear that both of these submissions were closer to the mark than any of the earlier medium responses. So in hindsight, I was glad we hadn't rushed through the process.

I had also received last-minute email notes from two mediums, responding to the query posed by Dr. Watson regarding what they might have written had they been in Robin's deathbed situation. Interestingly, these answers also proved much closer to Robin's code than any of the early responses. In hindsight, I could see that this is what Dr. Watson was hoping for. Framing the question in this way seemed to alleviate the sense of pressure tied to heightened expectations. This approach allowed the mediums to simply share what they felt without becoming overly concerned about results.

In his last response, George Dalzell offered, "Love is our direction, our transportation, our purpose, our destination and love is at the heart of our evolution, our creation, destruction, and resurrection."

Jamie Clark shared, "I love my family with all of my heart and Soul! I would let them know that I would be around and validate through many avenues that I am still around. I would also let them know that there is only GOD, that is all things seen and unseen, and that the only true reality is unconditional love in the big picture."

Although Bill Walker was unavailable, Dr. Watson, Dr. Williams, and I decided to reconvene one week after the opening of the envelope to read the late entries furnished by Alison Roepe and Gail Larmer. I remembered what Alison had told Dr. Williams earlier, sharing her impression that we did not have Robin's message but that she hoped to bring it through. Alison seemed right on the first count, as none of the early entries contained Robin's secret message. Now I wondered if the second half of her statement would prove true as well. Would she be the one to deliver Robin's secret message?

Dr. Watson opened Gail's envelope and read her message, "Life is not what you think it is. Life is what you make it." Her message wasn't a match, but we had one chance left.

Now, with what seemed our last hope for a direct hit resting in his hands, Dr. Watson opened Alison's envelope and removed her note. Just before reading it, he threw out a teaser, saying, "You'll like it, Mark."

Anxious yet hopeful, I paid close attention as he read Alison's note, which said, "Berney, the message I received Sept 7 from Robin—'It's all about love' and then, the Beatles song, 'All you need is love.' Allie Roepe"

While we didn't have a word-for-word match, Alison's communication seemed to really capture the essence of Robin's message. All three of us saw it as being very close, not just in words but in meaning. Now, looking back, it seemed even more noteworthy to consider Linda Williamson's earlier comments, "You need to give it a little bit of time. Don't set too short a cutoff point, because she'll get more through to you…. I do feel that you will get this from your sister, *but it may come in from unexpected quarters, or in unexpected ways.*"

A last-minute response from an intuitive I'd never heard of, delivered one day prior to the envelope opening? I guess you could call that "unexpected."

In reviewing the late responses, I noticed a few other interesting tidbits. For one thing, Alison brought up a Beatles song, which is something I had actually anticipated as a possibility—just not this song. From the time we were children, Robin and I loved the Beatles, and it seemed natural for her to include a reference to their music in conjunction with her theme. Then again, Dr. Williams thought that his comments about "Somewhere Over the Rainbow" may have steered Alison in the direction of a song. In his words, "I suspect that my comment to her about our having 'settled' on a song title may have unduly shaped Alison's decision." Despite the possibility that Dr. Williams was correct, I saw this particular song as matching up well with the theme of Robin's message.

Next I recalled Jamie Clark's comment, "I feel like you'll see at least five different things; like paragraphs, or lines, or words." While Robin actually wrote "LOVE is ALround US," it could be deduced that she probably intended to write "Love is all around us," which is a five-word phrase. Given that she was extremely ill and on narcotics at the time, such a spelling miscue would be easy to understand.

At the end of the process, we all decided that the experiment had been worthwhile, and each of us had learned a great deal. While we were debriefing, I said, "On one hand, I felt that I approached this too analytically and not intuitively enough. Maybe we just looked for consistent statements by various mediums and assumed that those pointed the way."

Dr. Williams replied, "Mark, your point here is very important and interesting." We then launched into a discussion and uniformly agreed that our approach in trying to guess the message probably relied too heavily on analysis and not enough on intuition. Correcting this might be easier said than done, but it was definitely worthy of consideration.

Said Dr. Williams, "I do believe we have assembled a good range of perspectives on how to approach such an investigation. I am reminded of Charles Tart's proposal forty-odd years ago, that we develop 'State-Specific Sciences.' A strictly cognitive-analytic approach is not focused (or defocused) appropriately."

On September 27, 2007, Drs. Watson and Williams presented information about our project at an IONS (Institute of Noetic Sciences) meeting in Lawrence, Kansas. Much of their discussion focused on "the tasks of trying to find patterns in the information." As Dr. Williams noted in an email after the IONS meeting, "The fact that Bill and I, being more 'blind' [to background information about Robin], focused on the same pieces to form a pattern is an interesting facet. Also, I believe I did not focus on the 'Love' aspects in the information, because very many medium sessions [tend to] convey love and love being the essence of being. I may have been led away from those pieces of information because I was looking for something 'unique'."

I followed up with Dr. Watson a few weeks after their presentation, and he indicated that the information was met with great enthusiasm and interest. I then uncovered the following in an article, which sheds some light on the IONS organization.

> It might be surprising that an organization seriously dedicated to the scientific study of phenomena such as spirit, transcendence and enlightenment thrives internationally, with nearly 30,000 members in over 50 countries. Founded by lunar astronaut Edgar Mitchell in 1973, the Institute of Noetic Sciences explores "frontiers of consciousness," attempting to establish new ways of thinking and shifting global worldviews. The immediate faculty of IONS boasts dozens of doctoral and medical degrees.[13]

Bernard "Berney" Williams, who is the president of the Lawrence IONS group, President of Holos University, and teaches Cultural and Physical Geography at the University of Kansas, says that a broad array of people are drawn to IONS. He notes that many attendees are "people who have had some frustration with the conventional assumptions with intellectual investigation. Many have had personal experiences that are contrary to (mainstream science)."[14] What IONS is attempting to do on a global scale, members try to do on a personal level, such as redefining how they think and reaching a higher level of understanding about the nature of their own consciousness and potential. Williams says it is encouraging for members to know there are others out there who have had what they considered abnormal experiences until learning of IONS.

According to Bob Nunley, a Kansas University professor and active member of IONS, "We are primarily an organization that forms the bridge between the mystically inclined scientists and the scientifically inclined mystics."[15]

Elaborating on the specific IONS session focused on our experiment with Robin's message, Dr. Williams noted in an email to me:

> We also received some notes from Gail [Larmer], prompted also by a personal meditation and postmarked prior to our opening the envelope. Gail's notes were not particularly close to the phrase in Robin's note. Gail DID, however, relate an interesting story about her process during a semi-formal presentation of our research project at a local IONS study group. Don and I presented the project, with contributions from Alison and Gail. During that discussion, Gail related that she had in fact been prompted to focus on love but pulled back from that impulse, because she felt that it was too universal a theme in mediumistic communications. The formal message Gail wrote and posted to us did NOT include the love aspect. She only informed us of her having "suppressed" an impulse to put love in the message during the presentation about the research project. Gail's discussion—although post hoc—was interesting, especially when considering how we seem to have demonstrated that analytic cognitive approaches are not the most effective methods in endeavors such as these.

So with a reasonably successful groundbreaking experiment in our pocket, we carved out some interesting new terrain that other people may choose to explore in different ways, modifying and enhancing the experimental methodology and learning new things. Last and by no means least, my sister Robin was able to contribute something of lasting importance to the world, establishing her own legacy.

Postscript: In the summer of 2008, I met another medium named Elizabeth Stanfield. After learning about my involvement in this field, she offered to provide a blind telephone reading for a person of my choosing that could serve as a sort of "test" of her abilities.

In accordance with her offer, I set up a call on July 3, 2008, during which Elizabeth was to read for an anonymous sitter. Unbeknownst to Elizabeth, the sitter I had selected was my mother, whose name is Shirley. The first time Elizabeth heard Shirley's name was when I introduced her at the beginning of the reading, which was facilitated via a telephone conference call.

While Elizabeth remained unaware of my mother's identity, she did a competent job and delivered a number of pertinent hits. Near the end of the reading, my curiosity got the best of me. I decided to mention the experiment involving Robin's secret message and asked Elizabeth if she'd like to take a stab at the code phrase. (By this point, at the very end of session, I had revealed that Shirley was my mother.)

Responding immediately, Elizabeth said, "I just heard *Carpe diem.*"

"Seize the day," I responded.

"She [meaning Robin] said, *Carpe diem* and then, *The soul survives.*"

After the reading, I told Elizabeth that she did not crack Robin's message, but I shared the fascinating fact that she had hit on the exact same phrase as another medium.

Elizabeth then said, "I just heard *Love lasts forever … love lasts always.*"

About a year later, I learned about an outstanding reading that Elizabeth had recently conducted with a grieving woman. In the reading, Elizabeth correctly identified that the woman had lost a son and that his name was Michael. Elizabeth then felt as if something big was about to come forth, so she became very quiet and listened intently. As Elizabeth shared with me later in a personal note, "Michael said one word—*grounded*. I'll never forget how the mother reacted when I first said that word. Her eyes flinched and then opened wide. I followed by asking, 'Is he saying this to mean that he had sometimes been grounded [as a form of punishment] or does this have another meaning?' The mother explained that she had always told Michael that he was a grounded individual and far more mature than his peers."

Continued Elizabeth, "Once the reading was over and we were discussing the information that came through, Michael's mother told me there was something she wanted to share about the final moments of his life. She told me that they had both been Houdini buffs, and before Michael died they agreed on a secret word that he would use if she ever went to a medium—to make sure that she knew it was him. I'll bet you can guess what that word was—yes, it was *grounded*."

CHAPTER 11

Synchronicity

In the years that have elapsed since Brandon's passing, my life has been filled with unusual events that have convinced me that synchronicity is real. This includes "chance" meetings with strangers where things lined up in unique and meaningful ways and a mutual benefit was invariably found. Many cases involved such astronomical chances for our meeting as to make "coincidence" the more implausible conclusion.

Renowned psychologist Carl Jung coined the term "synchronicity" and defined it as "temporally coincident occurrences of acausal events." More simply, Jung described synchronicity as "meaningful coincidence."

An implication of synchronicity is that the universe operates in a harmonious manner and that life has meaning. Such a model stands in stark contrast to the view of those who assert that everything happens by chance and any notions of "purpose" are whimsy.

You might ask, what does synchronicity look like?

On the week of January 12, 2009, I was walking through my neighborhood when my cell phone suddenly rang.

"Hello," I said.

The male caller (I will call him Joel) asked if I was Mark Ireland. (Everyone in this chapter is referenced by their actual name unless I call it out in this manner for reasons of privacy.)

After I confirmed my identity, the man asked if I had a pair of tickets for the Arizona Cardinals–Philadelphia Eagles NFC Championship Game. I wasn't surprised by his question since I'd just posted these tickets for sale on the Internet. I wasn't sure if I'd be able to attend the game and had placed the ad to gauge demand for the tickets. Things were making sense thus far until the man's next query caught me off guard.

"Are you the Mark Ireland who lost a son and wrote a book?"

Puzzled by how the man knew so much about me, I responded tentatively, "Yes—that's me."

The man then chuckled, revealing a sense of befuddled amusement, and continued. "My name is Joel. My wife and I lost our twenty-year-old son to cancer about two years ago."

Things were starting to crystallize but I was still perplexed by the cross-pollination of football tickets, parents who had lost a son, and my book. These things were unrelated and I had not included my last name in the ticket advertisement.

Joel then elaborated, "My wife has had great difficulty in dealing with the grief since our son's death and she wanted a reading with a medium." He continued, "I've always felt that this life we are now living is all there is and that when it's over, it's over. So, I never believed in that sort of thing [the idea of an afterlife or mediums]. But my wife was suffering so much that I was willing to try anything—so I supported her appeal for a meeting with a medium."

Joel's story was captivating but I was still left wondering how all this tied to me.

"Earlier today, my wife returned from a reading with a medium named Debra Martin. As I told you before, I've never really bought into this stuff, but I listened to the tape from my wife's session and was stunned. There were several highly specific things that Debra talked about that no one but our son would know."

Joel then volunteered a few details. "For one thing, Debra said that my *son and his grandfather were playing with Mitzie*. That was significant, because it was just four months after my son's passing that his grandfather died—and we had owned a dog named Mitzie."

Joel then mentioned something else, meaningful to his wife and him.

"Debra told my wife, *Your son thanks you for bringing the blanket to him before he died.* Even though our son was a twenty-year-old man, he still slept with his baby blanket every night—nestled under his pillow. Just prior to his passing, my wife brought our son's baby blanket to the hospital and gave it to him."

Joel finally explained that Debra Martin had encouraged his wife to buy my book, *Soul Shift*, and it was his assignment to pick up a copy from the store. Upon returning home from the store with book in hand, Joel took a moment to check his email and found a note from a business associate that caught his attention. For the past few days, he had been asking around to see if anyone was selling tickets to the Cardinals–Eagles game. One message, from an associate named Julia, suggested that he contact "Mark Ireland," who had tickets to the game.

When he saw the name referenced in the email and compared it to the name on the cover of the book he'd just purchased, Joel could not believe his eyes. It was at this point that Joel called the number provided by Julia to see if the Mark Ireland who owned the tickets was also the author of the book he'd just purchased.

Now things made sense to me, as I recognized Julia as a woman who dated one of my friends—a person who knew that I had tickets to the football game. With this said, Julia had no connection to Debra Martin—and in fact had never even heard Debra's name before this happened. Considering that metropolitan Phoenix had over four million residents at the time this took place, coincidence would seem an anemic explanation for the rare and long odds involved in this case.

By virtue of Debra's "hits" and the synchronous event that led Joel to me, his skepticism seemed to be waning. I viewed the scenario as a *sign* that we were supposed to meet—and later spoke to Joel and his wife on the phone for about forty-five minutes in a process that was healing for all concerned.

In late spring 2009, I was visiting my dentist for a routine checkup when Karly the office manager pulled me aside to request a favor. She told me about another couple, the Andersons, who were also patients at the dental office and had just lost their son. She asked if I would sign a copy of my book for them. So I ran home, signed a copy, and returned it to her within about thirty minutes, and she put it in the mail a short time later.

What Karly and I didn't know was that Fred and Linda Anderson had already read my book. And while perusing my biography on the back cover the Andersons noticed that we lived in the same city, so they wanted to meet me. As things happened, my signed copy showed up in their mailbox the very day they had this discussion, so they called Karly and asked if I would be willing to meet them.

Obliging the request, I connected by telephone with Fred a few days later, arranging a lunch to include our wives. Susie and I always want to help other bereaved parents. We've met numerous families in this same situation and have found the process to be both rewarding and mutually healing. Having experienced a similar tragedy, we harbor the empathy and understanding necessary to serve others in this way. When others gain a sense of hope and lifting of spirit, our burden is also lightened and we share in their peace.

When we met the Andersons a week later, our two families immediately formed a bond. They were warm, caring people whose hearts had been broken, as their son, Michael, had passed just a couple of months earlier. Michael was a student at the University of Miami but during his sophomore year in early 2009 had enrolled for a semester abroad in Sydney, Australia, accompanied by two friends. While in Sydney, Michael became very ill, with symptoms that seemed to mirror swine flu, including vomiting and diarrhea. But after three days of illness—on the very day he reported feeling better—Michael collapsed in his apartment and died. The Andersons did not receive the autopsy results or any answers for several months. When the response eventually came, the Andersons learned that traces of kangaroo feces had been found in Michael's system, carrying a lethal bacterium akin to *E. coli*. The toxins could have been introduced via a meal at an unsanitary restaurant or perhaps were tied to a trip he'd recently made to the Sydney Zoo, but they might never know for sure.

Shortly after we became acquainted with the Andersons, they met with renowned medium George Anderson—and they came back with glowing reports. They said that talking to George was almost like conversing directly with their son. A bit later I recommended some other mediums for them to consider and they decided on Tina Powers, booking an appointment with her in the spring of 2010. The Andersons had heard about my reading with Tina and were so impressed that they didn't hesitate in picking her for their next sitting.

To help with stress and pain of grief from losing Michael, Fred also began meditating on a daily basis. It was a practice he'd learned in college but shelved until now. After many months of dedicated meditation, Fred had a very unusual experience. He reported leaving his body and floating up to the ceiling where he could view the entire room (including his body) resting in the chair below. Fred's description fit perfectly with the classic out-of-body experience, or "OBE" as they are commonly called. In an OBE, subjects feel separation from their physical body and become aware that they have a different, lighter, and more flexible body in which they may "astral walk," floating about and feeling no sensations from their physical body, observing happenings below. What followed about a week later was both shocking and healing as Michael's face suddenly appeared directly in front of him while Fred was meditating.

Later that day, just hours after Fred's milestone meditation in which Michael's face appeared, the Andersons drove two hours to Tucson for a meeting with Tina Powers. Early in the reading Tina turned to Fred and explained that he was in the process of opening up to some new experiences and psychic abilities. She then stopped herself in mid-sentence and said, "Your son wants you to know that the experience was real. That was really his face that came to you in meditation." Tina had absolutely no way of knowing the event had just happened. The Andersons had not shared the story with anyone.

This gave Fred tremendous confidence in his newfound abilities and was a great comfort to the couple. Tina's statement was the ultimate validation of his contact with Michael.

After this incident, Fred continued to meditate on a daily basis and encountered a series of new experiences. He started receiving information that could later be verified as true and accurate, including precognitive experiences. In one case, his deceased father-in-law appeared to him, telling Fred it was imperative that he check on his mother-in-law immediately. After his meditation, Fred made mention of this to his wife but she initially scoffed at the suggestion. Linda's mother was always healthy as a horse—she was in her early eighties but was very active and even snow-skied on a daily basis. So the message Fred had passed along didn't seem to make much sense.

Despite her doubts, Linda called her mother and found that she had been quite ill for several days. Linda flew to New York immediately to be with her and made arrangements for medical attention. After a series of diagnostic tests, it was determined that Linda's mother had lung cancer and also suffered from congestive heart failure—the latter of which would likely have taken her life within days if treatment had not ensued immediately. The two women came back to Scottsdale, Arizona, where Linda's mother went into treatment at the Mayo Clinic. The care proved highly effective and likely extended her life, as well as her high quality of life, for many additional years.

In another case, Fred met me for lunch one day and pulled out the front page from a *USA Today* newspaper dated June 1, 2010, pointing out a triad of headlines and saying, "I saw this exact cover page just two weeks ago." More importantly, he went on to say that he had seen advanced glimpses of each event including a deep-water oil rig that would burst into flames in the Gulf of Mexico, a North Korean sub firing a missile at a surface vessel, and Israeli commandos boarding a Turkish flotilla headed for Gaza.

Fred continued to have varied psychic experiences such as visiting other deceased loved ones and even seeing the domain where Michael now lives. And I would share Fred's description of this alternate dimensional reality with you, but this was a sacred experience—one difficult to express with words capable of conveying a sufficient degree of accuracy or richness. Because of these occurrences, Fred told me that he is now absolutely certain that there is life after death. He has no fear of death whatsoever. Fred never dreamed of manifesting these sorts of abilities and is about as grounded a person as you will ever meet. Was it just a coincidence that Fred and I met?

At the urging of my publisher, I set up an online social networking page in late 2008 to help promote my first book. And although I'd not previously contemplated using this platform, it proved useful for cultivating new connections.

Among the first people I met through this new online channel was a woman named Kim whose youngest son, William, had died a few years earlier. From the photos Kim had posted, I noticed that William bore a striking resemblance to Brandon. Given this similarity, I sent an introductory note to Kim and she responded a short time later, agreeing with my observation about the likeness of our sons.

Kim explained that William died from liver failure at the age of sixteen. She has since become a strong advocate for organ donation. William suddenly fell ill one day and she rushed him to the hospital. She had suspected something simple like a virus but was informed that her son's liver was failing; he needed a transplant within twenty-four hours to survive. Miraculously, a donated liver was found within the short time window and her son underwent successful transplant surgery. But Kim's joy was short-lived because the implanted organ failed five months later. William passed. As wrenching as the loss was for Kim, she was grateful for those additional months she had been able to spend with her son. It had been borrowed time.

Because Kim had learned about my positive experience with mediums, she expressed an interest in having a reading with Laurie

Campbell. When it took place six months later Laurie delivered some remarkable hits, which Kim shared with me the following day. Kim had mentioned nothing about me when scheduling the appointment or during the session.

Laurie correctly identified that William's death was tied to a liver problem and also noted that he had leukemia. Kim saw this as an astounding hit because William had contracted leukemia after his transplant. It was a secret she'd not shared with anyone. Kim had feared that people would wrongly assume William contracted this disease from the donated liver, deterring people from organ donation.

Laurie also identified that William's head had been shaved in the hospital. The doctors had to shear William's scalp so they could drill a hole in his skull to drain fluid and relieve pressure.

"So what is William doing now?" Kim asked Laurie.

"He's playing music with Brandon," Laurie stated, apparently unaware that she was speaking of *my* son Brandon. "He's with a group of really good kids from different backgrounds who have a common interest in music and they all get together to play." This was interesting for several reasons—first because Laurie didn't know that William was a guitar player, and second because she didn't know that Kim and I were acquainted.

Laurie also told Kim that she saw her son "hiking on mountains." This made us wonder if Brandon had possibly taken William under his wing. My son was an avid hiker and lived in the mountainous state of Arizona, while William was a surfer from Florida who had never lived anywhere else.

At the end of the reading Kim came clean with Laurie, mentioning my name for the first time and sharing that I had referred her. Kim then explained that she didn't know anyone named Brandon, except my son, and William never met my son before passing.

There is far more to this and other stories of synchronicity. At roughly the same time Kim and I crossed paths, I met another bereaved parent through an online social network, Denise Kennedy from New Mexico. Denise had lost her son Eric in an auto accident a year earlier and had become a chapter leader of a support group called Compassionate Friends.

Nine months from my initial contact with Kim and Denise, I learned that Denise and her daughter were traveling to the Compassionate Friends national conference in Portland, Oregon. During the convention, Denise and her daughter met another woman named Kristen, who had lost her daughter in an auto accident two years earlier. (Ironically, Denise's daughter is also named Kristen; however, any time I mention the name "Kristen" in the balance of this chapter I am referring to the bereaved mother.)

Denise told me that she kept crossing paths with Kristen during the conference, so they spent a lot of time together. Kristen opened up, telling Denise that she only believed in a material reality and held out no hope of ever seeing her daughter again. She had decided to attend the conference hoping it might help her "learn how to get through this." Despite her pragmatic leanings, Kristen showed some signs of open-mindedness in her interest in a conference workshop discussing "signs" as evidence for the afterlife—a topic with which she was completely unfamiliar. Denise told me that, in general, Kristen was not very far along in dealing with her grief.

After hearing these things, I told Denise that I'd like to send a copy of my book to Kristen and asked for her address. Oddly, after receiving the information I noticed that Kristen lived in the same Florida town as my other friend Kim, William's mom. This motivated me to include a note, suggesting that Kristen contact Kim since they had both lost children. After all, what were the odds of me coming into contact with two bereaved mothers living in the same place in Florida, linked by a woman from New Mexico, via a conference in Oregon?

About a week later, I received an email from Kristen thanking me for the book, but I was completely unprepared for the rest of what she had to say. Kristen explained that she already knew Kim but that the circumstances were difficult: her daughter had died from injuries sustained in an auto accident in which she was a passenger in a car that collided with a vehicle occupied by Kim's older son, William's older brother, whom I'll call Bruce.

If I thought my connection with Kim and Kristen was bizarre up to this point, things had now moved to an entirely different level. At the time of this writing there are about 310 million people in the United States, so the odds of a series of associations like this coming together in this way are nearly incalculable.

Initially I wasn't sure how to respond but decided to let my heart do the talking as I told Kristen, "I don't know how or why we connected in this way, but I'm sure it has something to do with healing."

After learning about this situation from Kristen's note, I called Kim to explain the almost unfathomable set of circumstances. I was initially a bit puzzled that Kim had never mentioned this information to me, but it seemed there was some residual tension between the two mothers. And I suppose that it was inevitable for some hard feelings to exist even in a case that was ruled an accident.

When I heard the story it seemed clear to me that reconciliation was in order. I wasn't sure how to force something like that or how long it would take to come about naturally. Once again, the solution was unexpected.

Denise contacted me a few weeks after the Compassionate Friends conference, telling me that she'd applied—on behalf of Kristen and herself—for a fully sponsored trip to a retreat for bereaved mothers. A short time later she wrote to say that both she and Kristen had been selected to attend. The retreat was for mothers who had lost children and was focused on helping them heal, including information on how they could connect with the spirit of their deceased child. I don't know the full scope of the curriculum, but I could tell it was effective after viewing the two emails that followed—one from Denise and one from Kristen. The note from Denise came first and told me that Kristen had undergone a spiritual transformation, moving from a place of despair to one of hope.

A day or two later I received a note from Kristen and she said, "Mark, I'm happy to say that I am now an Engineer." I immediately recognized that she was quoting from the last chapter of my first book where I explained the difference between physicists and engineers. The physicist wants to know *how* something works while the engineer is satisfied to know that it *does* work.

Shortly after Kristen returned home I learned that Kim had invited her to a function to benefit organ donation, and Kristen decided to attend. Within a month or so, Kristen started her own group to help parents who had lost children, exploring evidence for the continuation of consciousness and survival of personal energy after physical death. Kim was invited to the first session and has continued to attend ever since. Likewise, Kristen has been highly supportive of Kim's ongoing organ-donation work and still makes a point to attend her meetings.

I was later surprised to discover the impetus behind Kristen's decision to attend Kim's function and show support. As Kristen wrote, "Do you know why I decided to accept that invitation to attend Kim's organ-donation brunch? It was because of what you said to me about these 'coincidences'—with Kim and I connecting in so many ways—having a higher purpose. I thought to myself ... well, I might as well attend and see what the universe has in store for us!"

I've come to the conclusion that the best healing comes from helping others and extending forgiveness.

As a postscript to this story, I later learned about two noteworthy subplots. First, Kristen's daughter had known Kim's older son Bruce; they played pickup basketball in the neighborhood years earlier, and Kristen subsequently found a photo of this activity.

Second, the girlfriend of Bruce, who was also in the car at the time of the accident, reported seeing the spirit of Bruce's brother William—both at the accident scene and then later at the hospital. Initially skeptical of the report, Kim asked the girl what William was wearing and she responded, "Khaki cargo shorts and a white t-shirt." Kim was stunned. The description was precise. Prior to his death from liver failure, William regularly wore khaki cargo shorts and a white t-shirt. This girl had never met William, and none of the photos displayed in Kim's home showed him dressed this way.

Chapter 12

A Reading to Remember

In December 2007, my friend Loree Dinsmore insisted that I join her for a reading with a Tucson medium, Tina Powers. This is the story of my initial visit with Tina, referenced elsewhere in these pages. Loree saw Tina for the first time six months earlier and had been so impressed that she felt compelled to book a second session. She was vague about her reasons for taking me along, stating only that she "felt a strong pull from spirit" to get me there.

When we arrived Tina looked surprised to see me, as she was expecting Loree only, and I had come along unannounced. An attractive woman in her early forties, with blond hair and fair skin, Tina was relatively short in stature. She had a soft welcoming disposition and was a lover of pets. Her dogs seemed quite excited to see us, so she soon moved them into an adjacent room, allowing us to conduct the reading without interruption.

Then we sat down and Tina said a brief prayer, asking for God's guidance and protection, and for the communication to be facilitated "for only the highest good." Following that, Tina said just a few words to Loree about her work situation and then turned her attention to me. She apologized to my friend but explained that she had "people there who wanted to talk to me."

"Why are they showing you on the road?" Tina asked.

It was funny because I'd been wondering if it would be worth my while to make the two-hour drive from Phoenix to be part of this, and Tina immediately pointed out my commute. I then volunteered this information.

"Were you sending out prayers on the way down here?" she asked. "Because they want me to tell you that you were heard."

How interesting, this was exactly what I'd done. During the drive to Tucson I mentally relayed requests to my father and my son, asking them to communicate clearly and strongly during the session. I didn't know if I'd receive any messages because it was Loree's reading, but I was holding out hope that I'd hear something. I then told Tina "yes" without elaborating.

Tina continued, "Now I'm picking up a male energy on the other side for you. It feels like I'm getting your father's energy. And I'm seeing a piece of paper. Did you take care of some paperwork for your father? Sorting out something? Are there piles of it? I'm seeing piles."

"Yeah, it's everywhere," I said, while thinking of the huge volume of documents I'd inherited after my father's passing—ranging from a manuscript he'd written on psychic development, to ten volumes of trance-session transcripts, as well as other miscellaneous writings dating back to 1960.

She continued, "Did he write at all? I feel like there are all these unfinished books. Have you thought about picking any of these up and going forward with them?"

"I'm way down the road with that."

"I'm getting a thumbs up with this, so he's working with you on it. And he says this is going to be big but don't worry because *you have my support with this.* I think you know this [is going to happen] but he says that he is excited to tell you from this vantage point in time."

I thought this was interesting, as I was working on my first book at this time—seeking a publisher while simultaneously trying to figure out how and when to pursue publication of my father's materials, especially his book on psychic development. Other mediums had also told me that I was working on something that would be very big.

Tina resumed, "There's a *sorry* here for you. Because things weren't clear and you have been left to make decisions. He apologizes to you for not taking care of things." This was true, as my father was great at starting things but not always so good at finishing them—that was my specialty. Tina continued, "He is around you while you're doing this. But it's like there is a lump in his throat. And I'm hearing that song, 'Cat's in the Cradle'."

Tina then shared a message directly from my father, in his own voice, *"Tell my son first of all that I regret that we didn't bond more—that is my error. It was never a question of love, but I was selfish."* Reverting to her perspective and interpretation, Tina clarified, "He says *selfish without realizing so.* Now he gets an opportunity to look at his life and he sees the error that he made. You need to know how proud he is of you because he wasn't always able to verbalize this."

This has been a recurring topic in almost all of my good readings. My father was not around much when I was growing up, primarily because of his work and travel. It was also interesting that she made mention of him being "proud" of me because that was the very last thing he said to me when we were together just days before he died. I don't ever recall him saying that phrase before this visit.

Tina resumed, "I'm hearing the word *enterprising*—he had a lot of dreams that weren't fulfilled—he wants me to communicate that to you. He was a visionary. I'm picking up an extremely intelligent individual, who is very multi-faceted but couldn't quite deal with the common sense of everyday life. And there are some messages here about how he handled his life that he wants to speak about to you."

My father was a visionary. He had big dreams and ideas, but he wasn't very practical and his follow-through skills were mixed, so many of his ideas went unfulfilled.

"Did your father do the same work as me? I just heard that. I get the sense that he was a medium and pulled through information from the other side to help people."

I was really surprised that Tina had zeroed in on my father like this. Frankly, I was stunned.

"But he didn't work on his own issues," she went on. "Part of him wants to cry, because he could see for everyone else—he was this visionary—but he couldn't deal well with everyday life."

I piped in, "He lacked balance."

Tina's hit here was pretty remarkable. Few mediums have been able to identify the fact that my father was a psychic-medium, not to mention the related information about his ability to help others but failure to work on his own issues.

Tina resumed, "He's telling me *moments of extreme clarity and then moments of almost not being here.* He regrets this; he was very vacant."

She then touched on a sore spot: "I don't know if he drank. He's showing me this cloudedness. It was like an escape." It had been a problem for him. Like many empathetic people, especially psychics and mediums, my father had issues with alcohol. It can turn down their sensitivity for a while but when consumed excessively can become a habit that is detrimental to the person's well-being.

Tina's comment made me reflect on how alcohol affected my father's life. On one hand it seemed to contribute to his habitual tardiness, as well as severe health problems. But on the other hand it seemed to make him spontaneous and carefree—relaxed and fun to be around. When not drinking he would become very serious. It was an interesting dichotomy. But on the whole, alcohol was a negative factor in his life and he would have been better off without it.

Tina followed, "I just want to tell you I understand how that could happen while doing this work. It was his way of grounding and escaping. Because I feel like he was very, very good at what he did; many people were pulling on him and that he couldn't say no. He's telling me that he had a really hard time with boundaries. He let himself be spread thin for everyone else. It's like that physician who takes really good care of everyone else except his own family."

I understood. My father was a tremendous psychic and medium, and he had been relentlessly hounded by troubled people who sought to latch on. He felt great empathy for all people and never turned anyone away.

Tina changed course. "You have his abilities. Now we always have choices, you know what I mean. Part of the block is that you saw what it did to him and you want your own space and privacy."

I've been told by numerous mediums that I have some latent

psychic ability. It has manifested in modest ways, but I've yet to have the sort of breakthrough event I've anticipated. Similarly, Tina indicated that my ability was there under the surface but had not yet kicked in.

Returning to the topic of writing, Tina stated, "There's more than one book. Are these the piles? There's your own material too. It's not just about him."

"Right. There's my own stuff and then there's his stuff, and I've got to figure out how to pull his material together."

Tina said, "This [psychic] block may be why it might be hard for you to get this book out. Is it taking a while to do?" With this statement, she identified that I had my own book—the writing was not exclusively about my father or his work. Continuing on the topic of getting this work of my own published, Tina mentioned, "Your dad's showing me a brick wall. He's *not meaning to pressure you*, he just said."

I was putting a lot of pressure on myself but did feel like I was trudging through mud on the publishing front. In hindsight I may have been better off seeking publication of my father's book on psychic development along with some of his other materials prior to trying to publish my own book. But both have since been published, so it's now a moot point.

Tina switched subjects. "He wants to talk about his brother all of a sudden. His brother is over there too. And he laughingly said, *My brother also had the curse.*" It now appeared that my father was turning over the reins as Tina said, "Your uncle is now here to say hello. And why are they showing me—I'm across the country, I'm across the world—is it Ireland? I'm in Ireland."

I volunteered, "Probably so you could get my last name, which is Ireland."

Tina resumed, "Yeah, I'm in Ireland. It's a *wonderful way to be able to talk with you*, your uncle says. He loves you very much and he is also sending love to the family. Is there a church? I have visions of a church."

"Yes, they both had churches. My father founded the University of Life church in Phoenix, and my uncle founded *Y-our* Church in Tucson."

Tina then said, "They are having a great time and are glad you made it here today. There was a question as to whether you would make it. You know … another medium, another reading."

When I'd walked in the door Tina probably thought I was the last person in the world who would have seen a medium before, initially assuming I was a skeptic. Now she was onto the fact that I'd met with *many* of them. And it wasn't a sure thing that I would be able to make it to this reading, because it required a four-hour round trip on a work day.

Tina moved on. "They just showed me a dog; whose dog is that? Did anybody have a little dog? I'm seeing a little dog running around that has crossed over. I don't know if it's theirs or yours."

Responding coyly, with Brandon in mind, I said, "This could be leading to something I've been told before—about another male who is on the other side. I wonder if they're using this as—"

Tina finished my sentence, "As a way to get me to say that? Maybe so, because they definitely want me to say the word *dog.*"

I was prodding Tina in hopes she'd reveal more. While this is not something I can prove as being *true*, it was the fourth time that a "dog in spirit" had been mentioned during a reading. In each preceding instance it was specifically noted that this was a "small dog" and it was suggested that it belonged to my son—although I didn't immediately volunteer this.

Tina indicated that the dog didn't belong to me. I then volunteered, "Then this dog belongs to some other male that's close to me, at least based on the feedback I've had."

"Yeah, I've got a green light. Is this person someone who died suddenly?"

"It was pretty quick."

"I just feel like it's very quick when they cross."

I was champing at the bit. "I'll just tell you—it's my son."

"Oh, goodness."

"I don't know if that's the same person you're getting."

"Oh, so if you're getting that [about the small dog] a third or fourth time, that's pretty cool," Tina said.

This reference to my son "having a small dog on the other side" was previously mentioned by Allison Dubois, Laurie Campbell, and Jamie Clark, all three accomplished mediums.

Tina then looked at me with a sense of deep empathy as tears welled in her eyes and she continued, "And I'm hearing that song 'Amazing Grace.' I hear that there's been a grace for you, 'Dad.' You're also doing something for him—there's this writing about your son. He acknowledges this; it's his story. This is to help people and to help parents cope with this. He's writing this with you. That almost makes me want to cry and I'm not a good messenger when I cry. You were also talking to him in the car and he says he was right there on the drive down."

At this point I don't know if I was more stunned by the detailed nature of what Tina shared or touched by it. I was barely able to keep from sobbing. Brandon's story was the cornerstone of my book, *Soul Shift*. In the time that has passed since the book was released, thousands of copies have been sold and I've been contacted by countless people, most of whom were bereaved parents. Almost invariably, they tell me that the book was invaluable to them in their healing process after losing a child. Some went so far as to say that the book helped them more than any other single thing.

Tina resumed, "Did you also start some sort of foundation for him, or are you thinking of doing it? He's just showing me that it would use his name and it helps others."

"It's been a thought."

"He thinks it's a good idea and you should go for it."

Many mediums have actually brought this up, suggesting exactly the same thing. And today, several years after this reading, in partnership with a woman named Elizabeth Boisson, I have co-founded an organization to assist people who have lost children called "Helping

Parents Heal." The organization doesn't feature Brandon's name, and it's not yet a formal 501(c)3 nonprofit foundation, but that designation is within our sights.

Moving on, Tina asked, "Was there ever a tree planted for him? He wants me to talk about the tree."

I replied, "His school planted a tree for him as a memorial." The tree featured a metal sculpture in front of a bass guitar.

Tina then delivered another hit: "What is it about Angels? He just showed me an angel. Somehow you're going to get an angel, whether somebody gives it to you, but it's from him from the other realm. Does mom call him her angel? He won't let me let go of the word *angel*. He most certainly was not an angel, he's saying. There's some way he's going to get an angel to you, so you'll have this object to laugh at and hold onto."

At the time of Tina's statement I saw no relevance, other than the fact that my wife had occasionally referred to Brandon as "her angel." After returning home and telling my wife about this, she showed me an angel figurine with Brandon's name engraved on it—given to us by friends after his passing. The figurine was exactly as described, fitting into the palm of my hand. Somehow the figurine had been displayed in the same spot in our kitchen, in plain view for four years since Brandon's passing, yet I'd never noticed it.

Tina asked me if I'd ever done counseling for other parents.

"I've been doing it recently, but not officially." In saying this I was just acknowledging that I am not a licensed counselor.

She elaborated, "He says that you're doing this. You're being called in to help certain individuals. It's like you're able to drop everything just because you know what it is to go through this, and you go. It's like a vocation."

"I'm not employed that way but I feel it's very worthwhile."

"Your son says that you're able to go to that moment with them. And he's with you when you are doing this counseling. Also, when you do this counseling he is with the person who crossed, on the other side. So it's like you are with the family and he is with their loved one."

Continued Tina, "Now he's showing me a candle associated with some sort of ceremony. I feel like I'm in a church. I don't necessarily get the feeling that you're religious, but more spiritual. Is your wife's family more religious?"

I'm not big on church but I am definitely a believer. My wife was raised in a much more conventional religious tradition, and her family regularly attended Lutheran church. I feel that the essence of church resides within me and has nothing to do with brick and mortar. I am presented with opportunities to minister to people every day, in every imaginable setting—that is my church.

Tina went on, "I feel like I'm at a church service and somebody lit candles for him. He's just showing me these candles and wants to say thank you, but I feel it's on Mom's side."

This stirred a memory and I responded, "There was a Christmas Eve service we attended at my wife's church. My son and I sat side by side and everyone lit candles." This service left an indelible memory for me; it occurred just three weeks before Brandon passed. I sat next to Brandon at that particular service and shared the flame of my candle in order to light his and then he used his flame to light Susie's candle and so on. Everyone in the congregation held a lit candle as we sang "Silent Night."

Tina concluded, "That's where he was trying to get me. It definitely felt like holidays—either a Midnight Mass or Christmas celebration. I'm also hearing, *Light a candle for me, Dad*."

Twelve days later, in recognition of Brandon's request made through Tina, I lit two candles on Christmas Eve, 2007. Right after that I received an email from my medium friend Jamie Clark, who said, "Brandon says thanks for lighting the candles." Jamie knew nothing about Tina's statement.

Tina resumed, "You know, he's really an evolved soul. He is using the word *teacher*, so he's doing teaching on the other side." This is obviously not something that can be proven, but I have been told in virtually every reading prior to this one that Brandon is an "old soul" or "spiritually advanced."

Tina then moved on to something that is too sensitive to share in totality here, as it would likely hurt the feelings of the person mentioned. But since it was so impactful, I will share what I can. Tina asked if I'd done some work with a woman and identified her occupation. She then asked if the woman had a "harsher" energy, further solidifying my knowledge of who was being discussed. Tina explained the exact nature of my problem with the woman and—while assuming my son's voice—proceeded to say, "She didn't get it, *Dad.*" Tina delivered this phrase in the *exact* manner that Brandon would have. In fact, it felt like I was talking directly with him. This was the most emotionally touching part of the entire reading.

Speaking of my story—the crux of my book—Tina said, "There's a chance that this may turn into a movie to help people heal. So don't be surprised if that comes knocking—more movies like this are needed to help people heal. As your world expands, don't be afraid. Expand with it because there's a very private part of you [that sometimes wants to avoid the attention associated with all of this]. *We're all doing it together* is what I'm to tell you."

This was interesting because some students from Arizona State University's Cronkite School of Journalism subsequently taped a documentary, *The Inner Light*, featuring my story. Whether Tina was referencing this film or a larger commercial effort is not yet known.

Tina switched subjects again. "I've got your father here. Did he do readings on a platform?"

"Yes," I said.

"He says that he's going to help me because I've done it a few times but I really don't like it. And I'm also seeing a blindfold. Is it the blindfold billet stuff? Who did this? Is this your uncle?"

Flabbergasted, I replied, "Both my father and my uncle did it."

Tina was furnishing some amazing details, the likes of which I'd never received before in any prior reading. She has been the only medium to identify that my father worked from a platform and that he did blindfold billet demonstrations.

"I feel like it was their forte. So they could definitely pull spirit through but they were also very psychic."

I replied, "Yeah, big time," knowing that blindfold billet was certainly my father's and uncle's strong suit.

"Did people study them? There's an Edgar Cayce sort of feeling here. I don't know if there's a library yet or some sort of foundation for them."

"Well, I'm trying to dig up research information from where my dad was supposed to have been tested years and years ago, but it's been hard for me to get my hands on any of this."

"I feel like it's real obscure. That's what I'm getting. The word spread about your family, or *the brothers*, I'm hearing. And I'm also back east somewhere. There's some sort of institute I'm seeing that has some work on them. I feel like I'm pulled across the country, definitely. Yeah, there's a huge documentary in the making here on everyone—on the family."

Throwing out a guess, I asked, "I don't know, but Duke University is in North Carolina. Was it Duke?"

Tina responded, "I just heard the song 'Duke of Earl,' so I believe there is a lead there. I'm hearing that testing also occurred at other places that were obscure."

Tina's mention of "obscure places" rang true. I'd located a document written in 1962 by a P. H. Waldraff, PhD, who observed my father's abilities during a California Parapsychology event hosted by Kay Sterner, president of the organization. In fact, this document was apparently written in order to be sent to J. B. Rhine at the Duke University parapsychology lab.

Recounting other places my father was supposed to have been tested, I shared, "Vienna is one that I've heard of."

"You will find something there. You may make a trip to Vienna. I see you walking around there."

(Jumping forward in this recounting, I contacted Dr. Peter Mulacz well after my reading with Tina, because he was someone I learned had been conducting research with the Austrian Society for

Parapsychology in Vienna since 1966. I was encouraged by the fact that Dr. Mulacz recognized my father's name and by his indication that my father may well have been tested there. To help him narrow the scope of his search, I explained that testing would most likely have occurred sometime in the 1960s. Dr. Mulacz told me that the Austrian Society for Parapsychology was located at the Technical University of Vienna from 1964 until 2000, when it moved to Vienna University. He said that there was one professor at the University of Innsbruck–Tyrol, Hubert Josef Urban, who'd been heavily involved in psi research around the time my father most likely would have been there. Dr. Mulacz also speculated that in another possible scenario, tests may have been carried out by one professor on his own initiative. Overall, he didn't seem too optimistic about the chances of finding any related documents at this point but said that he would put feelers out.)

Tina confirmed, "And they're saying *Duke University*. There will be something there, but very obscure—like it's tucked away in a box somewhere. So you may have to go there [to North Carolina]. They're showing your father's papers [mixed in] with many other papers in this room. I'm seeing that you may very well have to go through them."

A week after the reading, I contacted my father's friend Jerry Conser, who knew Sally Rhine-Feather, the daughter of J. B. Rhine. Shortly afterward, Jerry, Sally, and I had a three-way conference call. I was stunned to hear Sally say that the Rhine Institute had hundreds of boxes of documents stored in their North Carolina warehouse. She noted that the materials were poorly cataloged in boxes or stacked onto skids, making it difficult to locate any specific documents. With that said, she did indicate that we were welcome to come to the warehouse and go through the boxes. I found this amazing, seeing that it precisely matched Tina's depiction of the situation. Sally also indicated that all materials prior to 1965 were housed by Duke University, instead of her facility.

After the reading I came upon an article from an Alabama paper, the *Tuscaloosa News*, dated March 12, 1972, in which J. B. Rhine's right-hand man, Helmut Schmidt, explained how he had tested my father in a public setting. Schmidt wrote a three-digit number on a piece of paper, sealed it in an envelope, and delivered it to my father, whose eyes were already taped and blindfolded. Without opening the envelope, my father called out the correct number "385" and told him the color of ink used to write it. Schmidt had said, "The odds against just such an occurrence are higher than anybody can count."

Tina changed subjects. "Is there film of him doing what he does? I feel like I'm looking at video of him."

"Yes, I'll get you a copy of it," I said, recognizing the reference to my father's 1970 appearance on "The Steve Allen Show."

"There may be interest in this from some research organization— I see some sort of video story that somebody puts together. People would be very interested in the brothers and piecing together something. You're not one to brag, are you? It's hard for you to promote this because it's so close to your heart. You want to put it out there, but it's almost like you need a mouthpiece to run around and to generate some interest."

"It's not the SPR, is it?"

"I feel like they might have some interest, but they also feel very bogged down today—like they don't have enough people, or something."

After the reading I reached out to Guy Lyon Playfair of the Society for Psychical Research in London, and he told me that this description was exactly right. The organization is spread thin today and resources are limited.

"I'm seeing a TV excerpt on them. They are showing me that there's so much on your plate that it can get very frustrating to you. Just know that this is all going somewhere; they're showing me this bouquet of flowers. So it does bloom; it does come to fruition. It's just not always in the timeframe we would like. I'm seeing this funny visual of people in stands. It's like you have a cheering section over there and you need to know that they are helping and that there is higher work to all of it."

Switching gears, I asked, "Do you have anything from my son for his brother?"

Tina told me that Brandon was showing her a guitar. "Your younger son says, *Tell him that I hear the music.* Has his brother actually recorded some music?"

"He has a good friend, someone like a brother, who recorded some music recently." In saying this I was referring to Stu Garney, Brandon's best friend. And I was aware that my older son Steven had contributed a melodic line to one of the songs recorded by Stu and his band.

Tina continued, "Somehow, your [deceased] son has a hand in this—if that makes sense. Now I'm also seeing it looks like a CD or DVD."

"Yeah, it was Stu, who was my son's best friend and almost like a brother. Stu and some friends were able to get studio time and recorded a CD." One of the songs recorded, "See Through Disguise," was written and practiced by Brandon and Stu before Brandon's death—it was also the title track on the album.

Tina responded, "The recording is important and somehow he knows about it. But I also feel like I'm to talk about music for you— music that you listen to that brings you back to him. He says he *comes through the music,* meaning his energy comes through. So he's with you when you are listening to this."

What Tina was describing had multiple meanings for me. First, when I hear Pink Floyd's songs "Wish You Were Here" and "Comfortably Numb," they remind me of Brandon. And when I hear or play songs on my guitar that we used to play together it reminds me of Brandon as well. Perhaps more to the point, the song called "The Other Side" is one that we believe was channeled from Brandon through James Linton. (See chapter 2.)

Tina resumed, "There is this big banner that just got unraveled and it says, *I love you.* And *I'm right here, right beside you.* It's to the left of you often."

It was interesting that Tina specifically said the words "right beside you." The song "The Other Side" includes the words "forevermore by your side." Also, about a year after Brandon's passing I experienced something I would describe as "supernatural" when I observed bright flashing white lights to my left while sitting idly in my den.

"I also see a guitar pick."

"I play too," I said, "but I've not done much since he's been gone because we used to jam together."

"Did you write a song? He says that there's a song about him. He also says the word *together.* Did you write a song together?"

While I had not written a song with Brandon, there was a song I had written called "Blue Night" that we used to play together a lot. But I suspect the reference may have been to the aforementioned song, "The Other Side," or possibly "See Through Disguise," which he had co-written with Stu Garney.

"*Dad, take up the guitar, I'll be right there,* he's telling me," Tina said. "He'll be right there beside you. He says that music was really important to him; it was a big part of his life. He enjoyed this and had dreams of being in a rock band on tour. He says when you're ready, you should pull out the guitar and he will help you write a song."

I later got confirmation that if not for his passing Brandon may have ended up playing in a band and touring with his former instructor, Todd Hogan.

"I'm just getting this really beautiful holiday picture. Especially close right now, during this December timeframe. Exceptionally close. I'm hearing the word *family.* So I don't know if it's a family photo taken at Christmas time or if it's a Christmas card. It's beautiful and it looks like family around the holiday."

I shared, "That was the last picture we ever had taken with him. It was of the four of us together at Christmas time." The photo is a fixture in our home and was used for our Christmas cards in 2004.

"Oh, he loves this picture. And I feel like it's up, you can view it, other people can view it."

"It's on a table in our family room."

"They are saying, *You have a lot of support over here—just know that. God bless you.*"

That was the end of our reading. Four days later Tina called to share one additional message, which she said had come from my father.

"Please tell my son that I am ever so grateful for his interest in my life and preserving for history what is possible for the human mind."

The statement definitely sounded like my father.

Ultimately, what made this reading most convincing to me was the fact that Tina furnished a significant number of highly specific hits, far beyond what could have been possible even if she had known my identity. These validations came in the form of detailed information known only to me. And again, I was a complete stranger to Tina when I walked in her door.

CHAPTER 13

The Combination–Lock Experiment

In early 2010 I received an email entitled "Acquainted with Dick Ireland" from a man named Bob Ferguson, who met my father at a parapsychology conference in 1968. In his note, Bob said that my father's demonstration of clairvoyance was so phenomenal that no other psychics wanted to follow him at the symposium. Bob's initial note opened the door to an ongoing dialog between the two of us.

He told me about an unusual photograph taken of him during the conference and sent me a scanned image so I could see it first-hand. The picture showed Bob speaking from a podium and included a remarkably clear image of another man as an etheric presence, positioned directly behind him. As soon as Bob saw the photo he immediately recognized the image as that of his deceased brother, Walter. Per Bob, the picture was taken on a Polaroid camera by a Reverend Robert Evanston, who was visiting from Tucson, Arizona. This was before the advent of personal computers and digital image-enhancement software—and Bob received the photograph immediately after his talk, so there was no opportunity for anyone to manipulate the image. Also, Reverend Evanston never left the room.

In our next dialog, Bob mentioned that he knew the late Reverend Florence Becker, who had founded the Golden Gate Spiritualist Church in San Francisco. Bob raved about Becker and shared his opinion that she was probably the best psychic-medium of all time, but also mentioned my father in the same breath.

Bob then told me a memorable story about his first encounter with Reverend Becker, which occurred when he was nineteen years old, while serving in the Navy. Bob was intrigued by the concept of life after death, having attended a spiritualist church in Denver. This is where he first heard about Florence Becker, who was described as a "phenomenal medium from California." While stationed in the Bay Area, Bob decided to visit the Golden Gate Church. He departed alone from his station at Treasure Island and told no one where he was going that day.

Bob arrived late for the service and entered the sanctuary quietly. Reverend Becker was already sharing messages with parishioners. Bob hoped to remain unnoticed as he slithered into a seat, but Reverend Becker stopped in her tracks and announced, "Bob, your brother, Walter Deforest Ferguson, says that you shouldn't be late for church." Bob was stunned. Becker had just accurately stated the first, middle, and last name of his brother who had been killed in World War II. Bob had never met Becker before, or ever visited her church, and no one else knew he was attending the service.

Switching back to my dialog with Bob in early 2010, it was clear early on that he was comfortable talking with me. Within a short time he began to share messages that proved accurate. His first such message was, "I keep hearing a young man's voice repeating the phrase *band-aids.*" For the previous six days my wife had been dressing a nasty wound on my back, placing a large band-aid over it. About a week earlier, I'd scratched myself rather deeply while asleep and the wound had been slow to heal. Bob explained that he once worked as a psychic-medium but was retired from such service.

After another note with a touching validation, the messages started to get a bit more complicated. On February 13, 2010, just a couple of weeks after our first contact, Bob sent me a noteworthy email. While relaying information he believed was coming from my father, Bob wrote, "I received that I should relay a bit of 'proof' to Mark that hasn't been written about in published writings. He wanted you to remember the incident concerning *the tumblers in the lock.*"

I didn't know what he was talking about. I politely tried to relay that I was unable to identify the significance of his comments but would let Bob know if something were to surface later on. At this point, however, I assumed there wasn't anything here.

Just one day later Bob sent me the following message: "I don't want to take up your time, but the [reference to the] lock and the tumblers I received in a message refers to an event where your dad and your uncle thought they needed to/wanted to pick a lock—not for any illegal purposes, of course."

Now I was really confused because Bob seemed so focused on this subject of opening a lock, and none of it made any sense to me. Not seeing a clear connection, I wrote back suggesting to Bob that the messages may be symbolic in nature and would probably need to be decoded.

Bob was not backing off—or perhaps a particular spirit would not let go of his attention. One week after his initial communication on the subject, Bob sent me another note indicating that a spirit had continued to "bug him" about my father and uncle and what he described as "the lock-picking adventure." He then explained that it had something to do with this person's interest in Harry Houdini, Margery (the Boston medium), and other related issues.

With everything Bob was sharing, it seemed I had a lot to digest and possibly to learn. So with his messages in mind, I conducted a little research to see what I could find about the connection between Houdini and the medium "Margery," whose real name was Mina Crandon. Through my digging, I learned that Margery was Houdini's greatest nemesis and renowned for her participation in a contest sponsored by *Scientific American* magazine, which offered a $2500 prize to any medium able to demonstrate real psychic ability. Houdini was retained as a debunker, to observe those applying for the prize and to call out any instances of fraud. Crandon didn't trust Houdini, and her critics suggested that she may have been as clever as her adversary.

During a séance investigated by panel members assembled by *Scientific American*, Margery was placed in a wooden box that had holes cut out for her head and arms so her hands could be held throughout the process. A bell was also placed in the case, which Margery had been asked to ring through supernatural means..After she entered a trance state, Margery's spirit guide, Walter—speaking through her—proclaimed that Houdini had tampered with the bell so it would not ring. It was then found that a piece of rubber had been wedged against the clapper, preventing it from ringing, but there was no way to prove that Houdini was responsible for it. In a subsequent séance, Walter indicated that Houdini had placed a collapsible carpenter's ruler inside the box so he could accuse the medium of cheating. The ruler was found, and years later Houdini's assistant later admitted to placing the object in the box on the Magician's instruction. This caused Houdini to be discredited, and many people came to doubt his earlier cases of "proving" fraud.

As I tried to assemble the puzzle pieces to determine how the subject of Margery and Houdini related to me, I started to get the sense that some spirit—perhaps my father, my uncle, some deceased scientist, possibly even Houdini himself—wanted evidence of the afterlife to come forward in the world today.

Houdini was seen as a "debunker" in his day, yet he was also clearly fascinated by the idea of eternal life—as evidenced by the secret code he left with his wife at the time of his death. This code was apparently brought through by the medium Arthur Ford, but controversy about this erupted, so we have no clear-cut answer to this puzzle today (as described in chapter 10). So I wondered, *Might this be another code-breaking exercise?*

Bob added that he had received a message completely unrelated to the "lock bit." He said it was about the twentieth-century dancer Isadora Duncan, who Bob said communicated *through* my father "in a language he did not speak." I found this quite intriguing because my mother had told me about a trip that she and my father made to Europe in 1966, which included a stop in Denmark. The small Scandinavian nation was my mother's ancestral home—where her father had been born—yet my father had never been to Denmark and had no ties to the country.

As my mother explained it, my parents were riding in a cab in Copenhagen when my father spontaneously began speaking Danish to the driver. It was clear to my mother that my father's linguistic exploits were successful, based on the ongoing two-way nature of the dialog and because they arrived at their desired destination without delay. Since my father didn't know how to speak a word of Danish, my parents attributed this phenomenon to a channeled communication.

On February 21, 2010, I exchanged emails with Dr. Emily Kelly, a parapsychologist at the University of Virginia's Division of Perceptual Studies. I was explaining to her the experiment involving the secret message left behind by my sister. And after reading my account of the experiment, Dr. Kelly made mention of a test with better controls, designed by Dr. Ian Stevenson before his death a few years earlier. (Stevenson is highly respected for his extensive and scrupulous investigation of reincarnation cases, as mentioned in chapter 6.) When Dr. Kelly described Stevenson's experiment to me, the light bulb immediately went on. She wrote,

> Dr. Stevenson suggested setting a combination lock—one picks a word or phrase that is highly meaningful, and that one would be likely to remember after death, and then the word or phrase is translated (by a process Ian describes in his paper) into the number that the combination lock is set to. This way, the results are unambiguous—the lock either opens or it doesn't—and one can also make numerous attempts with numerous mediums to try to obtain the word or phrase that will unlock it.

Dr. Kelly went on to write in a subsequent email that Dr. Stevenson actually left such a lock behind, as did several other people, but they've yet to receive the right code word (or words) to open them. As she noted, "We have quite a few locks here that people have set over the years—including one by Ian himself. Unfortunately, although since Ian's death some people have reported dreams or impressions they have had about this, we haven't yet unlocked the lock."

She then asked if any of the mediums I knew would be interested in trying to obtain Dr. Stevenson's word or phrase. She spelled out the specific requirements: "All I know is that it is a six-letter word or a six-word phrase, since it takes six letters to translate into the six-digit combination. If a medium could get this, it would obviously be fantastic!"

Unless this was just a crazy coincidence, it sure seemed that my father and uncle and possibly others in the spiritual realm wanted me to reach out to the mediums I knew to see if they could obtain a code to open one or more locks. Bob Ferguson's three messages about "picking a lock" and "Houdini," who'd left a secret code before his death, came before I'd ever heard of Dr. Stevenson's experiment. They also seemed to describe this very process—in explicit detail.

So I embarked on this mission with zeal, reaching out to a number of mediums that I knew. I asked them to try to connect with Ian Stevenson or any of the other people in his circle who left locks behind, explaining that the code could be a single word consisting of six letters, or a phrase consisting of six words.

I clarified that if it were a single word containing more than six digits, only the first six digits would be decoded into numbers for the lock. Likewise, I explained that if it were a phrase, the first letter of each word would be used, and only the first six words of the phrase would be used. There was no time limit on the request, and they could provide as many responses as they wanted to, now or in the future. I also asked them to share the manner in which they received any information—whether by a vision, dream, clairaudience, a sense of direct contact with the deceased, etc.

In addition to contacting the mediums, I sought to "pull in" a word or phrase myself. While I don't consider myself a psychic or a medium, I occasionally receive intuitive insights that have proven accurate. So, while in a relaxed state, I mentally asked for help from Ian Stevenson, my father, and other deceased loved ones to assist in bringing me the word or phrase. Oddly, the word *Martin* popped into my head right away, although this made absolutely no sense to me. In fact, I almost decided against reporting the word because it seemed silly—like it was just my imagination—but I eventually decided to share it.

A short time later I began receiving responses from a number of mediums, and I started consolidating them into a document for Dr. Kelly. Aside from my personal submission, I received words and phrases from seven different people, with one medium sharing her response much later than the others. The last medium to submit indicated that she would do so "when the time was right," so it seemed that she had a sense of inner guidance about the matter.

A few days later I met with the last medium, Debra Martin, to talk about a few things and see if she was able to furnish a submission. Debra explained that she had been meditating and asked Dr. Stevenson to provide the code—and noted that a word came to her immediately. I then told Debra about how I had received the word *Martin* a few weeks earlier during a meditation but didn't know if it was of any value. She smiled and immediately pointed to herself, as if to say *duh*, reminding me, "Mark, my last name is Martin." This correlation had been staring me in the face the entire time, but I'd been oblivious to it. I was as excited as I was embarrassed for being so dense. Now I thought, maybe, just maybe, I had been given the word *Martin* to steer me to the person who might break the code—Debra Martin. And if she were able to furnish the correct code, it would seem to point toward a sort of "cross-correspondence" among Bob Ferguson, Debra Martin, and me.

To preserve the integrity of the process, I cannot share any of the medium responses. I am hopeful that the correct code has been or will be delivered—opening one of the locks—but for now you and I must wait patiently.

CHAPTER 14

More Signs

T his chapter is a collection of experiences that point to signs of connection, contact, and validation from loved ones who have passed. In some cases the signs were subtle, and in others they were overt, but my family and I were alert to all of them. Since some signs were so unmistakable and profound, we knew not to write off the less obvious ones as mere coincidence, but rather to appreciate the entire body of evidence.

People who have ADCs (After-Death Communications) and NDEs (Near-Death Experiences) are often reluctant to speak about them with others. In most cases their reticence is associated with fear that their account will be marginalized, they'll be scoffed at, or that they may be considered unstable. Because our modern society is so materialistic, that which may be deemed "reality" is typically limited to things that can be seen, felt, heard, tasted, or touched—in a purely physical sense. This is unfortunate because ADC and NDE accounts point to a deeper and more complex reality. If considered in earnest, such reports could help lead us to a better understanding of the total nature of the universe—perhaps one much grander than our current commonly held conception.

My wife Susie's good friend Annette recently disclosed information about an unusual occurrence that took place about a week after Brandon's death. At that time Annette had given Susie a call one evening and invited her to go on a walk the next morning. Prior to Brandon's passing, walking on the trails around our neighborhood was a regular activity for my wife, so she saw this as an opportunity to spend time with a good friend and get a small taste of normalcy.

The next morning arrived and Annette woke with a terrible headache, so she really didn't feel like going, but after contemplating what Susie was going through she felt obliged. They went on their walk, talked at length, and then returned to their respective homes. As she entered her house, Annette broke down in tears thinking about Susie's pain. Shortly thereafter, she stepped into her youngest son's closet and then sensed someone behind her. Annette heard the words, "Thanks for walking with my mom today." Greatly surprised, she turned to see who was speaking. She suspected her husband or one of her two sons, but no one was there. No one was even home. Annette had not shared this story any sooner because she was afraid it would cause us more pain. On the contrary, we were thrilled to hear about Annette's ADC.

Psychic-mediums sometimes share information that doesn't seem to make sense at the time it is given, yet later on the pieces come together and a meaningful affirmation comes to light.

Back in 2004, during my reading with Allison Dubois, she told me that anytime I heard the song "Fly Me to the Moon," it would signify that my father was present. When Allison made this statement, it didn't really mean much to me. I'm sure that my father liked Frank Sinatra, but I didn't remember this song being especially significant to him.

Six years later, on October 16, 2010, Susie and I joined our friends the Andersons for dinner. Recognizing that this was my father's birthday, I raised my glass and made a toast to him—and everyone joined in. Immediately after the toast had been made, a male entertainer who had been setting up prior to this point started his set with "Fly

Me to the Moon." Later on, between sets, I asked the singer if he had a set playlist. He didn't. Tommy Holloway said that he randomly picked whatever song came to him at the spur of the moment.

&

Some people gain a sense of connection to their deceased loved ones during quiet times or meditation. Others prefer to spend time in nature and feel the presence of their loved ones while enjoying a walk or other outdoor activity.

On the fifth anniversary of Brandon's passing, I went on a hike with my older son Steven and Stu, Gary, and Dave, three of Brandon's closest friends who had been with him on the day of his death. The four boys and I retraced the steps they'd all made five years earlier to honor Brandon and deal with some of the lingering pain. Everyone missed my youngest son's physical presence, though it was beautiful outside and the desert gave us a sense of peace, serenity, and holiness—reminding us of what drew Brandon here in the first place.

After ninety minutes of hiking we were well up the mountain. I began to feel fatigued and a bit nervous over the steep, treacherous terrain. I decided to rest, and Steven remained with me while Stu, Gary, and Dave continued on to build a makeshift memorial at the location where Brandon had passed. While the boys were constructing the memorial up the mountain I sat below, silently perched on a rocky spot. I sat praying and thinking about Brandon as tears welled up in my eyes. I was not sad, just taking in everything that reminded me of Brandon. I reflected on all the times of his life—first as a cute toddler, then as a gentle boy, and ultimately as a caring young man who made me proud. I also spoke to him in my mind, expressing love. A bit later Stu, Gary, and Dave returned down the mountain and they shared a photo of the memorial they had constructed for Brandon, consisting of a cross made of sticks and an arrangement of quartz stones forming his initials.

Shortly after returning home, I sent notes to friends and family telling them about the hike. I mentioned that I had paused during the climb, and that the boys had continued on to build a memorial, but I did not share any details about where I was sitting, or anything about what I had been thinking while resting. After sending my note, I received a response from Sally Owen, a friend who happens to be a medium. Sally wrote, "Brandon shows me that he stayed with you and 'heard what you said' as the others continued up."

About two hours after sending my note, I received a response from another friend, Elizabeth Stanfield, also a medium (whom I referenced at the end of chapter 10.) She shared some insights that seemed to indicate Brandon had been with us that day. She asked about the clothes I had worn on the hike. "Were you wearing shoes with an 'N' on them? Nike or New Balance?" I was blown away. The shoes I had worn were indeed New Balance and bore an "N" on the side. She had no way of knowing. While we had developed a friendship via email and telephone, Elizabeth had never actually met me in person, nor had she ever seen a photo of me other than a head shot. And hiking boots would have been the more obvious guess for mountain climbing, so it seemed she was dialed in.

The *coup de grâce* came as she asked for confirmation on the setting that day, speaking as if she'd been afforded a supernatural periscope to view the scene: "Were you sitting on a rock and remembering his baby-hood as the boys climbed up the hill?" This was exactly what I had been doing. Elizabeth's response was like reading an instant replay of what I had experienced while suspended on that jagged granite—contemplating all aspects of my son's life.

Elizabeth then moved on to something seemingly unrelated to the hike: "What about the red jacket?" When she said this I was initially a bit confused, as I recognized the jacket but I hadn't worn it that day. It was an old, red satin Phoenix Cardinals jacket that Brandon had borrowed from time to time. The garment was pretty dated—the team had changed its name to the Arizona Cardinals in the early 1990s.

Why would Brandon reference a jacket I had not worn on that day? For twenty-three years, I had been a die-hard fan of the Cardinals—a losing franchise. Although expectations were always low, later that very day, on January 10, 2009, the Cardinals pulled off an upset play-off victory over the Carolina Panthers—proceeding to win the NFC Championship and advance to the Super Bowl for the first time ever. It seemed Brandon had been afforded a sneak peek into this future scenario and knew that I'd be happy. I felt he was saying, *Hey dad, you're going to like this!*

People in grief often find that music can serve as a meaningful source of healing. A certain song or artist that was significant to the deceased person now becomes important to those left behind. And if the music plays at just the right time, the song may take on special significance, providing an unmistakable sense of connection with the deceased person.

In 2008 it was announced that the heavy-metal band Iron Maiden would be visiting Phoenix, and Steven and I decided that we would attend the concert along with a few of his friends. We knew that Brandon would have loved to come to this show with us. Brandon was big into music—both as a bass player and as someone who appreciated the work of other artists. He told me that his favorite band was Pink Floyd, and I'm pretty sure that his second favorite was Iron Maiden— rather interesting selections for someone born in the mid 1980s. The latter band is known for their heavy-metal sound, theatrics, and the epic storylines of their lyrics. Religious literalists must occasionally be reminded that for every song like "Sign of the Beast"—a musical encapsulation of the movie *Damien, Omen II*—there is a tune like "Sign of the Cross." Iron Maiden is about entertainment, and they often feature supernatural themes from books or movies and turn them into musical action stories. Less appreciated perhaps is the band's musical prowess. They feature three guitarists who play intricate solos in perfect harmony at breakneck speed, a precise bass-ist, thundering drums, and the searing vocals of Bruce Dickinson, who has amazing range and power.

Years earlier, at Brandon's request, I learned some guitar parts to a couple of Iron Maiden's less renowned songs, "The Clairvoyant" and "Dream of Mirrors." Brandon was clearly tired of playing the bass line to "Back in Black" and was pushing me to expand my musical repertoire.

Shortly before the concert, I sent a thought-prayer to Brandon, mentally relaying the message, "If Iron Maiden plays 'The Clairvoyant,' I will know that you're with us." My request seemed a stretch because the song was obscure, and I hadn't seen it in playlists from previous tours. In doing a bit of research, I noticed that it had been released on the 1988 album, *Seventh Son of a Seventh Son*, so it was now more than twenty years old.

As the evening unfolded, Steven, his friends, and I had a great time at the show. The sound was amazing, and the band reeled off a string of well-loved songs with precision. The energy was over the top as Dickinson wailed while running around the stage, jumping and climbing stage props like a young gymnast.

Near the end of the concert I got my wish, as the band launched into "The Clairvoyant." It was the second-to-last song played. For top-pers, the band's mascot, "Eddie"—a ghoulish character standing about twenty feet tall—marched out on stage right when "The Clairvoyant" began, signifying that this was the featured song of the set. I felt an electric pulse run up and down my torso and sensed it was Brandon's way of touching in.

To most travelers the world seems vast, yet our loved ones who have passed on are not limited by the same rules of time and space that govern our Earthly experience. Those who are near to our hearts yet no longer clothed in flesh are but a thought away no matter where we go. Love transcends the perceived limits of our physical world.

In late spring 2011, my wife and I went on a European vacation. We spent the latter portion of our trip in a small Italian town called Sestri Levante. While there we took a train down to the Cinque Terre, a chain of five beautiful, small seaside villages nestled into the cliffs on the Mediterranean coast, interconnected by walking trails. On the following day we decided to walk around Sestri Levante and scope out the town.

We enjoyed nearly perfect weather during most of our trip, but this particular day was overcast and drizzly. It started raining hard while we were walking around looking at shops and the local architecture, so we'd dodged into the first opening we could find. Unbeknownst to us, we had inadvertently entered an exhibit featuring the work of Storm Thorgerson, the artist responsible for Pink Floyd's album cover designs. Knowing that Pink Floyd was Brandon's favorite band we found this situation rather ironic, especially when "Wish You Were Here"—our signature song for Brandon—began playing as we entered. It seemed beyond unusual to stumble into such a place across the globe in a small Italian village, finding such an exhibit and a welcoming song.

Sometimes people come into your lives for a while but then they fall out and you lose touch. In some such cases you may reconnect at a later time, forging new and meaningful relationships. And in some of these instances the reconnection seems beyond chance and serves to complete a circle.

Brandon took bass lessons for six years and was still taking instruction at the time of his passing in 2004, even though he had become an accomplished player. It was about learning more and refining his skills, because he was serious about the instrument and wanted to be the very best he could be. Brandon appreciated his instructor, Todd Hogan, and Todd considered our son to be like a little brother. They would often "jam" together outside of lessons.

Speaking to Brandon's character as much as his musical prowess, Todd invited our son to join his band and they played together during several public performances. Todd had done very well in music after founding a band called Three Days Down that headlined in concerts where Lifehouse was the opening act. Unfortunately, some of his band-mates fell into substance abuse, so while Lifehouse went on to achieve major commercial success, Todd's group dissolved. When forming a new band, Todd planned to take a different approach and knew he could always depend on Brandon to avoid such pitfalls.

We were not alone in our suffering when Brandon died. Todd had already lost his band and had been in the process of losing both a wife and a daughter to a pending divorce. When Brandon was gone too, Todd was devastated. We didn't know him very well at the time, but we liked what Brandon had to say about Todd and always sensed that he had a warm and caring spirit.

Todd attended Brandon's funeral service and addressed the gathering of three hundred people. In his heartfelt testimony about our son, Todd stated, "Brandon is definitely in heaven," speaking about Brandon's "selfless nature" and "pure heart." After the service, we lost track of Todd for seven years. Susie and I continued to think about him fondly but didn't know where he was living or what he was doing.

Back in the late 1990s I took guitar lessons for about a year and a half then shelved the instruction for a long time thereafter. In early 2011, I decided to take a refresher course in hopes of sharpening my playing skills and acquiring some new techniques. I signed up with Stan Sorenson, a jazz guitarist, with whom my son Steven had recently studied. Stan was easy-going and had a good sense of humor, so I felt right at home with him. Since my lessons took place where Brandon had formerly studied, the person of Todd Hogan crept into my mind. At the end of my first session I asked Stan if he knew Todd's whereabouts.

Stan pointed to the door to an adjacent room and said, "He's right there, giving a lesson." Pleasantly surprised, I waited for Todd's session to conclude and then caught him. He was quite excited to see me and we spoke for about thirty minutes, enjoying a nice exchange. Reflecting on the past, Todd told me that no matter how dark things got in his life, Brandon used to cheer him up with his happy, calming disposition and his sage advice. As Todd put it, "Brandon always had a way of putting things into perspective and making me appreciate the good things in my life." This was especially helpful to Todd at his lowest points, when his marriage was disintegrating and his band falling apart.

One week later I brought Todd a copy of my book. Todd was a devout Catholic, so I wasn't sure how he would receive it, but during my thirty-minute music lesson he plunged into the book and devoured as much as he could. As I made my exit, I found Todd waiting anxiously at the door. Beaming with a revelatory grin, Todd shared that he had experienced paranormal things in his own life, especially during his childhood. His parents had sent him to a priest and a psychologist for counseling, and these "experts" concluded that he had an over-active imagination. After figuring out that it was taboo to discuss these sorts of things, Todd attempted to shut them out and no longer spoke about them when they did occur.

During our conversation Todd noted that some of these experiences had started up again and even heightened. He was sensing spiritual presences around him. I asked Todd if Brandon had visited him, and he said that this had occurred on several occasions. Todd also indicated that he had just received a message of encouragement from Brandon pertaining to his new music. The message conveyed that Todd's new album was "awesome" and that Todd "would be receiving unexpected help." In fact, Todd was offered a recording deal right after this message came through. I was also able to lend support by steering Todd to resources that enabled him to move forward with a recording contract. He recently completed and released an outstanding collection of original songs entitled *Nowhere in Between*.

Reconnecting with Todd was a blessing for my family and me, and the timing seemed beyond coincidence. Now remarried with a caring wife and two adorable children, and a budding musical career, Todd seems very happy.

CHAPTER 15

Summation

Before his near-death experience in 2008, Dr. Eben Alexander—who taught and performed neurosurgery at the Harvard Medical School—concurred with most of his fellow scientists by assuming that the brain produces consciousness. But after a close brush with death following a week-long coma, as a rare form of bacterial meningitis attacked his brain, Dr. Alexander's worldview changed.

According to prevailing theories on brain function, Dr. Alexander should have been incapable of consciousness during his coma, as the entire outer surface of his brain was covered with bacteria and puss. As Dr. Alexander notes in his book, *Proof of Heaven*, "… when varieties of *E. coli* that have picked up DNA strands that make them especially aggressive invade the cerebrospinal fluid around the spinal cord and brain, the primitive cells immediately begin devouring the glucose in the fluid, and whatever else is available to consume, including the brain itself." [1]

Describing the consequence of this *E. coli* attack on his brain, Alexander explained, "During that time, my entire neocortex—the outer surface of the brain, the part that makes us human—was shut down. Inoperative. In essence, absent. When your brain is absent, you are absent too." [2] Despite this dire scenario, Dr. Alexander actually experienced an expanded awareness, sensing an immensely loving connection with the divine source and knowledge of the interconnected nature of the universe. His biological recovery could be described as miraculous, since doctors did not expect Dr. Alexander to survive. I wondered if there was a bigger purpose at work here—why it was that a person with this particular background and stature happened to come back from the brink of death to tell his story.

I had the opportunity to speak with Dr. Alexander twice in 2012 and asked him a few questions about his experience. This prompted him to share his greatest revelation, previously expressed to colleagues in question form, *"Do you know what this means?!"* Dr. Alexander then shared his perspective, mirroring my view, that consciousness is primary and that matter and form are creative expressions produced by consciousness—and that the spiritual realm is real.

Dr. Alexander's story reinforces my contention that personal experience is the greatest catalyst for change in a person. But what about those who have yet to have such a life-altering event?

Via cultural conditioning, people come to see things through a particular lens that produces their reality. And sometimes people identify so strongly with an ideology—be it religious fundamentalism, scientism, atheism, or some other "ism"—that the creed itself becomes the key descriptor for the person's own self-image. Not only does this limit the scope of their exploration, it can create a false or incomplete sense of self.

For some, reassessing concepts about truth and reality can be a scary proposition. What if you'd lived your entire life alone on a remote island—assuming that the visible edge of the sea was the end of the world? Now suppose that you saw a ship for the first time and you were taken aboard it and subsequently transported to a plane. Now imagine that you flew in that plane and then saw the world from above when a large continent came into view. What if you landed in a city on that continent that was filled with large buildings, automobiles, and millions of people? How would you deal with the shock of it all? Would you plug your ears and close your eyes, pretending it was all a dream?

It may not be easy, but if people can open their mind to new information and evidence, it can be a first step in helping them recognize their own truth—to "Know Thyself," as suggested in the ancient Greek maxim. It is easy for an individual say "I believe that" or "I am this." It is more difficult to reflect deeply, assimilating an inner truth as opposed to espousing a commonly accepted ideology.

I'm not recommending that people abandon their chosen religion or spiritual philosophy. Rather, I am suggesting that a deep self-exploration—conducted earnestly and honestly—will expand a person's sense of awareness about themselves, their willingness to learn new things, and their ability to change. This process can enrich someone's religious or spiritual life as well as communal experience, making them more empathetic.

I want people to open their minds to the evidence I have presented, as well as a much larger body of proof available to the explorer. My hope is to help people work their way through the seemingly irreconcilable chasm between the culture of scientism—with its atheistic, secular-humanist ideology and denial of spirit—and traditional religious explanations that seem largely outmoded and implausible to many people. There is a middle ground.

I recognize that some will be closed off because the information conflicts with their worldview—whether or not they realize this as the source of their rejection. I earnestly encourage such persons to think deeply on these matters and consider whether they approached the evidence with an open mind or dismissed it without true consideration.

Among phenomena affirming the afterlife, I chose to focus on mediumship since it yields some of the most compelling evidence and because it can provide tremendous healing to bereaved persons. It is also the area with which I'm most familiar, as I was raised by a father with these abilities and have since met some of the top psychic-mediums in the world today.

In terms of the healing effects of mediumship, I have seen people who were completely distraught after losing a loved one, but they bounced back after experiencing an evidential reading. Hope was restored for these individuals because they were given sufficient evidence that they had actually connected with the living essence and personality of their deceased loved one. Without hope and sense of purpose, people can lose their will to live and therefore cannot contribute their gifts to the world. I see life as having purpose and meaning.

I've also come into contact with parents who were devout in their religious convictions until they lost a child, then questioned everything they had previously professed to believe. One such couple, now good friends of mine, pursued a different course after their son passed and they began to view things from an entirely new perspective, broader than before. After the death of their son, the church where they'd been quite involved for many years demonstrated little concern for their well-being and offered no support. The couple also found that their most outwardly religious friends were actually the least willing to discuss their deceased son and were the "most depressing people" to be around. Conversely, the couple received great support from unexpected quarters—a minister from another church and a few mediums who reached out in an unsolicited way, seeking no payment for their services. These mediums furnished highly evidential information, including some facts about their son's cause of death—unknown to anyone at the time but later validated. Prior to their son's passing, the couple didn't even know what a medium was, but they subsequently came to find that they didn't have to rely on blind faith alone. A session with a good medium can serve as a healing balm.

Some people like my friends never questioned church doctrine or traditionally accepted views before suffering a loss. But after the trauma associated with the death of their child, they explored matters more deeply—eventually expressing puzzlement over the reasons why churches often discount modern-day occurrences of phenomena that parallel scriptural accounts. Their loss served as a catalyst for a newfound curiosity about things that had never before drawn their interest, and this open-minded perspective resulted in a deeper search and more reflective personal introspective process. In the end many of these people didn't lose their faith despite the ultimate challenge to faith: why bad things happen to good people. Instead they adapted it into something they could truly believe and that resonated with them. They also felt a new sense of freedom about how to frame their beliefs while maintaining their membership in a church—or not.

I chose to explore the link between religion, spirituality, and psychic-medium phenomena because there is an important relationship that is rarely discussed. Scriptures mention many "miracles" that are most reasonably explained by precognition, psycho-kinesis, clairvoyance, clairaudience, and mediumship. Most churches are hesitant to admit this, although some members of the clergy will attest to these things when off duty. To ignore this seemingly obvious connection is to pander to materialists who contend that such stories are nothing but elaborate fables that tricked simple-minded people centuries ago, which now serve to discredit religion. Spiritual leaders would be wise to learn more about parapsychology, opening up to the possibility that at least some of the stories are congruent with said phenomena. Their added knowledge in this area would strengthen their arguments about the legitimacy of some miracle accounts in scripture, fostering more trust and belief among parishioners.

Within this project I also wanted to identify the "neutral ground" or common spiritual denominator to which most people can relate. I would suggest that this "place" is approximately two steps back of any particular religion or dogma—a space where all can meet and relate in a peaceful and mutually respectful way. I am motivated to draw light to the inter-relatedness of humankind and the critical need for us to strive for a greater unity among all peoples. My father helped me understand and embrace these concepts, and they remain a critical aspect of my perspective today. I would suggest that these principles are actually self-evident, even though humanity has shown a propensity to live in the opposite way.

Throughout history, extremists have insisted that their way is the only acceptable path, displaying little or no tolerance for alternate perspectives. This type of thinking has led some cultures and religions to demonize others whose views differed from their own—people whom they never sought to understand in the first place. Yet Jesus told his followers, "… Love your enemies and pray for those who persecute you" (Matthew 5:44). Based on how most people treat one another in the world today, this directive may seem a lofty and almost unattainable ideal. I recently saw a woman on TV who demonstrated forgiveness and love to a man who murdered her entire family. How rare is that? More commonly, I've met people who hold onto their anger toward others over infringements that are much less significant. But to forgive and love—or demonstrate compassion for—someone that you dislike requires empathy. And to empathize with a person you must first understand them. If we took more time to learn about people we dislike, we might come to see the underlying factors driving their undesirable behavior. And once you have some context, understanding the person's life experiences, you may well feel sorry for them.

Regarding the ongoing and debilitating dilemma manifesting as "us vs. them," I would suggest that it's critical to explore our points of commonality, as revealed within the universal principles of truth running through all faiths and ideologies. While the differences in belief sets have been extensively explored—sometimes with deadly consequences—the areas of accord have rarely been considered.

My father called the veracities found in all faiths "the golden strand of truth." At this point in history I see this as a critical topic. Now and then I encounter someone whom I call an Earth Angel, a person who glows with warmth and sincerity—one who places personal concerns below the welfare of others, living in congruence with the principle of the inter-relationship of all. Such people provide a worthy example for all to consider.

My personal view is that we are souls who ventured into physical embodiment for growth-yielding experiences. And in accordance with this idea I have come to see the importance of establishing a personal spiritual practice—one attuned to the individual. This can serve to open up possibilities inherent within a person for a direct connection to the divine—call it God, Source, Infinite Divine, Universal Intelligence, any other term you like, or no term at all.

Whether your concept of the divine is a personal God, an ineffable force, the Universe itself, or something else entirely, is ultimately up to you. The key is to recognize that a portion of this divine source is within you—accessible to you—and that another realm of being exists beyond this world of physical manifestation. It is important because the process of connection via prayer, meditation, contemplation, and other practices lends guidance and helps to reveal our life path. It can also give us strength to stay on course during difficult times. Finally, it can give you comfort and confidence to truly know that your vital essence will continue on in an expanded way after the physical body you now occupy is no more.

Postscript

At twenty-nine years of age, my father wrote the following letter to his dad, who was dying of cancer. As you read this, consider that my father and grandfather didn't have a very good relationship, yet it's clear that my father didn't want his dad to fear death.

I learned about the letter in 2004 when my uncle Robert first mentioned it, explaining that he had been in the hospital with my grandfather at the time it was delivered. My uncle told me that my grandfather thereafter repeatedly asked him, "Bob, would you please read Dick's letter to me again?" The letter, now in my possession, is a perfect fit for this book. It also demonstrates my father's sincerity and dedication to the "soul work" that was his life's mission.

April 2, 1962

Dear Dad,

Here I am in Detroit, and in an effort to catch up on my letter writing, I thought I'd send a letter off to you.

How fast time passes and how strange it is where the ship of life takes us. How little you or I could have thought, I would be a minister someday. If you can remember, as clear as I, and I'm sure you can, what a strange child I was; it makes it even more unusual that I should be a minister. I think it must have been my extreme interest in life that drove me on my search to find out why—life, death, the mystery of birth, and why man seemed always beset by trials and problems of every nature—that finally ushered me into this field. With no regrets, because I have had a chance which few people do to view life, close at hand, by meeting and dealing with every type of family problem, and every manner of difficulty that could arise. It's a wonderful feeling to know to help someone understand what they couldn't accept, or to help someone over a road they couldn't have traveled without your guidance. I have been devoted to my work, and feel sincerely thankful for my opportunity to contribute to man's needs, by what assurance is mine to give, no matter how small.

Life and death are extremely personal and therefore difficult to talk about, especially to those who are close to us. Perhaps this is why I couldn't say all the things I wanted to when I was home. The close of earthly life is a sure thing— for all of us—and we can't know just when it will come. How many times it has been close to you and passed you by, in the war, in your recent operations, every time you drove in the car, and now it seems near again.

We can all speculate on death—almost everyone has: the doctor, the body is all there is; the scientist, nothing is ever lost, just changed in form; and the most comforting, the minister, the soul is the real you and the body is only a mode of manifestation in the physical world, and when it is no longer a fit habitat for the soul, the soul withdraws and leaves an empty shell.

I don't mean to minister to you, for how can a son minister to a father? It's only that I want you to know, as I know, that the minister is right. I have no means to convey to you the experiences I have had with life after death—but *to me* it's real. I couldn't teach others to believe something I didn't know or was in doubt about. I didn't get my proof through any school or someone else; not even the logic of man's survival satisfied me; and by some grace of God, I was privileged to know for myself, by actually talking with and seeing those who have graduated into a higher school of life. This is my *personal* proof, and it has been a proof to thousands of others, mostly strangers to me, who have come and received *personal* proof about those they once loved, and by conveyance of facts known only to them they have been convinced.

When a new baby is born it comes from out of the great no-where into the some-where, and when the soul is born into another stage of life (through death) it returns to that great gulf it came from.

I know whenever you stand at that point, just between the two worlds, for a moment you'll know that everything is alright. When you begin to see with the sight of the soul (spirit) even before you leave the body, you'll see I'm right, and when Aunt Ellie, Grandma Birch, and especially your own dad become clearly visible, you'll be too anxious to join them to even think about the old worn-out body you'll be leaving behind.

And then you'll realize that you left behind four sons to carry on the job of living, rightly raised, and ready to help the world be a better place for our sons to live.

Have no regrets of the past, dad, and just remember I'll be seeing you again—here or there—it makes no difference. I can't make the trip with you, but I know it will be a pleasant one. Take my love and hellos to all my friends, and don't forget to come and visit me—you promised.

Love always, your son
"Dick"

Not the End

Endnotes

Chapter 1: The "Why"

1. Dr. Julie Beischel, research summary distributed as a pamphlet.
2. Dr. Julie Beischel, in *Winds of Change*, Windbridge Institute Newsletter, Vol. 6, Issue 1, Spring 2013.
3. Pim van Lommel, MD, *Consciousness Beyond Life* (New York: Harper One, 2010), p. 317.

Chapter 2: The Next Phase

1. www.kirlianresearch.com.
2. www.reiki-for-holistic-health.com/auracolormeanings.html.

Chapter 3: Seeing Things Differently

1. Chris Carter, "Does Telepathy Conflict with Science? Many are starting to think not," *The Epoch Times*, English edition, www.theepochtimes.com/n2/science/does-telepathy-conflict-with-science-211214.html.
2. Gregg Braden, *The Spontaneous Healing of Belief* (Carlsbad, CA: Hay House, 2008), p. xi.
3. http://en.wikipedia.org/wiki/Optical_illusion. "The copyright holder has irrevocably released all rights to it, allowing it to be freely reproduced, distributed, transmitted, used, modified, built upon, or otherwise exploited in any way by anyone for any purpose, commercial or non-commercial, with or without attribution of the author, as if in the public domain." Check URL named in "Source" for additional information.
4. Mark C. Baker and Stewart Goetz, *The Soul Hypothesis: Investigations into the Existence of the Soul* (New York: Continuum International Publishing Group, 2011).
5. http://education.jlab.org/qa/atomicstructure_10.html.

6. Sir Oliver Lodge, *Phantom Walls* (London: Hodder and Stoughton, Limited, 1929), p. 95.

7. Joannie Fischer, "The First Clone," *U.S. News & World Report* (November 25, 2001).

8. Radio interview with Dr. Robert Lanza, "Consciousness and the Universe," on "Coast to Coast AM," March 26, 2010.

9. Ibid.

10. www.huffingtonpost.com/robert-lanza/is-there-a-god-or-is -ther_b_639416.html.

11. Hans Holzer, PhD, *The Psychic Yellow Pages* (New York: Citadel Press, Kensington Publishing Corp., 2001).

12. www.aspsi.org/feat/life_after/_testimonials.php#Price.

13. www.spr.ac.uk/expcms/index.php?section=29.

14. Ibid.

15. Ibid.

16. *Proceedings of the Society for Psychical Research*, Vol. XII, pp. 5, 6.

17. Eleanor Sidgwick, "Psychology of Mrs. Piper's Trance Phenomena; Chapter V: Communicators," *Proceedings of the Society for Psychical Research*, Vol. XXVIII (December 1915): p. 204.

18. www.survivalafterdeath.info/articles/doyle/spr.htm.

19. www.survivalafterdeath.info/articles/saltmarsh/plan.htm.

20. Montague Keen, "Communicating with the Dead: The Evidence Ignored—Why Paul Kurtz is Wrong," *Journal of Scientific Exploration*, Vol. 17, No. 2 (2003): p. 292.

21. Michael Schmicker, *Best Evidence* (Lincoln, NE: Writers Club Press, 2002), p. 60.

22. Ibid., p. 63.

23. Robertson is the Immediate Past President of the Scottish Society for Psychical Research (in 2013). Roy, who died in 2013, was Professor Emeritus of Astronomy at the University of Glasgow, a Fellow of the Royal Society of Edinburgh, the Royal Astronomical Society, and the British Interplanetary Society, and Founding President of the SSPR.

24. Information obtained via personal correspondence with Tricia J. Robertson, SSPR, October 2010.

25. Skeptiko blog: Transcript 51, www.skeptiko.com/blog/?p=39 (September 18, 2008).

26. Personal communication, Tricia J. Robertson, SSPR, October 2010.

27. Ibid.

28. Michael Tymn, "The Very Strange Story of the Late George Pellew: The Man Who Proved He Wasn't Dead," *Atlantis Rising*, Issue 100, July/August 2013: pp. 39, 66–67.

29. Ibid.

30. Montague Keen, "Communicating with the Dead," p. 293.

31. Ibid.

32. *The Daily Grail*, "The Departed," interview with Dr. Julie Beischel, www.dailygrail.com/interview/julie-beischel-the-departed (September 11, 2009).

33. Michael Schmicker, *Best Evidence* (see note 21), p. 222.

34. Ibid., pp. 223–24.

Chapter 4: Interviews with Two Psychic-Mediums

1. Joel Martin and Patricia Romanowski, *We Don't Die: George Anderson's Conversations with the Other Side* (New York: Berkeley Books, 1988).

2. *The Epoch Times*, online edition, March 26, 2012. www.theepochtimes.com/n2/science/does-telepathy-conflict-with-science-211214-all.html.

Chapter 5: The Skeptical Neurosis

1. Dr. Don Watson, personal communication, 2008—this paragraph and the quotes that follow.

2. http://orwell.ru/people/koestler/ak_en. Koestler was being referenced by Watson in our conversation.

3. *Northern Journal of Medicine*, 1844, I 387.

4. http://ghosts-uk.net/modules/encyclopedia/entry.php?entryID=141, referencing Karl R. Popper, *Science: Conjectures and Refutations* (London and New York: Routledge and Keegan Paul, 1963), pp. 43–86.

5. www.victorzammit.com/index.html.

6. Tricia Robertson, "About Sceptics," article in *The Soul Shift Newsletter,* Issue 2 (May 2009). To subscribe to this newsletter (published by the author of this book) and access archives: www.markirelandauthor.com.

7. www.skepticalinvestigations.org/Observeskeptics/ CSICOP/30yearswar_6.html.

8. Marcello Truzzi, "On Pseudo-Skepticism," *Zetetic Scholar,* No. 12/13 (1987): pp. 3-4.

9. http://blavatskyarchives.com/zeteticism.htm.

10. www.tricksterbook.com/ArticlesOnline/CSICOPoverview.htm.

11. www.victorzammit.com/articles/montague.html.

12. Ibid.

13. Ibid.

14. Ibid.

15. Ibid.

16. www.skeptiko.com/51-dr-julie-beischel-responds-to-critics-of-psychic -medium-research/.

17. Richard Ireland, *The Phoenix Oracle* (New York: Tower Press, 1970), out of print.

18. Dr. Julie Beischel, "Contemporary Methods Used in Laboratory-Based Mediumship Research," *The Journal of Parapsychology,* Vol. 71 (Spring/ Fall 2007): pp. 50, 51.

19. www.sheldrake.org/D&C/controversies/wiseman.html.

20. www.dailygrail.com/features/the-myth-of-james-randis-million-dollar -challenge.

21. Ibid.

22. Ibid.

23. Tricia Robertson, "About Sceptics," see note 6 above. Source material: Collins and Pinch, *The Construction of the Paranormal.*

24. Ibid. Robertson's source material: Le Shan, *From Newton to ESP.*

25. Lyall Watson, *Beyond Supernature* (New York: Bantam, 1987).

26. Ibid.

27. www.skeptiko.com/46-dr-rupert-sheldrake-and-the-skeptics/.

28. Dr. Dean Radin, *The Conscious Universe* (San Francisco, CA: Harper San Francisco, 1997), p. 229.

29. Ibid.
30. http://iands.org/research/important-research-articles/80-penny-sartori
    -phd-prospective-study.html?start=2.
31. Anita Moorjani, *Dying To Be Me: My Journey From Cancer, To Near
    Death, To True Healing* (Carlsbad, CA: Hay House, Inc., 2012), pp. 63,
    80.
32. www.freedommag.org/english/vol28I2/page44.htm.

CHAPTER 6: Reflections

1. Dr. Richard Ireland, *The Phoenix Oracle* (New York: Tower Books,
   1970), p. 95.
2. Erlandur Haraldsson, "Persistence of Past-Life Memories: Study of
   Adults Who Claimed in Their Childhood to Remember a Past Life,"
   Journal of Scientific Exploration, Vol. 22, No. 3, 2008.
3. Mae West, *Mae West on Sex, Health, and ESP* (London and New York:
   W. H. Allen /Virgin Books, 1975).

CHAPTER 8: Psychic Phenomena and Mediumship in Religion and History

1. www.survivalafterdeath.info/articles/moore/christianity.htm.
2. http://daemonpage.com/socrates-daimon.php.
3. Pamela Davidson, *Russian Literature and its Demons* (Oxford and New
   York: Berghahn Books, 2000), p. 137.
4. Ibid.
5. Ibid.
6. Elaine Pagels, *The Origin of Satan: How Christians Demonized Jews,
   Pagans, and Heretics* (New York: Vintage Books /Random House, 1995).
7. Ibid.
8. Elaine Pagels, *The Gnostic Gospels* (New York: Vintage Books, 1979).
9. Elaine Pagels, *The Gnostic Paul: Gnostic Exegesis of the Pauline Letters*
   (Harrisburg, PA: Trinity Press International, 1975).
10. John Shelby Spong, *The Sins of Scripture: Exposing the Bible's Texts of
    Hate to Reveal the God of Love* (New York: Harper Collins, 2005).
11. www.survivalafterdeath.info/articles/moore/christianity.htm.

12. Ibid.

13. Courtesy of author Cullen Dorn: unpublished commentary.

14. Ibid.

15. Ibid.

16. *Phillip Gowins, Sufism: A Path for Today, The Sovereign Soul (Sarasota, FL: New Paradigm Books, 2006).*

17. John Spencer Trimingham, *The Sufi Orders in Islam* (New York: Oxford University Press, 1971), pp. 151, 158.

18. Ibid.

19. Robert W. Funk, Roy W. Hoover, and the Jesus Seminar, *The Five Gospels* (New York: HarperCollins, 1994).

20. Elaine Pagels, *The Gnostic Gospels* (see note 8), p. 142.

21. Elaine Pagels, *The Gospel of Thomas,* audio-book (CD) (Boulder, CO: Sounds True, 2006).

22. Ibid.

23. Helmut Koester, *Introduction to the Gospel of Thomas,* translated by Thomas O. Lambdin, www.theologywebsite.com/etext/naghammadi /thomas.shtml.

24. Ibid.

25. Elaine Pagels, *The Origin of Satan* (see note 6), pp. 70–71. NHC is an acronym referring to the Nag Hammadi library collection.

CHAPTER 10: Robin's Flight

1. Tijn Touber, "Life Goes On," http://north-ca-iands.org/index.html.

2. Ibid.

3. Pim van Lommel, *Consciousness Beyond Life: The Science of the Near-Death Experience* (New York: Harper Collins, 2010), p. 54.

4. Michael Sabom, *Light and Death* (Grand Rapids, MI: Zondervan Publishing House, 1998), pp. 37–38.

5. Allen Spraggett, *Arthur Ford: The Man Who Talked with the Dead* (New York: Signet, The New American Library, 1973), p. 10.

6. Ibid., p. 157.

7. Ibid., p. 132.

8. Ibid.

9. Ibid., p. 158.

10. Essays by Dr. Don Watson, shared in personal communication: "Are We Nothing but a Pack of Neurons?" and "Introduction to the Theory of Enformed Systems."

11. Ibid.

12. Ibid.

13. Sam Knowlton, "IONS Studies 'frontiers of consciousness'," *Lawrence Journal-World* (September 18, 2005).

14. Ibid.

15. Ibid.

CHAPTER 15: Summation

1. Dr. Eben Alexander, *Proof of Heaven: A Neurosurgeon's Journey into the Afterlife* (New York, Simon & Schuster, 2012), p. 50.

2. Ibid, p. 24.

About the Author

Mark Ireland is the son of Richard Ireland, a renowned twentieth-century psychic. He is the author of *Soul Shift: Finding Where the Dead Go* (North Atlantic Books, 2008), a moving account of his personal quest for answers about life after death, written after the passing of his youngest son Brandon. In 2012 Mark co-founded a Scottsdale, Arizona-based national nonprofit organization, Helping Parents Heal, dedicated to assisting parents who have lost children. Resources for healing include open and non-dogmatic discussion of spiritual experiences and evidence for the afterlife, for those interested in such exploration. Affiliate groups are expected to welcome everyone regardless of religious (or non-religious) background and allow for open dialog.

Mark edited *Your Psychic Potential: A Guide to Psychic Development* (North Atlantic Books, 2011), authored by his father in the 1970s but never released during his lifetime. Mark has carried out his own investigations of psychic potential and consciousness survival (assisted by Tricia Robertson of the Scottish Society for Psychical Research and neuroscientist Dr. Don Watson), as well as participated in mediumship research studies, including serving as a test sitter at the University of Arizona and the University of Virginia. He continues to delve into scientific research and other evidence for an afterlife.

Mark holds a Bachelor's degree from Arizona State University and lives in Scottsdale, Arizona, with his wife, Susie. People can subscribe to his *Soul Shift Newsletter* by visiting www.markirelandauthor.com.

North Atlantic Books
Berkeley, California

Personal, spiritual, and planetary transformation

North Atlantic Books, a nonprofit publisher established in 1974, is dedicated to fostering community, education, and constructive dialogue. NABCommunities.com is a meeting place for an ever-growing membership of readers and authors to engage in the discussion of books and topics from North Atlantic's core publishing categories.

NAB Communities offer interactive social networks in these genres:

NOURISH: Raw Foods, Healthy Eating and Nutrition, All-Natural Recipes

WELLNESS: Holistic Health, Bodywork, Healing Therapies

WISDOM: New Consciousness, Spirituality, Self-Improvement

CULTURE: Literary Arts, Social Sciences, Lifestyle

BLUE SNAKE: Martial Arts History, Fighting Philosophy, Technique

Your free membership gives you access to:

Advance notice about new titles and exclusive giveaways

Podcasts, webinars, and events

Discussion forums

Polls, quizzes, and more!

Go to www.NABCommunities.com and join today.